The Heritage of Freedom ESSAYS

ON THE RIGHTS OF

FREE MEN

EDITED BY WILFRED S. DOWDEN
AND T. N. MARSH Both of Rice University

HARPER & BROTHERS   Publishers
New York

The Heritage of Freedom

To Our Parents
Bessie S. and Roy H. Dowden
and
Ethel Reaugh Marsh

And I will war, at least in words (and—should
   My chance so happen—deeds), with all who war
With Thought;—and of Thought's foes by far most rude,
   Tyrants and sycophants have been and are.
I know not who may conquer: if I could
   Have such prescience, it should be no bar
To this my plain, sworn downright detestation
   Of every despotism in every nation.
              —Byron, *Don Juan,* IX, xxiv

CONTENTS

PREFACE

In view of the large and still growing number of textbooks for reading in college courses, the task of providing one that offers a different method and new material might at first seem hopeless; yet the editors of this text believe that its design and content are original. Its variety without diffuseness, diversity without incoherence, and stylistic difference without thematic disorganization are, we believe, innovations in college readers, and the new material is provided by the excellent, though by no means common, essays that are included—essays that range from the well-ordered prose of Mill and Bagehot to the delightfully familiar style of Elmer Davis.

With this principle of unity in mind, we have chosen essays that relate to the one idea of human freedom rather than to a variety of subjects, in the belief that both instructor and student can benefit from studying a book that has a central theme approached from various points of view. This ideal has enabled us to avoid the lack of direction common to many essay texts. Part of its value, therefore, is that all of the selections can be included in the syllabus, thereby avoiding the waste inevitable in longer texts with numerous essays on sharply divergent themes, simply because there is not enough time to cover them in class. We also hope that the selections will suggest further relevant reading in complete works which can be chosen by the instructor from many now easily available; this hope arises from our conviction that even beginning college students need not always expect their intellectual food to be predigested.

The organization is inherent in the subject, each section being devoted to one aspect of human freedom. The first section serves as an introduction, and those that follow indicate how the general concept of freedom is operative in the various aspects of human existence.

The book has two primary objectives. First, we have tried to provide examples of good writing. Special care has been exercised in the selection of these essays, therefore, and questions on composition and content are included at the end of each selection. In addition to these specific guides, a series of general questions and topics for discussion follows each section. The latter are designed to assist the student in determining the interrelation of the various essays in each group and to suggest ways in which he may pursue the study of these issues further.

Secondly, the book has been compiled not because we feel that our civil liberties are under attack and we view ourselves as their embattled defenders, but because we have detected in our students an apathy toward, and consequently a lack of understanding of, our basic freedoms. Most of these essays are philosophical rather than occasional, therefore, and thus the tone is of reasonable inquiry rather than petulant defense. This spirit also explains the almost equal balance of old and modern essays included in the text.

There remains only the pleasant duty of expressing our gratitude to those who have assisted in the preparation of this book: the Librarian and staff of the Fondren Library; the staff of the Development Office, Rice University; Professor R. A. Tsanoff (for revising his essay especially for this book); and to our friends and colleagues who have given us invaluable encouragement and criticism.

W. S. D.
T. N. M.

William Marsh Rice University
September, 1961

During the contest of opinion through which we have passed, the animation of discussion and of exertions has sometimes worn an aspect which might impose on strangers unused to think freely and to speak and to write what they think; but this being now decided by the voice of the nation, announced according to the rules of the constitution, all will, of course, arrange themselves under the will of the law, and unite in common efforts for the common good. All, too, will bear in mind this sacred principle, that though the will of the majority is in all cases to prevail, that will, to be rightful, must be reasonable; that the minority possess their equal rights, which equal laws must protect, and to violate which would be oppression. Let us, then, fellow citizens, unite with one heart and one mind. Let us restore to social intercourse that harmony and affection without which liberty and even life itself are but dreary things. And let us reflect that having banished from our land that religious intolerance under which mankind so long bled and suffered, we have yet gained little if we countenance a political intolerance as despotic, as wicked, and capable of as bitter and bloody persecutions. During the throes and convulsions of the ancient world, during the agonizing spasms of infuriated man, seeking through blood and slaughter his long-lost liberty, it was not wonderful that the agitations of the billows should reach even this distant and peaceful shore; that this should be more felt and feared by some and less by others; that this should divide opinions as to measures of safety. But every difference of opinion is not a difference of principle. We have called by different names brethren of the same principle. We are all republicans—we are federalists. If there be any among us who would wish to dissolve this Union or to change its republican form, let them stand undisturbed as monuments of the safety with which error of opinion may be tolerated where reason is left free to combat it. I know, indeed, that some honest men fear that a republican government cannot be strong; that this government is not strong enough. But would the honest patriot, in the full tide of successful experiment, abandon a government which has so far kept us free and firm, on the theoretic and visionary fear that this government, the world's best hope, may by possibility want energy to preserve itself? I trust not. I believe this, on the contrary, the strongest government on earth. I believe it is the only one where every man, at the call of the laws, would fly to the standard of the law, and would meet invasions of the public order as his own personal concern. Sometimes it is said that man cannot be trusted with the government of himself. Can he, then, be trusted with the government of others? Or have we found angels in the forms of kings to govern him? Let history answer this question.

—THOMAS JEFFERSON, from "The First Inaugural Address," March 4, 1801

I ～ The Idea of Freedom

OF THE LIBERTY OF
THOUGHT AND DISCUSSION
*John Stuart Mill

The time, it is to be hoped, is gone by, when any defence would be necessary of the "liberty of the press" as one of the securities against corrupt or tyrannical government. No argument, we may suppose, can now be needed, against permitting a legislature or an executive, not identified in interest with the people, to prescribe opinions to them, and determine what doctrines or what arguments they shall be allowed to hear. This aspect of the question, besides, has been so often and so triumphantly enforced by preceding writers, that it needs not be specially insisted on in this place. Though the law of England, on the subject of the press, is as servile to this day as it was in the time of the Tudors, there is little danger of its being actually put in force against political discussion, except during some temporary panic, when fear of insurrection drives ministers and judges from their propriety; and, speaking generally, it is not, in constitutional countries, to be apprehended, that the government, whether completely responsible to the people or not, will often attempt to control the expression of opinion, except when in doing so it makes itself the organ of the general intolerance of the public. Let us suppose, therefore, that the government is entirely at one with the people, and never thinks of exerting any power of coercion unless in agreement with what it conceives to be their voice. But I deny

From *Essay on Liberty* (1859), chap. II.

the right of the people to exercise such coercion, either by themselves or by their government. The power itself is illegitimate. The best government has no more title to it than the worst. It is as noxious, or more noxious, when exerted in accordance with public opinion, than when in opposition to it. If all mankind minus one were of one opinion, and only one person were of the contrary opinion, mankind would be no more justified in silencing that one person, than he, if he had the power, would be justified in silencing mankind. Were an opinion a personal possession of no value except to the owner; if to be obstructed in the enjoyment of it were simply a private injury, it would make some difference whether the injury was inflicted only on a few persons or on many. But the peculiar evil of silencing the expression of an opinion is, that it is robbing the human race; posterity as well as the existing generation; those who dissent from the opinion, still more than those who hold it. If the opinion is right, they are deprived of the opportunity of exchanging error for truth: if wrong, they lose, what is almost as great a benefit, the clearer perception and livelier impression of truth, produced by its collision with error.

It is necessary to consider separately these two hypotheses, each of which has a distinct branch of the argument corresponding to it. We can never be sure that the opinion we are endeavoring to stifle is a false opinion; and if we were sure, stifling it would be an evil still.

First: the opinion which it is attempted to suppress by authority may possibly be true. Those who desire to suppress it, of course deny its truth; but they are not infallible. They have no authority to decide the question for all mankind, and exclude every other person from the means of judging. To refuse a hearing to an opinion, because they are sure that it is false, is to assume that *their* certainty is the same thing as *absolute* certainty. All silencing of discussion is an assumption of infallibility. Its condemnation may be allowed to rest on this common argument, not the worse for being common.

Unfortunately for the good sense of mankind, the fact of their fallibility is far from carrying the weight in their practical judgment which is always allowed to it in theory; for while every one well knows himself to be fallible, few think it necessary to take any precautions against their own fallibility, or admit the supposition that any opinion, of which they feel very certain, may be one of the examples of the error to which they acknowledge themselves to be liable. Absolute princes, or others who are accustomed to unlimited deference, usually feel this complete confidence in their own opinions on nearly all subjects. People more happily situated, who sometimes hear their opinions disputed, and are not wholly unused to be set right when they are wrong, place the same unbounded reliance only on such of their opinions as are shared by all who surround them, or to whom they habitually defer; for in proportion to a man's want of confidence in his own solitary judgment, does he usually repose, with implicit trust, on the infallibility of "the world" in general. And the world, to each individual, means the part of it with which he comes in contact; his party, his sect, his church, his class of society; the man may be called, by comparison, almost liberal and large-minded to whom it means anything so comprehensive as his own country or his own age. Nor is his faith in this collective authority at all shaken by his being aware that other ages, countries, sects, churches, classes, and parties have thought, and even now think, the exact reverse. He devolves upon his own world the responsibility of being in the right against the dissentient worlds of other people; and it never troubles him that mere accident has decided which of these numerous worlds is the object of his reliance, and that the same causes which make him a Churchman in London, would have made him a Buddhist or a Confucian in Pekin. Yet it is as evident in itself, as any amount of argument can make it, that ages are no more infallible than individuals; every age having held many opinions which subsequent ages have deemed not only false but absurd; and it is as certain that many opinions now general will be rejected by future ages, as it is that many, once general, are rejected by the present.

The objection likely to be made to this argument would probably take some such form as the following. There is no greater assumption of infallibility in forbidding the propagation of error, than in any other thing which is done by public authority on its own judgment and responsibility. Judgment is given to men that they may use it. Because it may be used erroneously, are men to be told that they ought not to use it at all? To prohibit what they think pernicious, is not claiming exemption from error, but fulfilling the duty incumbent on them, although fallible, of acting on their conscientious conviction. If we were never to act on our opinions, because those opinions may be wrong, we should leave all our interests uncared for, and all our duties unperformed. An objection which applies to all conduct can be no valid objection to any conduct in particular. It is the duty of governments, and of individuals, to form the truest opinions they can; to form them carefully, and never impose them upon others unless they are quite sure of being right. But when they are sure (such reasoners may say) it is not conscientiousness but cowardice to shrink from acting on their opinions, and allow doctrines which they honestly think dangerous to the welfare of mankind, either in this life or in another, to be scattered abroad without restraint, because other people, in less enlightened times, have persecuted opinions now believed to be true. Let us take care, it may be said, not to make the same mistake: but governments and nations have made mistakes in other things, which are not denied to be fit subjects for the exercise of authority: they have laid on bad taxes, made unjust wars. Ought we therefore to lay on no taxes, and, under whatever provocation, make no wars? Men, and governments, must act to the best of their ability. There is no such thing as absolute certainty, but there is assurance sufficient for the purposes of human life. We may, and must, assume our opinion to be true for the guidance of our own conduct: and it is assuming no more when we forbid bad men to pervert society by the propagation of opinions which we regard as false and pernicious.

I answer, that it is assuming very much more. There is the greatest difference between presuming an opinion to be true, because, with every opportunity for contesting it, it has not been refuted, and assuming its truth for the purpose of not permitting its refutation. Complete liberty of contradicting and disproving our opinion is the very condition which justifies us in assuming its truth for purposes of action; and on no other terms can a being with human faculties have any rational assurance of being right.

When we consider either the history of opinion, or the ordinary conduct of human life, to what is it to be ascribed that the one and the other are no worse than they are? Not certainly to the inherent force of the human understanding; for, on any matter not self-evident, there are ninety-nine persons totally incapable of judging of it for one who is capable; and the capacity of the hundredth person is only comparative; for the majority of the eminent men of every past generation held many opinions now known to be erroneous, and did or approved numerous things which no one will now justify. Why is it, then, that there is on the whole a preponderance among mankind of rational opinions and rational conduct? If there really is this preponderance—which there must be unless human affairs are, and have always been, in an almost desperate state—it is owing to a quality of the human mind, the source of everything respectable in man either as an intellectual or as a moral being, namely, that his errors are corrigible. He is capable of rectifying his mistakes, by discussion and experience. Not by experience alone. There must be discussion, to show how experience is to be interpreted. Wrong opinions and practices gradually yield to fact and argument; but facts and arguments to produce any effect on the mind, must be brought before it. Very few facts are able to tell their own story, without comments to bring out their meaning. The whole strength and value, then, of human judgment, depending on the one property, that it can be set right when it is wrong, reliance can be placed on it only when the means of setting it right are kept constantly at hand. In the case of any person whose judgment is really deserving of confidence, how has it become so? Because he has kept his mind open to criticism of his opinions and conduct. Because it has been his practice to listen to all that could be said against him; to profit by as much of it as was just, and expound to himself, and upon occasion to others, the fallacy of what was fallacious. Because he has felt, that the only way in which a human being can make some approach to knowing the whole of a subject, is by hearing what can be said about it by persons of every variety of opinion, and studying all modes in which it can be looked at by every character of mind. No wise man ever acquired his wisdom in any mode but this; nor is it in the nature of human intellect to become wise in any other manner. The steady habit of correcting and completing his own opinion by collating it with those of others, so far from causing doubt and hesitation in carrying it into practice, is the only stable foundation for a just reliance on it: for, being cognizant of all that can, at least obviously, be said against him, and having taken up his position against all gainsayers—knowing that he has sought for objections and difficulties, instead of avoiding them, and has shut out no light which can be thrown upon the subject from any quarter—he has a right to think his judgment better than that of any person, or any multitude, who have not gone through a similar process.

It is not too much to require that what the wisest of mankind, those who are best entitled to trust their own judgment, find necessary to warrant their relying on it, should be submitted to by that miscellaneous collection of a few wise and many foolish individuals, called the public. The most intolerant of churches, the Roman Catholic Church, even at the canonization of a saint, admits, and listens patiently to, a "devil's advocate." The holiest of men, it appears, cannot be admitted to posthumous honors, until all that the devil could say against him is known and weighed. If even the Newtonian philosophy were not permitted to be questioned, mankind could not feel as complete assurance of its truth as they now do. The beliefs which we have most warrant for have no safeguard to rest on, but a standing invitation to the whole world to prove them unfounded. If the challenge is not accepted, or is accepted and the attempt fails, we are far enough from certainty still; but we have done the best that the existing state of human reason admits of; we have neglected nothing that could give the truth a chance of reaching us: if the lists are kept open, we may hope that if there be a better truth, it will be found when the human mind is capable of receiving it; and in the meantime we may rely on having attained such approach to truth as is possible in our own day. This is the amount of certainty attainable by a fallible being, and this the sole way of attaining it.

Strange it is, that men should admit the validity of the arguments for free discussion, but object to their being "pushed to an extreme"; not seeing that unless the reasons are good for an extreme case, they are not good for any case. Strange that they should imagine that they are not assuming infallibility, when they acknowledge that there should be free discussion on all subjects which can possibly be *doubtful,* but think that some particular principle or doctrine should be forbidden to be questioned because it is so *certain,* that is, because *they are certain* that it is certain. To call any proposition certain, while there is any one who would deny its certainty if permitted, but who is not permitted, is to assume that we ourselves, and those who agree with us, are the judges of certainty, and judges without hearing the other side.

In the present age—which has been described as "destitute of faith, but terrified at scepticism"—in which people feel sure, not so much that their opinions are true, as that they should not know what to do without them—the claims of an opinion to be protected from public attack are rested not so much on its truth, as on its importance to society. There are, it is alleged, certain beliefs so useful, not to say indispensable, to well-being that it is as much the duty of governments to uphold those beliefs, as to protect any other of the interests of society. In a case of such necessity, and so directly in the line of their duty, something less than infallibility may, it is maintained, warrant, and even bind, governments to act on their own opinion, confirmed by the general opinion of mankind. It is also often argued, and still oftener thought, that none but bad men would desire to weaken these salutary beliefs; and there can be nothing wrong, it is thought, in restraining bad men, and prohibiting what only such men would wish to practise. This mode of thinking makes the justification of restraints on discussion not a question of the truth of doctrines, but of their usefulness; and flatters itself by that means to escape the responsibility of claiming to be an infallible judge of opinions. But those who thus satisfy themselves, do not perceive that the assumption of infallibility is merely shifted from one point to another. The usefulness of an opinion is itself matter of opinion: as disputable, as open to discussion, and requiring discussion as much as the opinion itself. There is the same need of an infallible judge of opinions to decide an opinion to be noxious, as to decide it to be false, unless the opinion condemned has full opportunity of defending itself. And it will not do to say that the heretic may be allowed to maintain the utility or harmlessness of his opinion, though forbidden to maintain its truth. The truth of an opinion is part of its utility. If we would know whether or not it is desirable that a proposition should be believed, is it possible to exclude the consideration of whether or not it is true? In the opinion, not of bad men, but of the best men, no belief which is contrary to truth can be really useful: and can you prevent such men from urging that plea, when they are charged with culpability for denying some doctrine which they are told is useful, but which they believe to be false? Those who are on the side of received opinions never fail to take all possible advantage of this plea; you do not find *them* handling the question of utility as if it could be completely abstracted from that of truth: on the contrary, it is, above all, because their doctrine is "the truth," that the knowledge or the belief of it is held to be so indispensable. There can be no fair discussion of the question of usefulness when an argument so vital may be employed on one side, but not on the other. And in point of fact, when law or public feeling do not permit the truth of an opinion to be disputed, they are just as little tolerant of a denial of its usefulness. The utmost they allow is an extenuation of its absolute necessity, or of the positive guilt of rejecting it. . . .

A theory which maintains that truth may justifiably be persecuted because persecution cannot possibly do it any harm, cannot be charged with being intentionally hostile to the reception of new truths; but we cannot commend the generosity of its dealing with the persons to whom mankind are indebted for them. To discover to the world something which deeply concerns it, and of which it was previously ignorant; to prove to it that it had been mistaken on some vital point of temporal or spiritual interest, is as important a service as a human being can render to his fellow-creatures, and in certain cases, as in those of the early Christians and of the Reformers, those who think with Dr. Johnson believe it to have been the most precious gift which could be bestowed on mankind. That the authors of such splendid benefits should be required by martyrdom; that their reward should be to be dealt with as the vilest of criminals, is not, upon this theory, a deplorable error and misfortune, for which humanity should mourn in sackcloth and ashes, but the normal and justifiable state of things. The propounder of a new truth, according to this doctrine, should stand, as stood, in the legislation of the Locrians, the proposer of a new law, with a halter round his neck, to be instantly tightened if the public assembly did not, on hearing his reasons, then and there adopt his proposition. People who defend this mode of treating benefactors cannot be supposed to set much value on the benefit; and I believe this view of the subject is mostly confined to the sort of persons who think that new truths may have been desirable once, but that we have had enough of them now.

But, indeed, the dictum that truth always triumphs over persecution is one of those pleasant falsehoods which men repeat after one another till they pass into commonplaces, but which all experience refutes. History teems with instances of truth put down by persecution. If not suppressed forever, it may be thrown back for centuries. To speak only of religious opinions: the Reformation broke out at least twenty times before Luther, and was put down. Arnold of Brescia was put down. Fra Dolcino was put down. Savonarola was put down. The Albigeois were put down. The Vaudois were put down. The Lollards were put down. The Hussites were put down. Even after the era of Luther, wherever persecution was persisted in, it was successful. In Spain, Italy, Flanders, the Austrian Empire, Protestantism was rooted out; and, most likely, would have been so in England, had Queen Mary lived, or Queen Elizabeth died. Persecution has always succeeded, save where the heretics were too strong a party to be effectually persecuted. No reasonable person can doubt that Christianity might have been extirpated in the Roman Empire. It spread, and became predominant, because the persecutions were only

occasional, lasting but a short time, and separated by long
intervals of almost undisturbed propagandism. It is a piece of
idle sentimentality that truth, merely as truth, has any inherent
power denied to error of prevailing against the dungeon and the
stake. Men are not more zealous for truth than they often are
for error, and a sufficient application of legal and even of social
penalties will generally succeed in stopping the propagation of
either. The real advantage which truth has consists in this,
that when an opinion is true, it may be extinguished once,
twice, or many times, but in the course of ages there will generally be found persons to rediscover it, until some one of its
reappearances falls on a time when from favorable circumstances it escapes persecution until it has made such head as
to withstand all subsequent attempts to suppress it.

It will be said, that we do not now put to death the intro-
ducers of new opinions: we are not like our fathers who slew
the prophets, we even build sepulchres to them. It is true we
no longer put heretics to death; and the amount of penal in-
fliction which modern feeling would probably tolerate, even
against the most obnoxious opinions, is not sufficient to extirpate them. But let us not flatter ourselves that we are yet free
from the stain even of legal persecution. Penalties for opinion,
or at least for its expression, still exist by law; and their enforcement is not, even in these times, so unexampled as to
make it at all incredible that they may some day be revived in
full force. In the year 1857, at the summer assizes of the county
of Cornwall, an unfortunate man, said to be of unexceptionable
conduct in all relations of life, was sentenced to twenty-one
months' imprisonment, for uttering, and writing on a gate,
some offensive words concerning Christianity. Within a month
of the same time, at the Old Bailey, two persons, on two separate occasions, were rejected as jurymen, and one of them
grossly insulted by the judge and by one of the counsel, because they honestly declared that they had no theological belief; and a third, a foreigner, for the same reason, was denied
justice against a thief. This refusal of redress took place in
virtue of the legal doctrine, that no person can be allowed to
give evidence in a court of justice who does not profess belief
in a God (any god is sufficient) and in a future state; which is

equivalent to declaring such persons to be outlaws, excluded from the protection of the tribunals; who may not only be robbed or assaulted with impunity, if no one but themselves, or persons of similar opinions, be present, but any one else may be robbed or assaulted with impunity, if the proof of the fact depends on their evidence. The assumption on which this is grounded is that the oath is worthless of a person who does not believe in a future state; a proposition which betokens much ignorance of history in those who assent to it (since it is historically true that a large proportion of infidels in all ages have been persons of distinguished integrity and honor); and would be maintained by no one who had the smallest conception how many of the persons in greatest repute with the world, both for virtues and attainments, are well known, at least to their intimates, to be unbelievers. The rule, besides, is suicidal, and cuts away its own foundation. Under pretence that atheists must be liars, it admits the testimony of all atheists who are willing to lie, and rejects only those who brave the obloquy of publicly confessing a detested creed rather than affirm a falsehood. A rule thus self-convicted of absurdity so far as regards its professed purpose, can be kept in force only as a badge of hatred, a relic of persecution; a persecution, too, having the peculiarity that the qualification for undergoing it is the being clearly proved not to deserve it. The rule, and the theory it implies, are hardly less insulting to believers than to infidels. For if he who does not believe in a future state necessarily lies, it follows that they who do believe are only prevented from lying, if prevented they are, by the fear of hell. We will not do the authors and abettors of the rule the injury of supposing that the conception which they have formed of Christian virtue is drawn from their own consciousness. . . .

Let us now pass to the second division of the argument, and dismissing the supposition that any of the received opinions may be false, let us assume them to be true, and examine into the worth of the manner in which they are likely to be held, when their truth is not freely and openly canvassed. However unwillingly a person who has a strong opinion may admit the possibility that his opinion may be false he ought to be moved by the consideration that, however true it may be, if it is not fully, frequently, and fearlessly discussed, it will be held as a dead dogma, not a living truth.

There is a class of persons (happily not quite so numerous as formerly) who think it enough if a person assents undoubtingly to what they think true, though he has no knowledge whatever of the grounds of the opinion, and could not make a tenable defence of it against the most superficial objections. Such persons, if they can once get their creed taught from authority, naturally think that no good, and some harm, comes of its being allowed to be questioned. Where their influence prevails, they make it nearly impossible for the received opinion to be rejected wisely and considerately, though it may still be rejected rashly and ignorantly; for to shut out discussion entirely is seldom possible, and when it once gets in, beliefs not grounded on conviction are apt to give way before the slightest semblance of an argument. Waiving, however, this possibility—assuming that the true opinion abides in the mind, but abides as a prejudice, a belief independent of, and proof against, argument—this is not the way in which truth ought to be held by a rational being. This is not knowing the truth. Truth, thus held, is but one superstition the more, accidentally clinging to the words which enunciate a truth.

If the intellect and judgment of mankind ought to be cultivated, a thing which Protestants at least do not deny, on what can these faculties be more appropriately exercised by anyone, than on the things which concern him so much that it is considered necessary for him to hold opinions on them? If the cultivation of the understanding consists in one thing more than in another, it is surely in learning the grounds of one's own opinions. Whatever people believe, on subjects on which it is of the first importance to believe rightly, they ought to be able to defend against at least the common objections. But, someone may say, "Let them be *taught* the grounds of their opinions. It does not follow that opinions must be merely parroted because they are never heard controverted. Persons who learn geometry do not simply commit the theorems to memory, but understand and learn likewise the demonstrations; and it would be absurd to say that they remain ignorant of the grounds of geometrical truths, because they never hear any-

one deny, and attempt to disprove them." Undoubtedly: and
such teaching suffices on a subject like mathematics, where
there is nothing at all to be said on the wrong side of the question. The peculiarity of the evidence of mathematical truths
is that all the argument is on one side. There are no objections,
and no answers to objections. But on every subject on which
difference of opinion is possible, the truth depends on a balance to be struck between two sets of conflicting reasons. Even
in natural philosophy, there is always some other explanation
possible of the same facts; some geocentric theory instead of
heliocentric, some phlogiston instead of oxygen; and it has to
be shown why that other theory cannot be the true one: and
until this is shown, and until we know how it is shown, we do
not understand the grounds of our opinion. But when we turn
to subjects infinitely more complicated, to morals, religion,
politics, social relations, and the business of life, three-fourths
of the arguments for every disputed opinion consist in dispell-
ing the appearances which favor some opinion different from
it. The greatest orator, save one, of antiquity, has left it on
record that he always studied his adversary's case with as
great, if not still greater, intensity than even his own. What
Cicero practised as the means of forensic success requires to
be imitated by all who study any subject in order to arrive at
the truth. He who knows only his own side of the case, knows
little of that. His reasons may be good, and no one may have
been able to refute them. But if he is equally unable to refute
the reasons on the opposite side; if he does not so much as
know what they are, he has no ground for preferring either
opinion. The rational position for him would be suspension of
judgment, and unless he contents himself with that, he is
either led by authority, or adopts, like the generality of the
world, the side to which he feels most inclination. Nor is it
enough that he should hear the arguments of adversaries from
his own teachers, presented as they state them, and accompanied by what they offer as refutations. That is not the way to
do justice to the arguments, or bring them into real contact
with his own mind. He must be able to hear them from persons who actually believe them; who defend them in earnest,
and do their very utmost for them. He must know them in their

most plausible and persuasive form; he must feel the whole
force of the difficulty which the true view of the subject has to
encounter and dispose of; else he will never really possess himself of the portion of truth which meets and removes that difficulty. Ninety-nine in a hundred of what are called educated
men are in this condition; even of those who can argue fluently
for their opinions. Their conclusion may be true, but it might
be false for anything they know; they have never thrown themselves into the mental position of those who think differently
from them, and considered what such persons may have to say;
and consequently they do not, in any proper sense of the word,
know the doctrine which they themselves profess. They do
not know those parts of it which explain and justify the remainder; the considerations which show that a fact which
seemingly conflicts with another is reconcilable with it, or
that, of two apparently strong reasons, one and not the other
ought to be preferred. All that part of the truth which turns
the scale, and decides the judgment of a completely informed
mind, they are strangers to; nor is it ever really known, but to
those who have attended equally and impartially to both sides,
and endeavored to see the reasons of both in the strongest
light. So essential is this discipline to a real understanding of
moral and human subjects, that if opponents of all important
truths do not exist, it is indispensable to imagine them, and
supply them with the strongest arguments which the most
skillful devil's advocate can conjure up.

To abate the force of these considerations, an enemy of
free discussion may be supposed to say, that there is no necessity for mankind in general to know and understand all that
can be said against or for their opinions by philosophers and
theologians. That it is not needful for common men to be able
to expose all the misstatements or fallacies of an ingenious
opponent. That it is enough if there is always somebody capable of answering them, so that nothing likely to mislead
uninstructed persons remains unrefuted. That simple minds,
having been taught the obvious grounds of the truths inculcated
on them, may trust to authority for the rest, and being aware
that they have neither knowledge nor talent to resolve every
difficulty which can be raised, may repose in the assurance

that all those which have been raised have been or can be answered, by those who are specially trained to the task.

Conceding to this view of the subject the utmost that can be claimed for it by those most easily satisfied with the amount of understanding of truth which ought to accompany the belief of it; even so, the argument for free discussion is no way weakened. For even this doctrine acknowledges that mankind ought to have a rational assurance that all objections have been satisfactorily answered; and how are they to be answered if that which requires to be answered is not spoken? or how can the answer be known to be satisfactory, if the objectors have no opportunity of showing that it is unsatisfactory? If not the public, at least the philosophers and theologians who are to resolve the difficulties, must make themselves familiar with those difficulties in their most puzzling form; and this cannot be accomplished unless they are freely stated, and placed in the most advantageous light which they admit of. The Catholic Church has its own way of dealing with this embarrassing problem. It makes a broad separation between those who can be permitted to receive its doctrines on conviction, and those who must accept them on trust. Neither, indeed, are allowed any choice as to what they will accept; but the clergy, such at least as can be fully confided in, may admissibly and meritoriously make themselves acquainted with the arguments of opponents, in order to answer them, and may, therefore, read heretical books; the laity, not unless by special permission, hard to be obtained. This discipline recognizes a knowledge of the enemy's case as beneficial to the teachers, but finds means, consistent with this, of denying it to the rest of the world: thus giving to the *élite* more mental culture, though not more mental freedom, than it allows to the mass. By this device it succeeds in obtaining the kind of mental superiority which its purposes require; for though culture without freedom never made a large and liberal mind, it can make a clever *nisi prius* advocate of a cause. But in countries professing Protestantism, this resource is denied; since Protestants hold, at least in theory, that the responsibility for the choice of a religion must be borne by each for himself, and cannot be thrown off upon teachers. Besides, in the present state of the world, it is practically impossible that writings which are read by the instructed can be kept from the uninstructed. If the teachers of mankind are to be cognizant of all that they ought to know, everything must be free to be written and published without restraint.

If, however, the mischievous operation of the absence of free discussion, when the received opinions are true, were confined to leaving men ignorant of the grounds of those opinions, it might be thought that this, if an intellectual, is no moral evil, and does not affect the worth of the opinions, regarded in their influence on the character. The fact, however, is, that not only the grounds of the opinion are forgotten in the absence of discussion, but too often the meaning of the opinion itself. The words which convey it cease to suggest ideas, or suggest only a small portion of those they were originally employed to communicate. Instead of a vivid conception and a living belief, there remain only a few phrases retained by rote; or, if any part, the shell and husk only of the meaning is retained, the finer essence being lost. The great chapter in human history which this fact occupies and fills, cannot be too earnestly studied and meditated on.

It is illustrated in the experience of almost all ethical doctrines and religious creeds. They are all full of meaning and vitality to those who originate them, and to the direct disciples of the originators. Their meaning continues to be felt in undiminished strength, and is perhaps brought out into even fuller consciousness, so long as the struggle lasts to give the doctrine or creed an ascendancy over other creeds. At last it either prevails, and becomes the general opinion, or its progress stops; it keeps possession of the ground it has gained, but ceases to spread further. When either of these results has become apparent, controversy on the subject flags, and gradually dies away. The doctrine has taken its place, if not as a received opinion, as one of the admitted sects or divisions of opinion: those who hold it have generally inherited, not adopted it; and conversion from one of these doctrines to another, being now an exceptional fact, occupies little place in the thoughts of their professors. Instead of being, as at first, constantly on the alert either to defend themselves against the world, or to bring the world over to them, they have subsided into acquiescence, and neither listen, when they can help it, to arguments against their creed, nor trouble dissentients (if there be such) with arguments in its favor. From this time may usually be dated the decline in the living power of the doctrine. We often hear the teachers of all creeds lamenting the difficulty of keeping up in the minds of believers a lively apprehension of the truth which they nominally recognize, so that it may penetrate the feelings, and acquire a real mastery over the conduct. No such difficulty is complained of while the creed is still fighting for its existence: even the weaker combatants then know and feel what they are fighting for, and the difference between it and other doctrines; and in that period of every creed's existence, not a few persons may be found, who have realized its fundamental principles in all the forms of thought, have weighed and considered them in all their important bearings, and have experienced the full effect on the character which belief in that creed ought to produce in a mind thoroughly imbued with it. But when it has come to be an hereditary creed, and to be received passively, not actively —when the mind is no longer compelled, in the same degree as at first, to exercise its vital powers on the questions which its belief presents to it, there is a progressive tendency to forget all of the belief except the formularies, or to give it a dull and torpid assent, as if accepting it on trust dispensed with the necessity of realizing it in consciousness, or testing it by personal experience, until it almost ceases to connect itself at all with the inner life of the human being. Then are seen the cases, so frequent in this age of the world as almost to form the majority, in which the creed remains as it were outside the mind, incrusting and petrifying it against all other influences addressed to the higher parts of our nature; manifesting its power by not suffering any fresh and living conviction to get in, but itself doing nothing for the mind or heart, except standing sentinel over them to keep them vacant.

To what an extent doctrines intrinsically fitted to make the deepest impression upon the mind may remain in it as dead beliefs, without being ever realized in the imagination, the feelings, or the understanding, is exemplified by the manner in which the majority of believers hold the doctrines of Christianity. By Christianity I here mean what is accounted such by all churches and sects—the maxims and precepts contained in the New Testament. These are considered sacred, and accepted as laws, by all professing Christians. Yet it is scarcely too much to say that not one Christian in a thousand guides or tests his individual conduct by reference to those laws. The standard to which he does refer it, is the custom of his nation, his class, or his religious profession. He has thus, on the one hand, a collection of ethical maxims, which he believes to have been vouchsafed to him by infallible wisdom as rules for his government; and on the other a set of everyday judgments and practices, which go a certain length with some of those maxims, not so great a length with others, stand in direct opposition to some, and are, on the whole, a compromise between the Christian creed and the interests and suggestions of worldly life. To the first of these standards he gives his homage; to the other his real allegiance. All Christians believe that the blessed are the poor and humble, and those who are ill-used by the world; that it is easier for a camel to pass through the eye of a needle than for a rich man to enter the kingdom of heaven; that they should judge not, lest they be judged; that they should swear not at all; that they should love their neighbor as themselves; that if one take their cloak, they should give him their coat also; that they should take no thought for the morrow; that if they would be perfect they should sell all that they have and give it to the poor. They are not insincere when they say that they believe these things. They do believe them, as people believe what they have always heard lauded and never discussed. But in the sense of that living belief which regulates conduct, they believe these doctrines just up to the point to which it is usual to act upon them. The doctrines in their integrity are serviceable to pelt adversaries with; and it is understood that they are to be put forward (when possible) as the reasons for whatever people do that they think laudable. But anyone who reminded them that the maxims require an infinity of things which they never even think of doing, would gain nothing but to be classed among those very unpopular characters who affect to be better than other people. The doctrines have no hold on ordinary believers—are not a power in their minds. They have an habitual respect for the sound of them, but no feeling which spreads from the words to the things signified, and forces the mind to take *them* in, and make them conform to the formula. Whenever conduct is concerned, they look round for Mr. A and B to direct them how far to go in obeying Christ.

Now we may be well assured that the case was not thus, but far otherwise, with the early Christians. Had it been thus, Christianity never would have expanded from an obscure sect of the despised Hebrews into the religion of the Roman empire. When their enemies said, "See how these Christians love one another" (a remark not likely to be made by anybody now), they assuredly had a much livelier feeling of the meaning of their creed than they have ever had since. And to this cause, probably, it is chiefly owing that Christianity now makes so little progress in extending its domain, and after eighteen centuries is still nearly confined to Europeans and the descendants of Europeans. Even with the strictly religious, who are much in earnest about their doctrines, and attach a greater amount of meaning to many of them than people in general, it commonly happens that the part which is thus comparatively active in their minds is that which was made by Calvin, or Knox, or some such person much nearer in character to themselves. The sayings of Christ coexist passively in their minds, producing hardly any effect beyond what is caused by mere listening to words so amiable and bland. There are many reasons, doubtless, why doctrines which are the badge of a sect retain more of their vitality than those common to all recognized sects, and why more pains are taken by teachers to keep their meaning alive; but one reason certainly is, that the peculiar doctrines are more questioned, and have to be oftener defended against open gainsayers. Both teachers and learners go to sleep at their post, as soon as there is no enemy in the field.

The same thing holds true, generally speaking, of all traditional doctrines—those of prudence and knowledge of life, as well as of morals or religion. All languages and literatures are full of general observations on life, both as to what it is, and how to conduct oneself in it; observations which everybody knows, which everybody repeats, or hears with acquiescence, which are received as truisms, yet of which most people first truly learn the meaning when experience, generally of a painful kind, has made it a reality to them. How often, when smarting under some unforeseen misfortune or disappointment, does a person call to mind some proverb or common saying, familiar to him all his life, the meaning of which, if he had ever before felt it as he does now, would have saved him from the calamity. There are indeed reasons for this, other than the absence of discussion; there are many truths of which the full meaning *cannot* be realized until personal experience has brought it home. But much more of the meaning even of these would have been understood, and what was understood would have been far more deeply impressed on the mind, if the man had been accustomed to hear it argued *pro* and *con* by people who did understand it. The fatal tendency of mankind to leave off thinking about a thing when it is no longer doubtful, is the cause of half their errors. A contemporary author has well spoken of "the deep slumber of a decided opinion."

But what! (it may be asked) Is the absence of unanimity any indispensable condition of true knowledge? Is it necessary that some part of mankind should persist in error to enable any to realize the truth? Does a belief cease to be real and vital as soon as it is generally received—and is a proposition never thoroughly understood and felt unless some doubt of it remains? As soon as mankind have unanimously accepted a truth, does the truth perish within them? The highest aim and best result of improved intelligence, it has hitherto been thought, is to unite mankind more and more in the acknowledgement of all important truths; and does the intelligence only last as long as it has not achieved its object? Do the fruits of conquest perish by the very completeness of the victory?

I affirm no such thing. As mankind improve, the number of doctrines which are no longer disputed or doubted will be constantly on the increase: and the well-being of mankind may almost be measured by the number and gravity of the truths which have reached the point of being uncontested. The cessation, on one question after another, of serious controversy, is one of the necessary incidents of the consolidation of opinion;

a consolidation as salutary in the case of true opinions, as it is dangerous and noxious when the opinions are erroneous. But though this gradual narrowing of the bounds of diversity of opinion is necessary in both senses of the term, being at once inevitable and indispensable, we are not therefore obliged to conclude that all its consequences must be beneficial. The loss of so important an aid to the intelligent and living apprehension of a truth, as is afforded by the necessity of explaining it to, or defending it against, opponents, though not sufficient to outweigh, is no trifling drawback from, the benefit of its universal recognition. Where this advantage can no longer be had, I confess I should like to see the teachers of mankind endeavoring to provide a substitute for it; some contrivance for making the difficulties of the question as present to the learner's consciousness, as if they were pressed upon him by a dissentient champion, eager for his conversion.

But instead of seeking contrivances for this purpose, they have lost those they formerly had. The Socratic dialectics, so magnificently exemplified in the dialogues of Plato, were a contrivance of this description. They were essentially a negative discussion of the great question of philosophy and life, directed with consummate skill to the purpose of convincing anyone who had merely adopted the commonplaces of received opinion that he did not understand the subject—that he as yet attached no definite meaning to the doctrines he professed; in order that, becoming aware of his ignorance, he might be put in the way to obtain a stable belief, resting on a clear apprehension both of the meaning of doctrines and of their evidence. The school disputations of the Middle Ages had a somewhat similar object. They were intended to make sure that the pupil understood his own opinion, and (by necessary correlation) the opinion opposed to it, and could enforce the grounds of the one and confute those of the other. These last-mentioned contests had indeed the incurable defect, that the premises appealed to were taken from authority, not from reason; and, as a discipline to the mind, they were in every respect inferior to the powerful dialectics which formed the intellects of the "Socratici viri"; but the modern mind owes far more to both than it is generally willing to admit, and the present modes of education contain nothing which in the smallest degree supplies the place either of the one or of the other. A person who derives all his instruction from teachers or books, even if he escape the besetting temptation of contenting himself with cram, is under no compulsion to hear both sides; accordingly it is far from a frequent accomplishment, even among thinkers, to know both sides; and the weakest part of what everybody says in defence of his opinion is what he intends as a reply to antagonists. It is the fashion of the present time to disparage negative logic—that which points out weaknesses in theory or errors in practice, without establishing positive truths. Such negative criticism would indeed be poor enough as an ultimate result; but as a means to attaining any positive knowledge or conviction worthy the name, it cannot be valued too highly; and until people are again systematically trained to it, there will be few great thinkers, and a low general average of intellect, in any but the mathematical and physical departments of speculation. On any other subject no one's opinions deserve the name of knowledge, except so far as he has either had forced upon him by others, or gone through of himself, the same mental process which would have been required of him in carrying on an active controversy with opponents. That, therefore, which when absent, it is so indispensable, but so difficult, to create, how worse than absurd it is to forego, when spontaneously offering itself! If there are any persons who contest a received opinion, or who will do so if law or opinion will let them, let us thank them for it, open our minds to listen to them, and rejoice that there is someone to do for us what we otherwise ought, if we have any regard for either the certainty or the vitality of our convictions, to do with much greater labor for ourselves.

It still remains to speak of one of the principal causes which make diversity of opinion advantageous, and will continue to do so until mankind shall have entered a stage of intellectual advancement which at present seems at an incalculable distance. We have hitherto considered only two possibilities: that the received opinion may be false, and some other opinion, consequently, true; or that, the received opinion being true, a

conflict with the opposite error is essential to a clear apprehension and deep feeling of its truth. But there is a commoner
case than either of these; when the conflicting doctrines, instead of being one true and the other false, share the truth
between them; and the nonconforming opinion is needed to
supply the remainder of the truth, of which the received doctrine embodies only a part. Popular opinions, on subjects not
palpable to sense, are often true, but seldom or never the whole
truth. They are a part of the truth; sometimes a greater, sometimes a smaller part, but exaggerated, distorted, and disjointed
from the truths by which they ought to be accompanied and
limited. Heretical opinions, on the other hand, are generally
some of these suppressed and neglected truths, bursting the
bonds which kept them down, and either seeking reconciliation
with the truth contained in the common opinion, or fronting it
as enemies, and setting themselves up, with similar exclusiveness, as the whole truth. The latter case is hitherto the most
frequent, as, in the human mind, one-sidedness has always
been the rule, and many-sidedness the exception. Hence, even
in revolutions of opinion, one part of the truth usually sets
while another rises. Even progress, which ought to superadd,
for the most part only substitutes, one partial and incomplete
truth for another; improvement consisting chiefly in this, that
the new fragment of truth is more wanted, more adapted to the
needs of the time, than that which it displaces. Such being
the partial character of prevailing opinions, even when resting
on a true foundation, every opinion which embodies somewhat
of the portion of truth which the common opinion omits, ought
to be considered precious, with whatever amount of error and
confusion that truth may be blended. No sober judge of human
affairs will feel bound to be indignant because those who force
on our notice truths which we should otherwise have overlooked, overlook some of those which we see. Rather, he will
think that so long as popular truth is one-sided, it is more desirable than otherwise that unpopular truth should have one-
sided assertors too; such being usually the most energetic, and
the most likely to compel reluctant attention to the fragment
of wisdom which they proclaim as if it were the whole.

This, in the eighteenth century, when nearly all the in-

structed, and all those of the uninstructed who were led by
them, were lost in admiration of what is called civilization,
and of the marvels of modern science, literature, and philosophy, and while greatly overrating the amount of unlikeness
between the men of modern and those of ancient times, in-
dulged the belief that the whole of the difference was in their
own favor; with what a salutary shock did the paradoxes of
Rousseau explode like bombshells in the midst, dislocating the
compact mass of one-sided opinion, and forcing its elements to
recombine in a better form and with additional ingredients.
Not that the current opinions were on the whole farther from
the truth than Rousseau's were; on the contrary, they were
nearer to it; they contained more of positive truth, and very
much less of error. Nevertheless there lay in Rousseau's doctrine, and has floated down the stream of opinion along with
it, a considerable amount of exactly those truths which the
popular opinion wanted; and these are the deposit which was
left behind when the flood subsided. The superior worth of simplicity of life, the enervating and demoralizing effect of the
trammels and hypocrisies of artificial society, are ideas which
have never been entirely absent from cultivated minds since
Rousseau wrote; and they will in time produce their due effect,
though at present needing to be asserted as much as ever, and
to be asserted by deeds, for words, on this subject, have nearly
exhausted their power.

In politics, again, it is almost a commonplace, that a party
of order or stability, and a party of progress or reform, are both
necessary elements of a healthy state of political life; until
the one or the other shall have so enlarged its mental grasp
as to be a party equally of order and of progress, knowing and
distinguishing what is fit to be preserved from what ought to be
swept away. Each of these modes of thinking derives its utility
from the deficiencies of the other; but it is in a great measure
the opposition of the other that keeps each within the limits of
reason and sanity. Unless opinions favorable to democracy
and to aristocracy, to property and to equality, to co-operation
and to competition, to luxury and to abstinence, to sociality
and individuality, to liberty and discipline, and all the other
standing antagonisms of practical life, are expressed with

equal freedom, and enforced and defended with equal talent and energy, there is no chance of both elements obtaining their due; one scale is sure to go up, and the other down. Truth, in the great practical concerns of life, is so much a question of the reconciling and combining of opposites, that very few have minds sufficiently capacious and impartial to make the adjustment with an approach to correctness, and it has to be made by the rough process of a struggle between combatants fighting under hostile banners. On any of the great open questions just enumerated, if either of the two opinions has a better claim than the other, not merely to be tolerated, but to be encouraged and countenanced, it is the one which happens at the particular time and place to be in a minority. That is the opinion which, for the time being, represents the neglected interests, the side of human well-being which is in danger of obtaining less than its share. I am aware that there is not, in this country, any intolerance of differences of opinion on most of these topics. They are adduced to show, by admitted and multiplied examples, the universality of the fact, that only through diversity of opinion is there, in the existing state of human intellect, a chance of fair play to all sides of the truth. When there are persons to be found who form an exception to the apparent unanimity of the world on any subject, even if the world is in the right, it is always probable that dissentients have something worth hearing to say for themselves, and that truth would lose something by their silence. . . .

We have now recognized the necessity to the mental well-being of mankind (on which all their other well-being depends) of freedom of opinion, and freedom of the expression of opinion, on four distinct grounds; which we will now briefly recapitulate.

First, if any opinion is compelled to silence, that opinion may, for aught we can certainly know, be true. To deny this is to assume our own infallibility.

Secondly, though the silenced opinion be an error, it may, and very commonly does, contain a portion of truth; and since the general or prevailing opinion on any subject is rarely or never the whole truth, it is only by the collision of adverse opinions that the remainder of the truth has any chance of being supplied.

Thirdly, even if the received opinion be not only true, but the whole truth; unless it is suffered to be, and actually is, vigorously and earnestly contested, it will, by most of those who receive it, be held in the manner of a prejudice, with little comprehension or feeling of its rational grounds. And not only this, but, fourthly, the meaning of the doctrine itself will be in danger of being lost, or enfeebled, and deprived of its vital effect on the character and conduct: the dogma becoming a mere formal profession, inefficacious for good, but cumbering the ground, and preventing the growth of any real and heartfelt conviction, from reason or personal experience.

Before quitting the subject of freedom of opinion, it is fit to take some notice of those who say that the free expression of all opinions should be permitted, on condition that the manner be temperate, and do not pass the bounds of fair discussion. Much might be said on the impossibility of fixing where these supposed bounds are to be placed; for if the test be offence to those whose opinions are attacked, I think experience testifies that this offence is given whenever the attack is telling and powerful, and that every opponent who pushes them hard, and whom they find it difficult to answer, appears to them, if he shows any strong feeling on the subject, an intemperate opponent. But this, though an important consideration in a practical point of view, merges in a more fundamental objection. Undoubtedly the manner of asserting an opinion, even though it be a true one, may be very objectionable, and may justly incur severe censure. But the principal offences of the kind are such as it is mostly impossible, unless by accidental self-betrayal, to bring home to conviction. The gravest of them is, to argue sophistically, to suppress facts or arguments, to misstate the elements of the case, or misrepresent the opposite opinion. But all this, even to the most aggravated degree, is so continually done in perfect good faith, by persons who are not considered, and in many other respects may not deserve to be considered, ignorant or incompetent, that it is rarely possible, on adequate grounds, conscientiously to stamp the misrepresentation as morally culpable; and still less could law presume to interfere with this kind of controversial misconduct. With regard to what is commonly meant by intemperate discussion, namely invective, sarcasm, personality, and the like, the denunciation of these weapons would deserve more sympathy if it were ever proposed to interdict them equally to both sides; but it is only desired to restrain the employment of them against the prevailing opinion; against the unprevailing they may not only be used without general disapproval, but will be likely to obtain for him who uses them the praise of honest zeal and righteous indignation. Yet whatever mischief arises from their use is greatest when they are employed against the comparatively defenceless; and whatever unfair advantage can be derived by any opinion from this mode of asserting it, accrues almost exclusively to received opinions. The worst offence of this kind which can be committed by a polemic is to stigmatize those who hold the contrary opinion as bad and immoral men. To calumny of this sort, those who hold any unpopular opinion are peculiarly exposed, because they are in general few and uninfluential, and nobody but themselves feels much interested in seeing justice done them; but this weapon is, from the nature of the case, denied to those who attack a prevailing opinion: they can neither use it with safety to themselves, nor, if they could, would it do anything but recoil on their own cause. In general, opinions contrary to those commonly received can only obtain a hearing by studied moderation of language, and the most cautious avoidance of unnecessary offence, from which they hardly ever deviate even in a slight degree without losing ground: while unmeasured vituperation employed on the side of the prevailing opinion really does deter people from professing contrary opinions, and from listening to those who profess them. For the interest, therefore, of truth and justice, it is far more important to restrain this employment of vituperative language than the other; and, for example, if it were necessary to choose, there would be much more need to discourage offensive attacks on infidelity than on religion. It is, however, obvious that law and authority have no business with restraining either, while opinion ought, in every instance, to determine its verdict by the circumstances of the individual case; condemning everyone, on whichever side of the argument he places himself, in whose mode of advocacy either want of candor, or malignity, bigotry, or intolerance of feeling manifest themselves; but not inferring these vices from the side which a person takes, though it be the contrary side of the question to our own; and giving merited honor to everyone, whatever opinion he may hold, who has calmness to see and honesty to state what his opponents and their opinions really are, exaggerating nothing to their discredit, keeping nothing back which tells, or can be supposed to tell, in their favor. This is the real morality of public discussion: and if often violated, I am happy to think that there are many controversialists who to a great extent observe it, and a still greater number who conscientiously strive towards it.

QUESTIONS

1. In the second paragraph of his essay, Mill says, "It is necessary to consider . . . these two hypotheses. . . ." What are the two hypotheses?
2. List the arguments Mill gives in favor of freedom of expression.
3. How does Mill answer the argument that, since we must "assume our opinion to be true for the guidance of our own conduct . . . it is assuming no more when we forbid bad men to pervert society by the propagation of opinions which we regard as false and pernicious"?
4. What point does Mill establish by remarking that "the Reformation broke out at least twenty times before Luther, and was put down"?
5. What does Mill think of a truth held in the mind without having been subjected to contradictory argument or opinion? Explain.
6. Using the last five paragraphs as a guide, prepare a sentence outline of Mill's essay.
7. What methods of transition does Mill use between paragraphs? Does he always use "transitional phrases or clauses"? What inference about "logical development" can be drawn from the fact that many of the paragraphs lack traditional transitional elements?
8. Mill's essay was written over a hundred years ago. Do you note any difference in his punctuation from that commonly

used today? Note especially his use of colons and semicolons.

9. Compare Mill's essay with those of Smith and Barth, which follow. Which has the longest paragraphs? Can you account for the difference in length? Choose two of Mill's longest paragraphs and try to determine the "topic sentence" in each. Is it stated, or made clear by implication?

10. Make a list of five expressions used by Mill which you think would not be idiomatic today. Compare your list with those made by several of your classmates and ask your instructor to check it for you. Is your list composed of expressions which are not now idiomatic, or are they merely unfamiliar to you?

THE BILL OF RIGHTS AND
OUR INDIVIDUAL LIBERTIES
✎ T. V. Smith

If America is today skirting another Valley Forge, as many think, it may revive our spirits, will certainly give us perspective, if we recall Thomas Paine's stirring words at the first Valley Forge. "These are the times that try men's souls. The summer soldier and the sunshine patriot will, in this crisis, shrink . . . ; but he that stand it *now* deserves the love and thanks of man and woman. . . . What we obtain too cheap, we esteem too lightly . . . and it would be strange indeed if so celestial an article as *freedom* should not be highly regarded."

These words were spoken during dark revolutionary days, days tremulous with hope of freedom from a foreign yoke. They may quite as fittingly be spoken now of freedom for all high constitutional ends. But let us take our bearings with the aid of this distinction between freedom *from* and freedom *for*.

From the American Declaration of Independence to the Bill of Rights in the Federal Constitution was only some dozen years, as the calendar measures. But it is like a trip around the world, as ideas go. It represents the vast social distance between the uttermost of action and the innermost of reflection and meditation. The Declaration of Independence is a preface to heroic action, culminating with man's right to the "pursuit of happiness." But this pursuit of *happiness* was itself in large the happiness of *pursuit*.

A *Freedom Agenda* pamphlet published by the Carrie Chapman Catt Memorial Fund, Inc. (New York, 1954).

Revolutionary days, that is, called for deeds; and a dynamic document emerged to mark in moving rhetoric a new nation's "hour of truth."

Independence from somebody must normally come to mean freedom for something else. Things worthwhile are not restricted to the muscular, nor are they monopolized by those who must always be up and doing. In man, at least, the thyroid is subordinate to the cerebrum. There is a quieter side no less precious than the active side of human nature.

The difference here intended is in no small part that between the childhood and the manhood of the race. President Herbert Hoover once remarked from the White House that the boy is an animal who takes exercise on every possible occasion. Be it said, for it is so. But the fully-grown man is one who can, with William Wordsworth, breathe deeply the prayer:

> Thanks to the human heart by which we live,
> Thanks to its tenderness, its joys, and fears,
> To me the meanest flower that blows can give
> Thoughts that do often lie too deep for tears.

But as the active child is father of the reflective man, so the Constitution proper carries forward the emphasis of the Declaration upon action, changing it from the idiom of revolution to the tempo of evolution. It sets up the machinery of effectiveness as touching the things which are to be done by citizens acting together. It supplements the art of sweet reasonableness with the technique of compromise for tensional times. The Constitution arose to rectify a government too weak to govern; but our Fathers did not forget that one's own government, only somewhat less than a foreign master, might go too far and make a mockery of human rights. The American Constitution made so nice an adjustment of the three departments of power—legislative, executive, judicial—that both the will to power and the temptation to complacency are kept under control. Revolutionary times made uppermost the fear of too much government, as our times warn against a government too weak to command respect. It was realistic in our Fathers and it remains prudent in us to remember that the legislative may encroach, the executive may trespass, and even the judicial may err. Protection was required, and is required, to safeguard man's right *to be* no less than his right *to do*.

It is precisely this intimate protection which the Bill of Rights (the first ten amendments to the Constitution) seeks to provide. It adds a new dimension to aspiration by recognizing man as something more than an animal full of activity. The private side of man needs protection from the public. It was this all important matter which Justice Brandeis had in mind when he declared that the Bill of Rights "conferred as against the government the right to be let alone—the most comprehensive of rights and the right most valued by civilized men."

It is this tenderness toward the intimate as over against the overt which we have in mind, or ought to have in mind, when we make a shibboleth of the sacredness of the individual. However moving may be the outer show of marching men, of humanity in action, there is something more majestic still which goes on in the citadel of the soul. Immanuel Kant, the German philosopher, spoke of first things in elevating the "moral law within" above even the "starry heavens at night." However we describe the inward, the show behind the scenes beggars the glittering spectacle before the footlights of history or spread across the canopy of nature. "In the greenwood of man's soul," as Ralph Hodgson says, "a little eye keeps shining." It is inwardly, in the absoluteness of thought, where each individual celebrates what to him is the high design of life.

Now what a man does with his privacy is not public business. It is his sovereign privilege to refuse, with Thoreau, to join up with other men at all; it is indeed his right to do nothing at all—but nothing—save to sit down and think things over. This right and this capacity to meditate, to contemplate, indeed to worship, yea to find in the solitary enterprise the very meaning of life itself, spells out man's sacred right "to be let alone." It is this double-edged freedom—to live alone and to luxuriate in it—which the Bill of Rights is mostly about. Through it we come face to face with man's inviolable right *to be*.

In fashion less abstract, it is these two dimensions of life which we celebrate in the historic distinction between what a citizen may think and what he may do. Belief and action, these two, represent the poles of our human enterprise; but these poles are so far apart that some intermediate medium is required to make negotiable the gulf between them. How far apart thought and action are may be seen in recalling that in the field of thought the sky is literally the limit, whereas in the field of action there is hardly anything that may not become the business of others, and so be subject to veto if it trenches upon their equal right to act.

Since thought, however, never physically interferes with thought, the inner process may be left fitly and fruitfully free. There is something about this fearful freedom that is as austere as it is majestic. The isolation which can result from its exercise may breed loneliness, and may even turn to tragedy; but it never spells crime, nor warrants seizure or search. There can never be justification for the vulgar practice of making "easy simplicity of lives not our own." As Emily Dickinson, our most probing poet, prescribes:

> The soul selects her own society,
> Then shuts the door;
> On her divine majority
> Obtrude no more.

What men may *do*, on the other hand, is always subject to question; and the machinery of government exists to find answers to conflicts, to reach agreements, and to provide penalties for transgressing the boundaries set by the equal right of all to act.

The medium which we have broached as intermediate between the poles of thought and action, is speech. Speech is of course a sort of action, though of the mildest sort. The frequency and the intensity of mouth-exercise among us might lead one to think otherwise. Laryngeal exercise is always engaging, at least to him who takes it; but it hardly makes the world go round. Talk after all is talk. It is wisdom publicly to interfere with private speech as little as possible; but there is no society so open but that libel is regarded as unlawful invasion of the rights of others, and indeed there is no society so free of talk that a citizen may upon some whim of libertarianism shout "fire" in a crowded hall. Still speech partakes more of thought than of action. Not only does it (ordinarily) enshrine some previous reflection (none but the shallowest of men talk merely to see what they are going to say!); but speech leads back to thought, fertilizing the process out of which it arises.

With these three domains now clearly before us, we may dare now to suggest proper distribution of the precious commodity of freedom with reference to each: the domain of thought, the domain of action, and the intermediate domain of speech. The three-fold formula follows: in thought freedom is absolute, in action freedom is severely limited, in speech freedom is limited but limited with utmost circumspection. Not all constitutions would so say; for not all governments recognize freedom as our being's end and aim. But democratic governments always recognize some such distinctions, and the American Constitution has its chief reason for being in the honest commitment to implement this three-fold freedom. The Bill of Rights is that part of our Constitution which puts the emphasis upon freedom as absolute as possible, and so elevates the rights of thought above speech and the rights of speech above action.

The first form in which our Constitution spells this insight out concretely is in its doctrine of separation between church and state. As this is all important, it gets first mention in the Bill of Rights. We shall see that what is intended is the broader distinction between man's will to power, in which limits are legitimate and necessary, and man's will to perfection, where there are no legitimate limits on freedom. Though the distinction permeates the whole realm of privacy, the Bill of Rights uses the religious idiom to make concrete our larger abstractions of value. The opening sentence is precisely this: "Congress shall make no law respecting an establishment of religion, or prohibiting the free exercise thereof."

A few simple words, well chosen and widely accepted, can make the deepest difference. For ages mankind had been stuck in the bloody bog of supposing it legitimate, and even requisite, for some men to prescribe what other men are to believe, or are not to believe. At the best this made religion a formal thing, at the worst a suppressive thing. A new insight was born of American experience: the notion, radical then but conservative now, that it is not governmental business what anybody believes, not even what he believes about religion. That is a man's own business, his and God's.

The result of other men's presuming upon privacy, said Thomas Jefferson, was "to make one half the world fools, and the other half hypocrites." Not all our governmental Fathers, and few of our religious Fathers, went as far as Jefferson; but they tended, especially the governmental Fathers, to regard orthodoxy as singularly loose-jointed among men that are generous. The Founding Fathers were generous men, and so the Bill of Rights registers the clear imputation that God should be regarded at least as good as the best men, tolerating if not rewarding originality. In such a divine economy, they believed, you get more harmony, not to say in the end more uniformity of belief, by putting orthodoxy to the supreme test of competition without the aid of government, or without overt resort to power at all. Truth is able to stand alone; it gets its exercise and growth by being required to do so.

It is clear, at any rate, that to establish one religion would be to disestablish every other religion, and this would be to carry limitations proper to action into the improper sphere of feeling and thought. Religion is attitude before it is action: it is worship; it is at the least what a man "does with his solitariness." Religion begins, however it ends, with something so truly individual that it lies quite beyond any legitimate reach of the public censor.

As Congress, under our Constitution, cannot act to prescribe orthodoxy (not even setting what is held to be "true" over what is denominated "false"), so the legislative branch cannot act to proscribe heterodoxy: cannot, that is, "prohibit the free exercise," of even adverse faith. At the minimum, our Bill of Rights proclaims tolerance for all the (various) forms of religion. At the maximum, it goes much further than this leeway. Toleration implies that somebody knows what is "true" but will not invoke his superior knowledge against those he holds to be in "error." The Bill of Rights arose not only from the colonial failure of toleration but from the inadequacy of toleration as a philosophy. It arose not out of any presumption of superior knowledge, but from political necessity and out of the modesty of what appears to be man's glaringly incomplete knowledge of final things.

It is a pressing and sad query, born of our own American experience, whether any church, or even religion, has been or will be whose virtue could survive a concession to it of a monopoly of power, against even vice or error. For men to discover, with Justice Holmes, that they are not God, is to disclose the most solid ground from which to extend to all the complete freedom which is proper to all thought and is allowable to every religious conviction. This advance of at least some of our Fathers from toleration of error to the acceptance of variety as a positive good, was their greatest advance. Upon this broad base rests at last, and rests most securely, the freedom of our Bill of Rights. There is a dignity about intellectual modesty, even in the religious field, which shames any presumption of human omniscience.

We have earlier remarked that the freedom guaranteed by the first amendment reaches well beyond religion in any specific sense. It reaches and covers every manifestation of thought. Variety is come to be the spice of all life. This amendment protects science against superstition; it protects art against provincialism; it protects politics against partisanship; it protects education against indoctrination. In truth it safeguards with the mantle of sacredness the whole inner life of man, extending its gracious exemption even to the right to disbelieve.

Nothing that a citizen thinks (so long as he but thinks it) is any business of government, or any legitimate excuse for anybody to proceed against him. This is the grand pay-off of our old and tried distinction between belief and action; and it is illustrated though by no means exhausted, in the separation provided by the Bill of Rights to protect both church and state. By it politics is saved from sectarian fanaticism; by it religious belief is made, as against intervention, privileged communication between God and man.

This deep-going distinction between idea and act also explains, and in the event justifies, our American tenderness of approach to that third domain, of speech. The Bill of Rights goes on from religious freedom to declare in the same sentence that Congress shall not abridge "the freedom of speech, or of the press." This protection elevates speech to a niche barely under that of thought in the pantheon of man's highest privileges. We have seen why this might be so and shall now see why it should be so.

Speech is, let us repeat, both action and thought. As we would safeguard the action of each citizen from the encroachment of others, so we must keep the medium of speech uncompromised by the license which libel is; but as we would also safeguard thought against any interference, we must have a special sensitivity toward its main medium, that of speech. It is not merely because the other fellow deserves to speak freely, but equally because we ourselves require candid criticism in order to become responsible in the exercise of our own rights and to remain responsive to the rights of others.

Without the operative right to speak freely, to publish without fear, to communicate without let or hindrance, the truth that we hold will turn into dogma which, by further prohibition, will cease to be true. Truth must grow or die. To take the easy way with it, the way of authority, is to doom to be stillborn any further issue from the womb of time. Only by comparing notes with one another in all modesty, only by criticism in candor, only through controversy courteously maintained, can the dynamic thing known as truth be made vital and be kept full of health and growth. The freedom of each man's individual "truth" rests only in the state's vast and generalized neutrality, proclaimed in this amendment.

The third right guaranteed by this amendment is that of assembly and petition. The right to talk, of which we have been speaking, implies the privilege of an audience, and even of a standing (organized) audience, so to say. So: it is the right of free people "peaceably to assemble, and to petition the government for a redress of grievances." This double right, like that of speech, is a limited right. The right to an audience is limited to means that are voluntary. Of course nobody has a right to compel others to listen to him, not even those who warn of dire things to come. We cannot enact boredom by statute. "The egotist," so runs the wisecrack, "is but the man who tells you all the things about himself that you were going to tell him about yourself, *if* he had given you a break." But the egotist quickly reaps in a free society the rewards befitting egoism: he loses his audience. Justice will out!

To make privacy fully fruitful, however, men must have the right to flee it. Positively, they must be able to get together with other men, to compare notes, to protest; and to organize as well as to agitate. The right to organize—to bargain collectively in economics and to bicker collectively in every field of life—this gives thought a goal more concrete than mere thinking; this gives speech a guerdon beyond babbling and gossip; this yields to action the strength of concert.

Oratory, which is the traditional medium of collective action, has always thriven in American life: all the way from public amusement after dinner to collective endeavor at the polls and in the market place. The effectiveness of our freedoms of speech and thought is measured largely by organization, which is the final fruit of oratory.

Modern dictators have made themselves effective by outlawing all organizations that might compete with them. Jealousy of other organizations than the state is a sure early sign that tyranny is a-brewing. "All within the state, nothing without the state, all for the state"—so runs the maturation of such jealousy. Thus tyrants dry up speech by prohibition of audition and thus they abort thought by drying up speech. When all men become captive auditors of but one organization, little attention goes longer into voluntary listening. When orators can say only what has been formulated in advance, oratory loses its soul of fire; when newspapers can print only what is pre-digested, the press loses its vitality; when thought can but repeat the pattern of what has been perpetrated, thinking loses both its fun and its fecundity.

By the simple device of prohibiting assembly and of forbidding organization, dictators have invoked effective attrition against both speech and thought. Forbid rain, and fountains dry up. Under our Bill of Rights every man is entitled to an open ear, but no man to a captive audience.

These several guarantees in our Bill of Rights are noble words, dedicated to great ends. And there are others like them—to the extent of ten initial amendments—each to be read and treasured for its own sake. It is enough here to try to catch and project the spirit of the document as a whole. Such safeguards, however, are but words—like the individual guarantees of the Soviet constitution—if citizens have grown too busy to treasure them or too timorous to maintain them. What some men die for other men must live for: that is man's only effective security. There is not a single guarantee in the entire Bill of Rights which a heedless legislature might not ignore, or a rash executive brush aside, or even a listless court forego.

This much our Fathers learned from foreign domination. It remains for us to convert their freedom *from* oppression into freedom *for* achievement. If our differentiation (not separation) of powers does not lead to a continuous concert among the three branches of government, we could lose our liberties as easily from complacency as from presumption. It is a balance of forces, a moving and operative equilibrium, which liberty requires.

There are citizens today (and many American well-wishers abroad) who think that we are in dire danger of losing our liberties through hysteria. They seem to forget that demagogues have passed this way before, indeed in every previous decade, trooping through their own noise to oblivion. They say that we are fighting communism by methods that either are, or will become, subversive of our ancient heritage. Others estimate the external threat (already internalized, they say) to be so clear and present that no methods will do save to fight fire with fire.

Meantime, between this hysteria and that counter-hysteria, the great body of our citizenry stands, not unbaffled but definitely uncowed. Their trust is not in parchment but is in what our imperishable parchment proclaims: liberty absolute for all thought, liberty limited for action, liberty as large as is humanly possible for speech. Not the Nay of fear but the Everlasting Yea of hope: this is clearly the accent of America. This is the calm voice lifted above troubled waters.

The Fathers have made it easier for us to remain calm by bequeathing to us the technique which kept them resolute. They learned not to take counsel of their fears. Fears are natural enough, but to contain them is spiritual. We have inherited not only that resolute attitude but this far-reaching theory as to the nature of our constitutional equilibrium.

Amendments X and IX (reading them in that order) provide that rights which are not specifically assigned to the central government belong to "the states or to the people themselves." And, further, the enumeration of these given rights shall not "be construed to deny or to disparage others retained by the people." To summarize: sovereignty in America is popular, first and last; government always exists for the people; and the only tenable law of progress is to allow as much freedom as possible to as many people as will stoutly possess themelves of it. "Walk from the people," as the wise proverb runs, "and you walk into night." Our historic eye is on the *people*: "The People, Yes."

It is in this presence that we stand, upon the old and sturdy platform of freedom for all the people with maturing responsibility, upon this we stand with more than a century and a half of tradition to steady us. This tradition should keep us from indulging trigger-happy anxiety. All experience hath shown that men do not throw off their collective habits in a day, or even in a day and night. Customs are the sturdiest of human reliances. Our American theory of liberty is sound, our practice of that liberty is stably grounded. This freedom is our fate. Those who know not what to trust, they trust they know not what. We have only to keep our powder dry, our wits about us, and our courage within us in order to acquit ourselves like men. "To acquit ourselves like men"—little more can be asked at the crossroads of history. Steady confidence is the only way to make conservatism truly conservative, the truest way to keep liberalism liberal. Dangers from without are seldom crucial until reinforced by fears from within. Resolute utilization of our present opportunities is the only guarantee which the future will honor, the only assurance which free men require.

QUESTIONS

1. What is the literary significance of the fact that Smith followed his quotation from Wordsworth's "Ode; Intimations of Immortality" with the statement "But as the active child is

father of the reflective man . . ."? List all the other literary allusions or quotations you can find in the essay.

2. What protection does the Bill of Rights seek to provide?

3. Smith once delivered a lecture in which he maintained that the "public ownership of human privacy" was the real issue between the United States and Soviet Russia. Relate this idea to this essay, forming thereby a concise statement of the central theme.

4. We noted in the essay by Mill that his paragraphs were much longer than those in the other two selections in this section. Comment on paragraphs 4 and 13 in Smith's essay.

5. "Belief and action, these two, represent the poles of our human enterprise. . . ." Why did the author include "these two" in this sentence? Do you think it adds anything to the sentence? Would he have left the same impression with the reader if he had not put this phrase in? Can you find other examples of this type of construction? Can you identify the Biblical ancestor of this phrase?

6. "So: it is the right of free people 'peaceably to assemble. . . .' " We raised the question about Mill's use of the semicolon and colon. Comment on the colon in this sentence. Why did Smith place it there? Is it commonly used in this manner? Is it incorrect? What inference can one draw about the author's style from such use of punctuation marks? Is it colloquial, formal, or rhetorical?

THE UTILITY OF FREEDOM
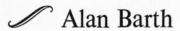 Alan Barth

Individual freedom . . . presupposes a tolerance of ideas which are thought to be mistaken, disloyal, and even dangerous. Tolerance of opinions which are thought to be innocuous is as easy as acts of charity that entail no sacrifice. But the test of a free society is its tolerance of what is deplored or despised by a majority of its members. The argument for such tolerance must be made on the ground that it is useful to the society.

The proposition to be proved, in short, is that free societies are better fitted to survive than closed societies. This is a proposition peculiarly relevant to the present struggle between the United States and the Soviet Union. Here the struggle is between a nation committed to the idea of individual freedom, and therefore to the principle of tolerance, and another nation which, in effect, denies the significance of the individual personality and the value of freedom.

Tolerance of diversity of opinion gives rise, undoubtedly, to what Madison called the spirit of faction. As long as men are permitted to express diverse opinions they will do so. As long as they are permitted to join in voluntary associations for the advancement of purposes they hold in common, there will be jostling for group advantage, pressure for special interests. Such conflicts are in greater or less degree disruptive. The resolution of them is the business of the democratic process. It is a process that has worked effectively for the American people in the past and can be counted upon to work in the future, so long as there is general acceptance of certain fundamental values and an underlying mutual trust among members of the society.

It is true that opinions challenging fundamental values and corroding mutual trust present a threat to social stability. To tolerate an organization like the Communist Party, which operates outside the democratic process and would destroy that process if it ever came to power, is to tolerate what must seem a seed of destruction. Similarly, to countenance the nihilism of a Senator McCarthy is to countenance methods that ignore standards of decency and poison the springs of confidence. Undoubtedly national unity—and therefore national security—suffers from such attacks on either side. But, paradoxically, loyalty in a free society depends upon the toleration of disloyalty. The loyalty of free men must be freely given—which is to say, that those who give it must be genuinely free to withhold it. Nothing is more fundamental to freedom than that this choice be a real one. The premise on which every free society rests, the American society more explicitly than any other, is that only through such freedom can loyalty be evoked and counted on to endure.

Moreover, to forbid disloyalty is to let it triumph. At bottom, the Communists and the Americanists are frighteningly similar: they are believers in the suppression and punishment of dissent. That they would suppress and punish different sorts of opinion is less significant than that, alike, they would suppress and punish. At bottom, they are alike also in being sick men: they are men who would relish a chance to use whip and club. It is necessary, therefore, to keep whips and clubs out of their hands—that is, to enforce the laws forbidding acts of violence, whether by them or against them. It is, however, equally necessary to enforce the laws which guarantee them the right to speak as they please. To suppress and punish their opinions is to embrace their opinions; it is to practice what they preach; and the end of that practice is the destruction of all diversity.

If tolerance of diversity involves an admitted element of risk to national unity, intolerance involves a certainty that unity will be destroyed. Unity does not grow out of uniformity; it grows out of resolved conflict. "Like the course of the heavenly bodies," Mr. Justice Brandeis once observed, "harmony in national life is a resultant of the struggle between contending forces. In frank expression of conflicting opinion lies the greatest promise of wisdom in governmental action; and in suppression lies ordinarily the greatest peril."

While speech can be silenced by authority, and silence may give the appearance of assent, thought cannot be wholly controlled by any instrument of suppression yet devised. Thought that is silenced is always rebellious. It can be won to an acceptance of contrary opinion only if it has been accorded a chance to be heard and assured of a future chance to win acceptance for itself. Majorities, of course, are often mistaken. This is why the silencing of minorities is necessarily dangerous. Criticism and dissent are the indispensable antidote to majority delusions. Afforded free expression, they serve as the self-regulating mechanism of a democratic community.

There is a persistent and prevalent myth that totalitarian societies are somehow more efficient than free societies. A dictatorship can move more swiftly, it is true, than a government which depends upon the voluntary consent of the governed. This is merely to say that the policies of irresponsible leaders are more speedily translated into action—which may be disastrously mistaken—than the policies of democratic leaders. Leadership is as necessary in a democratic as in a totalitarian state; and when leadership is lacking or inept or misguided, the consequences may be very costly. But free men have a means of correcting mistakes by a change of leadership. The incorrigible defect of dictatorship lies in the absence of any remedy for error on the part of the dictator.

This defect was revealed in numerous ways in the course of the war. For all its vaunted efficiency in the techniques of total war, Germany never fully mobilized its resources or its people. There was nothing like the all-out effort of Britain. Neither the industrial capacity nor the manpower of the country was ever wholly integrated. Unnecessary consumer goods were produced in plants that might have been converted to war

production; the luxury of domestic servants was widely enjoyed throughout the war, especially by Nazi Party officials.
. . .

These fatal inefficiencies in German mobilization grew directly out of the nature of totalitarian rule. There was no one to tell the Führer that the war effort was not being administered satisfactorily. To have questioned his wisdom would have been tantamount to treason. The mistakes therefore went uncorrected and in the end proved disastrous to the German people. The Strategic Bombing Survey reached the conclusion that these mistakes were rooted in a fundamental miscalculation about the strength of the nations ranged against Germany.
. . .

Faulty intelligence produced faulty planning all along the line in Germany. The belief that victory could be achieved quickly and cheaply produced an emphasis, in the composition of the German air force, on fighters and bombers of a type suitable to close co-operation with ground armies; Germany lacked, in consequence, the long-range bombers necessary to win the Battle of Britain. The development of jet planes, in which German technicians pioneered, was "much hindered," according to the Strategic Bombing Survey, "by Hitler's insistence that the aircraft be used as a fighter bomber." The assumption that Britain and the United States could mount only a limited air attack—"Allied production figures were disbelieved"—resulted in totally inadequate civilian-defense precautions. And when the mass air raids struck Germany, their psychological impact was compounded by Nazi propaganda which had stressed the infallibility of the Führer. A government based on coerced consent and the suppression of diversity lacked the capacity of a government based on voluntary consent to call for all-out effort and sacrifice on the part of the governed. It could command no comparable loyalty. It could achieve no comparable unity. It possessed no resiliency in disaster, comparable to that of the British after Dunkerque or the Americans after Pearl Harbor, to correct errors and restore confidence.

The validity of what has been said here is not lessened by

the fact that totalitarian Russia was among the victors and democratic France among the vanquished in the war. The Soviet dictator demanded, and received, heroic sacrifices from the Russian people; no nation waged war so totally. Russia mobilized tremendous strength, although wastefully in many respects; and her soldiers and civilians alike stood with magnificent fortitude at Stalingrad and Moscow, rallying after losses that, to the world outside, seemed catastrophic. But this qualification should be noted: the Russians were invaded, and by an enemy so stupidly ruthless as to leave them no alternative to resistance save extermination; even so, great numbers in the Ukraine and elsewhere showed themselves willing to join the Germans in fighting against their own government. In the vast unconquered land mass of the Soviet Union, however, the Nazi attack solidified devotion to leaders whom the people had no choice but to follow; and no doubt this attack from the outside forged a loyalty, beyond anything the Communist propagandists had been able to create, to a political system which with all its faults was their own.

France collapsed for a variety of reasons, perhaps the most fundamental of which was that she lacked in the 1930s the acceptance of common values and the underlying mutual trust which have been suggested as prerequisites to the working of the democratic process. The French people were united only in devotion to France as a geographical entity. They were rent by a political factionism that went beyond mere rivalry for public office or mere conflict as to policy; the Cagoulards and the Croix de Feu and the Monarchists and the Catholics and the Socialists and the Communists reflected deep cleavages respecting the nature of French society and the role of the State. There was no agreement among them as to first principles; agreement had to be forged, at last, through the anguish of defeat and regeneration. There is a profound warning for Americans in the French experience.

It has not been intended to suggest here that free societies are necessarily and invariably stronger than totalitarian societies. The point is simply that freedom is a source of strength if it is used wisely. It cannot provide a guarantee against ruinous mistakes; but it can provide a means of correcting

mistakes, a means denied to those who live in a society where
dissent is silenced.

There were many blunders, of course, in both British and
American planning of the war effort. They were subject, however, to unremitting and caustic criticism. Gradually, as a
result, they were overcome. . . . The process commonly called
"trial and error" is peculiarly democratic; it can work success-
fully only where opposition parties and the press and individuals are free to expose error, and where trial is always open to
protest. Criticism is liable to seem captious or crackpot or disloyal to those in authority, and often, no doubt, they are quite
right about it; but it is an invaluable goad and tonic all the
same. For all its excesses and inconveniences, societies that
tolerate criticism unconditionally tend to be stronger and more
stable than those that do not.

The contrast between the German and American experi-
ences in the development of atomic energy affords perhaps the
most dramatic illustration of the pragmatic uses of tolerance.
Some of the most brilliant German scientists, driven from their
homeland because they were Jewish or because they were politically unorthodox, found asylum in the United States and
in Britain and made important contributions to our primacy
in perfecting an atomic bomb. German science, once pre-
eminent, was crippled even more by the tendency to entrust
authority over research to politically "reliable" scientists—to
scientists who were more political than scientific. Doctrinaire
insistence on Nazi fetishes of race supremacy accelerated the
deterioration. The outcome, in strictly practical terms, was
to impair German national security.

A similar process seems to be taking place today in the Soviet
Union. In a number of fields, science is being cramped by orthodoxy. There is no reason to think that purges will promote
efficiency there any more than they did in Germany. Moreover,
the Russians, like the Germans, appear to be victims of their
own doctrinaire assumptions. It is a part of Russian doctrine
—as it was so mistakenly a part of German doctrine a decade
ago—that the United States is hopelessly divided and deca-
dent. No one who reports on conditions in this country dares,
therefore, to call the doctrine into question. Intelligence is

bound to be faulty when the bearer of bad tidings fears that he will fall into disfavor; and faulty intelligence is likely to produce mistaken policy. . . .

Democracies may unconsciously embrace their own peculiar form of totalitarianism through extra-legal pressures for conformity. If their members all talk alike and think alike, they run the serious risk of being plunged alike into disaster. The Gadarene swine had their own species of democracy when they rushed down the hillside together into the sea—acting with perfect unanimity, all agreeing, none contradicting.

From the point of view of national security, tolerance of diversity has proved itself to be a powerful asset. It has been the real "secret" of American strength. It has welded the diverse elements of the American people into a union in the genuine sense of the term; and, more than any other single factor, it has kept that union invulnerable to outside attack. The whole of the American experience refutes the notion that tolerance is a luxury to be enjoyed only in untroubled times. It is the genius of American growth. It is needed most, and most urgently, precisely in times like the present when the nation is subject to extraordinary stress. It may well be that for a long time to come we shall find ourselves ranged against the Soviet Union in a conflict of endurance which is not war in the conventional sense but which involves, nevertheless, a test of the survival value of the two societies. Those who hold that time is against us and therefore urge an immediate attack on Russia —preventive war is the phrase in fashion—betray a loss of faith in our own institutions. The American society—if it remains free—possesses a greater capacity for growth, a greater resourcefulness in meeting new problems and changing situations, than any closed society. Time is not against us; it is on our side. In the long run, the free have triumphed over the enslaved. We shall grow in strength as we exploit our freedom. . . .

The discussion of freedom in this book has been in utilitarian terms—in terms of its value for the security of the United States. But there is no disposition here to ignore its significance from the point of view of the individual. If, as we profess to believe in the United States, the nation exists only as an instrument to promote the welfare of its citizens, tolerance of diversity is imperative, because without it, without the personal liberty and individualism that flow from it, life would lose its savor. Progress in the arts, in the sciences, in the patterns of social adjustment springs from diversity and depends upon a tolerance of individual deviations from conventional ways and attitudes. The totalitarian society is not only less efficient than the free society in terms of its own survival; it is also stultifying and degrading to the human beings who live in it. Freedom gives a release to the human spirit, provides the indispensable condition for the realization of its limitless potentialities.

Individual freedom is, then, a means, an invaluable means, toward national security and survival. But it is an end as well —the supreme end which the government of the United States was instituted to secure. Faith in freedom as a means and as an end must be the ultimate touchstone of American loyalty, of the loyalty of all free men.

QUESTIONS

1. Relate the title of Barth's essay to the proposition he wishes to prove.
2. How does Barth refute the myth that totalitarian societies are somehow more efficient than free societies?
3. How does he answer the argument that, since totalitarian Russia was among the victors and democratic France among the vanquished in World War II, totalitarian governments are more efficient?
4. What aspect of the American philosophy of government has been the real "secret" of American strength?
5. How does Barth relate his argument for "the utility of freedom" in governmental operations to the individual in a free society?
6. What means of transition between paragraphs does Barth employ? Study each paragraph with this in mind. Are you ever left with a doubt concerning his references in any given paragraph?
7. Choose several of Barth's paragraphs and study them from the standpoint of organization. Is the topic sentence usually stated

or implied? Where does he most often place the topic sentence—at the beginning, middle, or end of the paragraph?

8. A "periodic sentence" is one in which the sense is held up until the end. Make a list of several sentences of this type, and try to determine whether Barth used this kind more frequently than the "loose sentence," i.e., the type in which the full sense is not so delayed. What is the value of the "periodic sentence"?

9. What correlation is there between his sentence structure and his paragraph organization?

QUESTIONS ON PART I

1. Why do all the writers in this section place so high a value upon "diversity"? What exactly do they mean by it? Is it a real value in democratic life?

2. What similarities do you find in all three essays about the need for opposing points of view to be not only held but voiced?

3. Which of Smith's opinions seem to you to be derived, directly or indirectly, from Mill's essay?

4. Write an essay in which you either attack or defend the principle that a free man must be free to be wrong as well as to be right.

II ❧ Freedom of the Press

NEWS AND
THE WHOLE TRUTH
✐ Elmer Davis

Each spring the members of the American Newspaper Publishers Association assemble in convention and spend a good
deal of their time eulogizing themselves. Conventions of editors and reporters, whether for newspapers or radio news, are
more practical and less complacent. The American news business, press and radio, certainly deserves some eulogies; it is
the most copious in the world, and I think its average quality
is at least as good as any others. But it is not yet good enough.
Too often we tell the customers not what is really going on,
but what seems to be going on. And I am not referring to the
small minority of newspapers, and the smaller minority of
newspapermen, who don't want to tell the truth, but to the
great majority who do want to tell the truth but often fall short.

Too much of our news is one-dimensional, when truth has
three dimensions (or maybe more); we still have inadequate
defenses against men who try to load the news with propaganda; and in some fields the vast and increasing complexity
of the news makes it continually more difficult—especially for
us Washington reporters—to tell the public what really happened. Some of these failings are due to encrusted habits of
the news business, which can be changed only slowly, but
which many men are now trying to change; some of them will

be harder to cure because they are only the reverse side of some of our greatest merits, and it is difficult to see how to get rid of them without endangering the merits too.

The merits which entail the worst drawbacks are competition and the striving for objectivity, and we should be much worse off without either. But objectivity often leans over backward so far that it makes the news business merely a transmission belt for pretentious phonies. As for competition, there is no doubt that the nation is much better served by three wire services—the Associated Press, the United Press and the International News Service, sometimes supplemented by the English Reuters—and by several radio networks than it would be by monopoly in either field. But competition means an overemphasis on speed, as has been noted by the Associated Press Managing Editors (not the editors of the AP but the men who use its service); and sometimes it leads to an exaggerated build-up.

Like most radio newsmen, I am heavily dependent on the wire services. I am supposed to be aware of all the world's news and to report what seems to me most important or that to which I can add something in the way of interpretation. But I can't cover it all myself—not even all that happens in Washington; usually I cover about one story a day on foot, get angles or elucidations on half a dozen others by telephone, and must depend on the wire services for the rest. Experience has taught me, when the versions of the same story given by two wire services differ materially, to prefer the less exciting; the other might have been souped up to beat the competition.

President Truman announced his decision not to run again at the end of his speech at the Jefferson-Jackson Day dinner on March 29, 1952—an extemporaneous addition to a script distributed several hours in advance. All the wire services sent out the text, of course; early editions of the Sunday papers were going to press and had to have it at the earliest moment. The UP and INS merely sent out the text; the AP, desirous of making everything clear (and maybe of getting the jump on the competition), prefaced it with a lead saying that the President made no disclosure of his intentions. Papers carrying that lead were on the street as he was disclosing his intentions.

At least one radio station—a good one, too—writing its eleven-o'clock news out of the AP, went on the air and said that he had made no disclosure of his intentions; whereas many of the listeners a few minutes earlier had heard the President say he wouldn't run.

I do not suppose that any of the wire services ever consciously sacrifices accuracy to speed; but speed is what counts most, because what every wire service wants is to get newspapers to use its story rather than its competitors' stories. I have seen many service messages on press-association wires boasting about how many minutes or even how many seconds, they were ahead of the competition, how their story got the play. I have seldom if ever seen a message saying, "While our story was unfortunately a few minutes behind time, it had more truth in it." Yet these outfits live, and must live, by competition; and we are better off with that competition, whatever its shortcomings, than we should be without it. One of the wire services has a motto, "Get it there first—but first get it right." I am sure they all try to do that; I am not sure that a wire service which actually succeeded in doing it would last long against the competition.

Nine days before the Germans surrendered in 1945 there was a great, though brief, flurry over an AP report from San Francisco—where the constituent assembly of the United Nations was then meeting—that they had surrendered and an announcement could be expected at any moment. The story was sent by one of the ablest reporters in the country; he got it from a person described as a high American official, who wouldn't let his name be used—something that happens every day; and it may have been mass self-delusion that persuaded many people that the high official was the Secretary of State, who would have known. Actually it was Senator Connally; but he might have known too; and if the reporter had stopped to check up with the Secretary of State or anybody else, the competition might have got the story out ahead of him. So it was left to the President of the United States to do the checking up and find out that the story was false.

That time, the AP got a beat on a surrender that didn't happen; nine days later it got a beat on the one that did happen—

because one of its correspondents broke a release date that fifteen other correspondents observed. Now some of those hold-for-release regulations of the SHAEF public-relations officers —imposed in an endeavor to get simultaneous release in all Allied capitals—may have seemed ridiculous; the German radio was already announcing the surrender. Nevertheless the sixteen correspondents who had covered the actual ceremony had all promised to hold the story till a certain hour. Fifteen of them did; one of them did not. If that incident had been repeated once or twice it would have made it extremely difficult for any correspondent to get any news.

Here the fault clearly lay with the pressure of competition. I am told, by a man who should know, that the three principal AP correspondents on the Western front had identical instructions; besides competing with everybody else they were competing with one another, presumably on the theory that that would keep them on their toes. It is not surprising that one of them got so far up on his toes that he fell over on his face.

It was the United Press that ended the old war four days early in 1918—an incident now remembered chiefly because Roy Howard, who was responsible for what was then the greatest boner in American news history, was able enough to live it down. He happened to be in a position to see, quite legitimately, what appeared to be an official dispatch; and he flashed it without checking up on it. It was in contradiction to the known intention of ending the war four days later; but I do not suppose there was or is a reporter for any wire service, American or foreign, who would not have done what Roy Howard did. It is hard to say how much actual harm was done, aside from taking the edge off the celebration of the real armistice; but there is some reason to believe that the message that fooled Howard was planted by a German agent in Paris, who presumably hoped that it would do harm.

Now these were not bad reporters; they were all good reporters, among the best; but they were all in too big a hurry, for fear somebody else would beat them to it. We have seen many forecasts of what will happen in the next war, if we have one. I do not know what the course of operations will be; the

one thing I feel safe in predicting is that some American reporter will end it a few days before it actually ends, and the
families of men who were killed after he said it was over will,
for the rest of their lives, be convinced that you can't believe
what you see in the papers.

Most Russian propaganda nowadays needs no fumigation
in this country; it defeats itself. The Russians appear to regard
us as enemies, and their routine propaganda is put out with
no expectation that it will have any effect on us but may only
help to keep other nations as neutral as possible as long as possible. There is one outstanding exception—the occasional
answers that Stalin used to vouchsafe to inquiries from American correspondents.

Certainly an "interview" with Stalin would have been a great
journalistic achievement. But the many reporters who tried it
never interviewed Stalin, asking him questions face to face.
They had to send in their questions through diplomatic channels; and Stalin answered them or not, according to whether
the answers would do some good to Stalin. The kind of questions he would answer were the kind asked him by Kingsbury
Smith of the INS in January 1949 and by James Reston of the
New York *Times* in December 1952. To Smith he said that
Russia would join the United States in a declaration that we
had no intention of going to war with each other (a promise
which, in somewhat different form, was a staple of Russian
propaganda—and Russia had made such promises to other
nations and broken them); that Russia would join us in gradual disarmament to that end (the Russians always say they
are for disarmament, on their terms); that Stalin had no objection to meeting President Truman—a meeting which the
President was known to regard as useless; and that Russia
would lift the Berlin blockade if the Western powers would
postpone the establishment of a West German state—preven-
tion of such establishment being the obvious purpose of the
Berlin blockade. The blockade was lifted some months later,
and endeavors have been made to represent Smith's questions
as at least partly responsible—which seems open to doubt in
view of the fact that the Allies had gone ahead and set up the
West German state before the blockade was lifted.

To Reston, Stalin said that he believed Russia and the United States could live together peacefully (if he had said they couldn't, that *would* have been news); that the source of the present trouble in the world was the cold war against the Soviet Union (all our fault, none of it his); that he would like to meet President Eisenhower to help ease world tensions; and finally that he would co-operate in new diplomatic approach to end the Korean war. And indeed some months later the Korean war was ended; but the diplomatic approach that led up to that result was begun only after Stalin was dead.

From both these sets of answers you got the picture of good old benevolent Uncle Joe, who wanted to live in peace with everybody; and you got vast publicity for certain propaganda arguments that Stalin wanted to get before the world. He could have got them before the world by a statement in *Pravda*, but that would have attracted far less attention than answers to well-known American reporters. Most editorials analyzed the Stalin statements for what they were; but their analyses were read by far fewer people than saw the news stories on the front page.

Now Smith and Reston, while of course they wanted answers from Stalin, did not want these particular answers; indeed these were not the questions they wanted to ask him. Each man had sent him several previous sets of questions which he ignored. Like a smart batter facing a pitcher who is trying to cut the corners of the plate, he refused to reach for the wide ones and finally made them lay it in the groove. It is an effective technique; Malenkov has not yet tried it, at this writing, but he probably will if he lasts long enough.

Reporting of the Korean war was in general very good— some of it, such as Homer Bigart's dispatches in the early months to the New York *Herald Tribune*, exceedingly good; but we let the enemy slip a few fast ones past us. There were two English-speaking Communist correspondents, the Englishman Alan Winnington and the Australian Wilfred Burchett, who had been with the Communist armies and then came down to Panmunjom to cover the truce talks. British and Australian correspondents would have nothing to do with them; but some of the Americans were innocent enough to suppose, at first, that they were just newspapermen like themselves, and quoted them as authorities not only for conditions behind the enemy lines but for what was going on in the truce-talk tents. I am told by correspondents returned from Korea that sometimes they had to use what they got from Winnington and Burchett because they could get nothing out of our public-information officers. But what did they get out of Winnington and Burchett? Not objective truth, you may be sure, unless by accident.

Enemy propaganda in Korea also made hay with photographs—many of them taken by an American, Frank Noel, an AP photographer who was a prisoner; but transmitted to our side of the lines, of course, by the Communists. According to those photographs the life of a prisoner of war in North Korea was indeed a happy one. We saw groups of prisoners, warmly dressed against the Korean winter—fat, well fed and smiling. Well—a man who knows that his picture is going to be printed in the American papers where his family will see it wants to look cheerful; they feel bad enough about his being a prisoner and would feel worse if they thought he was mistreated.

There were plenty of American prisoners who were not well fed and warmly dressed, but Noel was not allowed to take their pictures; his guides hurried him right past them till they found somebody whose picture, when passed on for publication in the American press, would be good propaganda for the Communists. In the circumstances it is no wonder they allowed a camera for Noel to be sent in through the lines; and some doubt remains as to whether this display of journalistic enterprise really served a useful purpose. These pictures were the truth, of what they depicted; but they certainly were very far from the whole truth about the prison camps in North Korea.

The United Nations Commission on Freedom of Information has been trying to work out an international code of ethics for newsmen—not an easy task in view of the different concepts of news (and of ethics) on the two sides of the Iron Curtain. The first and I believe the only one so far adopted (by a vote of six to nothing with five abstaining) says only that reporters, editors and commentators shall do their best to make sure that the information the public receives is factually accurate, with no fact willfully distorted and no essential fact deliberately suppressed.

I don't know why the American delegate abstained from voting for that innocuous declaration, unless for the reason that it doesn't go far enough. What is factual accuracy? Not merely what a man says, for sometimes he has said the contradictory thing in times past; and sometimes, indeed, what he says is known to be false. Truth has three dimensions; but the practices of the American news business—practices adopted in a praiseworthy ambition to be objective—too often give us only one-dimensional news—factually accurate so far as it goes, but very far indeed from the whole truth.

There was not much objectivity in the American press through most of the nineteenth century; if a story touched on the political or economic interest of the editor or owner, it was usually written so as to make his side look good. Some papers still follow that practice; but most of them, for some decades past, have accepted the principle that they ought to try to be objective in the news columns, leaving argument to the editorial page. Publish everything that is said on both sides of a controversial issue and let the reader make up his mind. A noble theory; but suppose that men who talk on one side (or on both) are known to be lying to serve their own personal interest; or suppose they don't know what they are talking about. To call attention to these facts, except on the editorial page, would not, according to most newspaper practice, be objective. Yet in the complex news of today how many readers have enough personal knowledge to distinguish fact from fiction, ignorance from knowledge, interest from impartiality?

This practice is perhaps not quite so prevalent now as it was twenty-five years or so ago—in the golden age of Calvin Coolidge, when it was the general opinion that things are what they seem. In those days, if the Honorable John P. Hoozis was an important person, you were likely to see him quoted at length in the newspapers on almost any subject, with no indication that he knew nothing at all about it, or no indication that he had a strong personal interest in getting people to believe what he said—even if the editor who printed the story happened to know it. He was an important man; he had made a statement; and it would not have been objective not to print it. We have been getting away from that deadpan objectivity of late years—or were, till the rise of Senator McCarthy.

He may be a unique case, but he is far from the only case in which the press (and radio) misinforms the nation through the habit of regarding anything that the Honorable John P. Hoozis says as news. Take an example more to the point, since there seems no question of any deliberate intention to mislead. In 1951 Pat Hurley was testifying in the MacArthur hearings —former Major General, former Secretary of War, former Ambassador to China Pat Hurley. About military affairs and Chinese politics he might have been supposed to know something—though even that may be open to doubt in view of his remark, some years ago, that Chinese Communists are just like Oklahoma Republicans except that they carry guns. Somehow he had got off the subject and into criticism of some hearings by Congressional committees, which had acquitted people whom he considered guilty.

"For instance," he said, "the hearings on the atomic energy organization. I read the report of the committee that heard that case, and it was a clean bill of health, a certificate of purity and patriotism for everybody in the organization. Yet less than six months, just a little after, Dr. Klaus Fuchs confessed in London; and the result is that they were not pure, they were not patriotic in that organization, and two of them are under sentence to death at this moment."

This of course was completely false, though the falsehood may presumably be charged to General Hurley's defective memory. Julius and Ethel Rosenberg, sentenced to death, did their spying (as Fuchs did practically all of his) when the atomic-energy program was operated by the Manhattan Engineering District under General Groves—two years or more before the Atomic Energy Commission (which had received the "certificate of purity" that Hurley mentioned) was established; indeed before it was even thought of. Furthermore, the Rosenbergs never worked even for Groves, let alone for the Atomic Energy Commission. Yet a prominent man had said that in an important hearing, so it was news; it ran in one or more editions of the evening papers, and doubtless on some news broadcasts, before it was corrected.

Who should have corrected it? Well, you would think any senator would remember that Hurley was completely wrong; but nobody said so. Two members of the committee who certainly knew, Senators McMahon and Hickenlooper, happened not to be in the committee room when Hurley made the statement. McMahon was told about it, came back while Hurley was still on the stand and managed to get it into the record that Hurley had made "a downright misstatement of facts." That duly got into the newspapers and on the radio; a senator had said it, so it was news.

Any competent news editor must have known that it was a downright misstatement of facts; yet I doubt if there was a newspaper in the country, printing Hurley's statement before McMahon's correction, that followed it with a bracketed insert, "This is not so." To do that would have been editorializing, interpreting the news, failing in objectivity. You could do it to Stalin and Hitler in their day, but tradition forbids doing it to one of our fellow citizens when he is engaged in controversy. Failure to make such a correction may salve a man's conscience about his loyalty to the ideal of objectivity. But how about his loyalty to the reader, who buys a newspaper thinking (or at least hoping) that it will tell him the truth? The newspaper is not giving him his money's worth if it tells him only what somebody says is the truth, which is known to be false.

It was the realization that objectivity had leaned so far over backward that it had become unobjective which led to the rise of the syndicated newspaper column, and a little later of the radio news commentary. These are both news and interpretation; our listeners, or readers, understand that we are saying, "This is the news and this is what I think it means." But even for us, with much more latitude than the ordinary reporter, it is becoming harder and harder to get at the three-dimensional truth in Washington—partly because the news becomes more and more complex, partly because so much of it is coming to consist of never-ending serial melodramas, like soap operas on the radio, or those newspaper cartoon strips that used to be comic.

Especially is this true of Congressional committee hearings, where the same witnesses appear and reappear. Adequate coverage of such stories entails reporting not only what a man says now, but the very different thing he may have said last year —or last week.

Most people may remember that McCarthy said there are 205, or 57, or 81 Communists in the State Department. But this is only one of McCarthy's many self-contradictions; who can keep track of them all? I have a stack of his speeches two feet thick on my office shelf; but when he says something that stirs a vague recollection that he once said something very different, I seldom have time to run through his speeches. I can't afford to hire a full-time specialist to keep up with what McCarthy has said; and if I had a McCarthy specialist I should also have to hire a Louis Budenz specialist and a Harold Stassen specialist. For these favorite witnesses of Congressional committees (Stassen is a favorite no longer, now that he has a government job; but he was) are, like McCarthy, gifted with self-refreshing recollections; if the first story doesn't stand up, they have no trouble remembering something better. And their talents have been given an open field by that new doctrine of Congressional jurisprudence, perpetual jeopardy.

It was written into the Fifth Amendment to the Constitution that no man shall be subject, for the same offense, to be twice put in jeopardy of life or limb. The men who wrote that did not foresee that Congressional committees would take over much of the judicial process and would not be bound by the constitutional limitation since they deprive no man of life or limb—only (unless he is foolish enough to perjure himself, or to refuse to answer their questions) of his good name and his opportunity to earn a living. Acting on the principle that nothing is ever settled till it is settled right, they can disregard the fact that a man has been examined and found guiltless by another Congressional committee—or by more than one— not to mention grand juries, loyalty boards and so on. They just keep on setting up committees till they find one that will get him.

Senator McCarran's Internal Security Committee seemed to

have undertaken to correct any errors that anyone else may have made in the direction of leniency; and it carried on the good work by procedures that are, so far, novel and indeed unique—at least on this side of the Iron Curtain. A witness before the McCarran committee—especially if he was a witness for the prosecution—knew what was expected of him. He didn't have to stop and think about his answer; it was usually handed to him wrapped up in the question: "You would say this is an indication of Communist sympathies, wouldn't you?" And this technique is made more effective by a new investigatory instrument known as the pertinent excerpt.

The pertinent excerpt is a refined and modernized version of our old friend, the sentence taken out of context. (One pertinent excerpt from a document used against Owen Lattimore turned out to be two sentences eleven pages apart, but put together.) Sometimes it is a line from a letter written fifteen years ago, read out of context to the man who wrote it (and didn't keep a carbon) with a demand that he explain what it means; but it is most effective when read to a man who didn't write it, indeed may never have seen it before, but is expected to say what it means with no idea of the reasoning of which it was a part. How does he know—or how does a reporter know who is covering the hearing—that in context it might have a quite different meaning?

Some years ago Lattimore wrote a book called *Solution in Asia*. John Carter Vincent had read it—years ago. When the McCarran committee had Vincent on the stand they read him a number of pertinent excerpts from chapters about Mongolia and Chinese Turkistan—statements about Russia, which they kept trying to get him to stigmatize as party-line stuff; and eventually he had to say that some of it did seem to indicate an inclination toward Communism. Not till that evening, when Vincent had a chance to look at the book again, did he realize that these pertinent excerpts came from a chapter which began, "To all of these peoples Russia and the Soviet Union has a great attraction. *In their eyes*," etc. (The italics are mine, not the McCarran committee's; which omitted that phrase altogether.) They had seemed to be asking him about what Lattimore thought; actually they were asking him about what Lattimore believed other people thought. I had read that book—but years ago, and hurriedly, as I have to read most books; I had forgotten all about it, and I doubt if any other reporter at the hearing had read it at all. So the story had to go out that evening that Vincent had found Communist leanings in Lattimore's book. Later, some admirers of the methods of the McCarran committee seemed to suspect that this particular handling of a pertinent excerpt might be open to criticism. Irving Kristol, writing in the *Twentieth Century*, explained that Lattimore was merely putting his own opinions into the mouths of Uzbeks and Mongols, "secure in the knowledge that they were not likely to write a protesting letter to the *Times*." I do not know how Kristol can be sure of that; Lattimore was there and talked to those people, Kristol was not. But if the reader can be persuaded that Lattimore was only conducting a dialogue with himself, that might distract attention from the omission of some rather pertinent words from this pertinent excerpt. (One of the senators on the committee, when I questioned him after the hearing about the relevance of some of these excerpts, explained, "Well, the main thing was that we got Vincent to say something against Lattimore.")

I am not here concerned with the ethics of this sort of thing —though that is a topic on which much might be said—but with its effect on a reporter's endeavor to give the public a reasonably accurate story. Reporters covering the McCarran hearings were continually in danger of giving the public a false report, not of what was actually said in their presence but of the three-dimensional truth of which what they hear is only one dimension. But who can read all the books or documents from which "pertinent excerpts" may be drawn? Who could remember them all, if he did?

William S. White of the New York *Times* happened to remember that there were material discrepancies, in emphasis if not in content, between General Wedemeyer's testimony before the McCarran committee and his testimony in the MacArthur hearings three months earlier—because White had covered them both and the memory had not had time to fade. What is remarkable about that episode is that the *Times* permitted White to report that discrepancy—something which many editors would regard as unobjective. But White seems to have more latitude than most reporters. Harold Stassen told the McCarran committee that at a conference of consultants to the State Department some years earlier, Lattimore had headed a "prevailing group" which recommended a ten-point program following the Communist line. When the stenographic record of the conference was published White analyzed it and demonstrated that there was hardly even a chemical trace of truth in Stassen's story. The *Times* published his analysis; few papers would.

But to analyze and find the truth requires not only a good memory but time. How does the average reporter get at the truth in cases like this if he has to sit all day in a committee hearing and then come back and write his story, with no time to check up on the witness's past testimony or on the validity of the pertinent excerpts? How do I do it, compelled as I am to keep an eye on all the world's news, pouring in at the end of the day, besides the story that is right in front of me? Yet, unless we try it, we give the public only one dimension of the truth—a mere surface, under which something very different may lie concealed.

The McCarran committee was very sensitive to anything that might seem an imputation against its motives. I know nothing of its motives; what concerns me is that its procedures made it extremely difficult for reporters to find out the truth and pass it on to the public. Objectivity requires me, however, to report that those procedures have been praised by many people, including the Daughters of the American Revolution and (though somewhat absent-mindedly) the American Bar Association.

I have dwelt at length on the McCarran committee because it was a remarkable phenomenon and so far unique. (Under Jenner its proceedings have not been quite so raw.) But it is not the only committee whose doings have encouraged, in reporting, another habit that is likely to mislead the public— the use of loaded words. One of those loaded words is "named." Now when a man is named as a Communist by Budenz, or named as a grafter by some of the witnesses before committees investigating corruption, that means nothing at all without corroboration. Yet if that man keeps appearing in the news the tag will stick to him; he has been named. A defendant on trial before a Congressional committee does not often, any more, say anything; he admits it, he acknowledges it. I have seen stories that came pretty close to saying, "The witness admitted that last year Christmas came on December 25."

Yet, searching my conscience while I was compiling these criticisms of others, I had to realize that lately I used an unloaded word when a loaded one would have been more accurate. That loaded word is "lobbying." There is nothing at all illegitimate about lobbying; there can be lobbying for good causes as well as bad, and by good or bad methods—though the most effective method, for the righteous as well as the wicked, is to convince a member of Congress that if he doesn't do what you want him to do, it will cost him votes. Nevertheless there has been so much lobbying for bad causes, by bad methods, that the word has become loaded; it means something evil.

The most effective job of lobbying that was done on Capitol Hill in 1952—out in the open, anyway—was done by the Citizens Committee for the Hoover Report, in persuading the Senate to accept the President's plan to put the Bureau of Internal Revenue under civil service. I happened to be in favor of that reform, as well as most of the recommendations of the Hoover Report; and when I reported these operations of the Citizens Committee, subconsciously realizing that "lobbying" has become a four-letter word, I said that they had reasoned with the senators. But I am afraid that if this had been an outfit that I didn't like, working for a measure I didn't favor, I should have called its operations lobbying—which they were. *Mea culpa*; I shall try to reform, and lead a better life.

One more example, which shows how the complexity of the news can lead to downright though quite unintentional misrepresentation. There are no more honest newspapers in the country than the New York *Times* and *Herald Tribune* and the Washington *Post*—perhaps no better newspapers either. Yet one morning in 1951 they all made the same mistake—and a mistake which happened to give support to their editorial policies. General Marshall had been testifying in the MacArthur

hearings about MacArthur's personal and unilateral peace pro-
posal of March 1951; and the next morning the top line of the
Times's eight-column head told us, "Marshall Says MacArthur
Upset Peace Move"; and the eight-column heads were substantially the same in the *Post* and *Herald Tribune*.

Now General Marshall hadn't said that; he had said that
MacArthur had lost "whatever chance there may have been"
of making peace at that time. This verbatim quotation appeared in the lead of every story, of course; but there was
room in the headline only for a very misleading simplifica-
tion. Misleading because actually the chance of making peace
at that time was infinitesimal—almost nonexistent. There was
no agreement among the nations with troops in Korea as to
what peace terms ought to be, and there is no indication that
the Chinese ever even thought about it till they had taken a
couple more first-class lickings. This fact was known to the
State Department reporters for the *Post*, the *Times* and the
Herald Tribune, but they weren't covering the MacArthur hearings; they were busy on their beats. It was not known to the
men who were covering the hearings, or to the men who edited
their stories, and it was nobody's business to tell them. I know
of no newspaper which has a regular system of lateral internal
communication by which one man tells another what he ought
to know (unless they are both assigned to the same story);
indeed he probably doesn't know the other man needs to know
it. And news has become so complex that it is just good luck
if any one man knows all he should know to cover his story
properly.

There was of course far graver distortion of the testimony
in the MacArthur hearings in some other newspapers. I have
selected this instance only because the papers involved are
technically among our best and ethically above suspicion of
slanting the news to support their editorial policies. Yet that
is what, quite inadvertently, they did.

What to do? More and more, from inside as well as outside
the trade, there is a demand for interpretive reporting, which
puts into the one-dimensional story the other dimensions that
will make it approximate the truth. But this entails serious
dangers. I have seen some undeniably well-intentioned en-

deavors to put in those other dimensions, but the dimensions were derived not from the evidence but from the opinions or prejudices of the reporter; and if the practice were to become general they might in some cases be derived from the opinions or prejudices of the publisher, as they so often used to be. One Chicago *Tribune* is enough. And even if a man's conscience is as rigorous, his mind as relentlessly objective, as the weights and measures in the Bureau of Standards, he may still fall short of doing as accurate a job as he means to do because he doesn't know all the angles, or hasn't time to get around to them under the pressure of covering what is in front of him and writing a story about it.

No wonder then that editors are slow to accept the need of interpretation. In the fall of 1951 Senator Alexander Smith of New Jersey, a very moral and religious man, was a member of a subcommittee passing on the fitness of persons nominated as delegates to the United Nations Assembly, including Philip Jessup. McCarthy and Stassen had accused Jessup of Communist affiliations and sympathies; and after two weeks of hearings, the committee rejected Jessup by a vote of three to two. Senator Smith said he had absolute confidence in Jessup's ability, integrity and loyalty; he explicitly repudiated any belief in the charges against him; yet, because Jessup was a "controversial figure" and for other reasons quite irrelevant to the issues before the committee, he voted against Jessup and for McCarthy.

The committee approved the appointment of Dr. Channing Tobias, Negro religious leader, against whom similar charges had been brought; he admitted that he was a joiner and had sometimes been careless about what he joined; but he brandished the Negro vote at them. Whether there is a Negro vote is open to doubt, but senators scare easily. It is impossible to escape the conclusion that Jessup too would have been approved if he had only been black.

One of the best reporters in Washington thought of beginning his report of that episode: "Yesterday afternoon Senator Alexander Smith wrestled with his conscience. He won." He didn't write that because he was afraid his paper wouldn't print it. But it might have printed it; in any case it seems to me an objective report of what happened. It is unthinkable that so high-minded a man as Senator Smith would have come to such a decision without wrestling with his conscience, and he certainly pinned it to the mat. Yet it could be argued that if that had been printed, it might have encouraged more free-wheeling interpretation by reporters of less ability or less integrity.

The good newspaper, the good news broadcaster, must walk a tightrope between two great gulfs—on one side the false objectivity that takes everything at face value and lets the public be imposed on by the charlatan with the most brazen front; on the other, the "interpretive" reporting which fails to draw the line between objective and subjective, between a reasonably well-established fact and what the reporter or editor wishes were the fact. To say that is easy; to do it is hard. No wonder that too many fall back on the incontrovertible objective fact that the Honorable John P. Hoozis said, colon quote—and never mind whether he was lying or not.

Yet more and more newsmen, in press and radio both, are coming to realize that we ought to do better than we are doing; and some of them are doing something about it. Dean Gordon Sabine of the University of Oregon School of Journalism has observed that the rise of McCarthy has compelled newspapers of integrity to develop a form of reporting which puts into context what men like McCarthy have to say. "Reporting all the dimensions of the news," he said, "we used to think of as dangerous. Today the lack of it creates the danger. And if this new approach brings the editorial page to the front page, if it mixes interpretation with naked fact, then we must realize simply that today we recognize the complexity of the news much more clearly than we did thirty or forty years ago, and we recognize the need for more capable newsgatherers and writers, and even more intelligent deskmen and editors."

We do indeed. A man who can be trusted with interpretive reporting must have both integrity and intelligence; even the New York *Times* seems to allow few if any of its reporters (except in the Sunday think-piece section) the freedom of interpretation that it accords to Bill White. Palmer Hoyt, publisher of the Denver *Post*, has issued to his staff a memorandum on how to treat the news about McCarthy so that the customers will not be deceived. "Many charges made by reckless or impulsive public officials," he says, "can not and should not be ignored; but news stories and headlines can be presented in such a manner that the reading public will be able to measure the real worth or value and the true meaning of the stories." A principle which he works out in some detail; "we are anxious," he says, "to take every possible step to protect the innocent."

And not merely the innocent victim of McCarthy, but the innocent consumer, who has little or no means of evaluating what he sees in print. All of us in the news business ought to remember that our primary responsibility is to the man who buys his newspaper, or turns on his radio, expecting us to give him in so far as is humanly possible not only the truth and nothing but the truth, but the whole truth.

QUESTIONS

1. Choose one or more important political events of the nineteenth century and find out how they were treated by several well-known newspapers of the time. Develop your discoveries into an essay on nineteenth-century "personal journalism."

2. What does Davis mean when he says that "truth has three dimensions"?

3. What is the tone of the essay? Why does Davis adopt this tone? Does it typify a particular view of modern life? How does this tone affect his style in general?

4. Define in detail Davis's attitude toward "objectivity."

5. How do you account for Davis's frequent use of the dash and the parenthesis? Replace, in one paragraph, dashes and parentheses wherever possible with other appropriate punctuation.

6. What is the rhetorical device used by Davis in the terms "Congressional jurisprudence" and "perpetual jeopardy"?

AN APOLOGY FOR PRINTERS
✒ Benjamin Franklin

Being frequently censur'd and condemn'd by different Persons for printing Things which they say ought not to be printed, I have sometimes thought it might be necessary to make a standing Apology for my self, and publish it once a Year, to be read upon all Occasions of that Nature. Much Business has hitherto hindered the execution of this Design; but having very lately given extraordinary Offence by printing an Advertisement with a certain N. B. at the End of it, I find an Apology more particularly requisite at this Juncture, tho' it happens when I have not yet Leisure to write such a Thing in the proper Form, and can only in a loose manner throw those Considerations together which should have been the Substance of it.

I request all who are angry with me on the Account of printing things they don't like, calmly to consider these following Particulars.

1. That the Opinions of Men are almost as various as their Faces; an Observation general enough to become a common Proverb, *So many Men so many Minds.*

2. That the Business of Printing has chiefly to do with Mens Opinions; most things that are printed tending to promote some, or oppose others.

3. That hence arises the peculiar Unhappiness of that Business, which other Callings are no way liable to; they who fol-

From *The Pennsylvania Gazette,* June 10, 1731.

low Printing being scarce able to do any thing in their way of getting a Living, which shall not probably give Offence to some, and perhaps to many; whereas the Smith, the Shoemaker, the Carpenter, or the Man of any other Trade, may work indifferently for People of all Persuasions, without offending any of them: and the Merchant may buy and sell with Jews, Turks, Hereticks and Infidels of all sorts, and get Money by every one of them, without giving Offence to the most orthodox, of any sort; or suffering the least Censure or Ill will on the Account from any Man whatever.

4. That it is as unreasonable in any one Man or Set of Men to expect to be pleas'd with every thing that is printed, as to think that nobody ought to be pleas'd but themselves.

5. Printers are educated in the Belief, that when Men differ in Opinion, both Sides ought equally to have the Advantage of being heard by the Publick; and that when Truth and Error have fair Play, the former is always an overmatch for the latter: Hence they chearfully serve all contending Writers that pay them well, without regarding on which side they are of the Question in Dispute.

6. Being thus continually employ'd in serving both Parties, Printers naturally acquire a vast Unconcernedness as to the right or wrong Opinions contain'd in what they print; regarding it only as the Matter of their daily labour: They print things full of Spleen and Animosity, with the utmost Calmness and Indifference, and without the least Ill-will to the Persons reflected on; who nevertheless unjustly think the Printer as much their Enemy as the Author, and join both together in their Resentment.

7. That it is unreasonable to imagine Printers approve of every thing they print, and to censure them on any particular thing accordingly; since in the way of their Business they print such great variety of things opposite and contradictory. It is likewise as unreasonable what some assert, "That Printers ought not to print any Thing but what they approve;" since if all of that Business should make such a Resolution, and abide by it, an End would thereby be put to Free Writing, and the World would afterwards have nothing to read but what happen'd to be the Opinions of Printers.

8. That if all Printers were determin'd not to print any thing till they were sure it would offend no body, there would be very little printed.

9. That if they sometimes print vicious or silly things not worth reading, it may not be because they approve such things themselves, but because the People are so viciously and corruptly educated that good things are not encouraged. I have known a very numerous Impression of Robin Hood's Songs go off in this Province at 2s. per Book, in less than a Twelvemonth; when a small Quantity of David's Psalms (an excellent Version) have lain upon my Hands above twice the Time.

10. That notwithstanding what might be urg'd in behalf of a Man's being allow'd to do in the Way of his Business whatever he is paid for, yet Printers do continually discourage the Printing of great Numbers of bad things, and stifle them in the Birth. I my self have constantly refused to print anything that might countenance Vice, or promote Immorality; tho' by complying in such Cases with the corrupt Taste of the Majority I might have got much Money. I have also always refus'd to print such things as might do real Injury to any Person, how much soever I have been solicited, and tempted with Offers of Great Pay; and how much soever I have by refusing got the Ill-will of those who would have employ'd me. I have hitherto fallen under the Resentment of large Bodies of Men, for refusing absolutely to print any of their Party or Personal Reflections. In this Manner I have made my self many Enemies, and the constant Fatigue of denying is almost insupportable. But the Publick being unacquainted with all this, whenever the poor Printer happens either through Ignorance or much Persuasion, to do any thing that is generally thought worthy of Blame, he meets with no more Friendship or Favour on the above Account, than if there were no Merit in't at all. Thus, as Waller says,

> Poets lose half the Praise they would have got
> Were it but known what they discreetly blot;

Yet are censur'd for every bad Line found in their Works with the utmost Severity.

I come now to the Particular Case of the N. B. above mention'd, about which there has been more Clamour against me, than ever before on any other Account.—In the Hurry of other Business an Advertisement was brought to me to be printed; it signified that such a Ship lying at such a Wharff, would sail for Barbadoes in such a Time, and that Freighters and Passengers might agree with the Captain at such a Place; so far is what's common: But at the Bottom this odd Thing was added, "N. B. No Sea Hens nor Black Gowns will be admitted on any Terms." I printed it, and receiv'd my Money; and the Advertisement was stuck up round the Town as usual. I had not so much Curiosity at that time as to enquire the Meaning of it, nor did I in the least imagine it would give so much Offence. Several good Men are very angry with me on this Occasion; they are pleas'd to say I have too much Sense to do such things ignorantly; that if they were Printers they would not have done such a thing on any Consideration; that it could proceed from nothing but my abundant Malice against Religion and the Clergy. They therefore declare they will not take any more of my Papers, nor have any farther Dealings with me; but will hinder me of all the Custom they can. All this is very hard!

I believe it had been better if I had refused to print the said Advertisement. However, 'tis done, and cannot be revok'd. I have only the following few Particulars to offer, some of them in my behalf, by way of Mitigation, and some not much to the Purpose; but I desire none of them may be read when the Reader is not in a very good Humour.

1. That I really did it without the least Malice, and imagin'd the N. B. was plac'd there only to make the Advertisement star'd at, and more generally read.

2. That I never saw the Word Sea-Hens before in my Life; nor have I yet ask'd the meaning of it; and tho' I had certainly known that Black Gowns in that place signified the Clergy of the Church of England, yet I have that confidence in the generous good Temper of such of them as I know, as to be well satisfied such a trifling mention of their Habit gives them no Disturbance.

3. That most of the Clergy in this and the neighbouring Provinces, are my Customers, and some of them my very good Friends; and I must be very malicious indeed, or very stupid,

to print this thing for a small Profit, if I had thought it would have given them just Cause of Offence.

4. That if I had much Malice against the Clergy, and withal much Sense; 'tis strange I never write or talk against the Clergy myself. Some have observed that 'tis a fruitful Topic, and the easiest to be witty upon of all others; yet I appeal to the Publick that I am never guilty this way, and to all my Acquaintances as to my Conversation.

5. That if a Man of Sense had Malice enough to desire to injure the Clergy, this is the foolishest Thing he could possibly contrive for that Purpose.

6. That I got Five Shillings by it.

7. That none who are angry with me would have given me so much to let it alone.

8. That if all the People of different Opinions in this Province would engage to give me as much for not printing things they don't like, as I can get by printing them, I should probably live a very easy Life; and if all Printers were everywhere so dealt by, there would be very little printed.

9. That I am oblig'd to all who take my Paper, and am willing to think they do it out of meer Friendship. I only desire they would think the same when I deal with them. I thank those who leave off, that they have taken it so long. But I beg they would not endeavour to dissuade others, for that will look like Malice.

10. That 'tis impossible any Man should know what he would do if he was a Printer.

11. That notwithstanding the Rashness and Inexperience of Youth, which is most likely to be prevail'd with to do things that ought not to be done; yet I have avoided printing such Things as usually give Offence either to Church or State, more than any Printer that has followed the Business in this Province before.

12. And lastly, That I have printed above a Thousand Advertisements which made not the least mention of *Sea-Hens* or *Black Gowns;* and this being the first Offence, I have the more Reason to expect Forgiveness.

I take leave to conclude with an old Fable, which some of my Readers have heard before, and some have not.

"A certain well-meaning Man and his Son, were travelling

towards a Market Town, with an Ass which they had to sell. The Road was bad; and the old Man therefore rid, but the Son went a-foot. The first Passenger they met, asked the Father if he was not ashamed to ride by himself, and suffer the poor Lad to wade along thro' the Mire; this induced him to take up his Son behind him: He had not travelled far, when he met others, who said, they are two unmerciful Lubbers to get both on the Back of that poor Ass, in such a deep Road. Upon this the old Man gets off, and let his Son ride alone. The next they met called the Lad a graceless, rascally young Jacka-napes, to ride in that Manner thro' the Dirt, while his aged Father trudged along on Foot; and they said the old Man was a Fool, for suffering it. He then bid his Son come down, and walk with him, and they travell'd on leading the Ass by the Halter; 'till they met another Company, who called them a Couple of senseless Blockheads, for going both on Foot in such a dirty Way, when they had an empty Ass with them, which they might ride upon. The old Man could bear no longer; My Son, said he, it grieves me much that we cannot please all these People. Let me throw the Ass over the next Bridge, and be no further troubled with him."

Had the old Man been seen acting this last Resolution, he would probably have been called a Fool for troubling himself about the different Opinions of all that were pleas'd to find Fault with him: Therefore, tho' I have a Temper almost as complying as his, I intend not to imitate him in this last Par-ticular. I consider the Variety of Humors among Men, and despair of pleasing every Body; yet I shall not therefore leave off Printing. I shall continue my Business, I shall not burn my Press and melt my Letters.

QUESTIONS

1. What fact is illustrated by the reference to Robin Hood's Songs and David's Psalms? Does this same condition exist today? Illustrate by examining the current "best-seller" list.
2. What restrictions or restraints does Franklin place on printers? In your opinion, do these restraints furnish grounds for a fed-eral or state censorship board?

3. What was the occasion for this essay? Note that Franklin does not indicate anywhere that he regrets having printed the advertisement with the fateful "N.B." Why not?
4. What is the tone of Franklin's introductory remarks?
5. Comment on the meaning of "indifferently" in paragraph 3. Make a list of other words in this essay that would probably not be used in the same sense today. Check your list in the *N.E.D.*
6. What stylistic effect is achieved by the fable at the end of the essay? Is it in the same tone as the opening remarks?

AREOPAGITICA

✍ John Milton

They, who to states and governors of the commonwealth
direct their speech, high court of parliament! or wanting such
access in a private condition, write that which they foresee may
advance the public good; I suppose them, as at the beginning
of no mean endeavour, not a little altered and moved inwardly
in their minds; some with doubt of what will be the success,
others with fear of what will be the censure; some with hope,
others with confidence of what they have to speak. And me
perhaps each of these dispositions, as the subject was whereon
I entered, may have at other times variously affected; and
likely might in these foremost expressions now also disclose
which of them swayed most, but that the very attempt of this
address thus made, and the thought of whom it hath recourse
to, hath got the power within me to a passion, far more welcome than incidental to a preface.

Which though I stay not to confess ere any ask, I shall be
blameless, if it be no other than the joy and gratulation which
it brings to all who wish to promote their country's liberty;
whereof this whole discourse proposed will be a certain testimony, if not a trophy. For this is not the liberty which we can
hope, that no grievance ever should arise in the commonwealth: that let no man in this world expect; but when com-
plaints are freely heard, deeply considered, and speedily reformed, then is the utmost bound of civil liberty obtained that
wise men look for. To which if I now manifest, by the very

Abridged. First published 1644.

sound of this which I shall utter, that we are already in good part arrived, and yet from such a steep disadvantage of tyranny and superstition grounded into our principles, as was beyond the manhood of a Roman recovery, it will be attributed first, as is most due, to the strong assistance of God, our deliverer; next, to your faithful guidance and undaunted wisdom, lords and commons of England! Neither is it in God's esteem, the diminution of his glory, when honourable things are spoken of good men, and worthy magistrates; which if I now first should begin to do, after so fair a progress of your laudable deeds, and such a long obligement upon the whole realm to your indefatigable virtues, I might be justly reckoned among the tardiest and the unwillingest of them that praise ye. . . .

For he who freely magnifies what hath been nobly done, and fears not to declare as freely what might be done better, gives ye the best covenant of his fidelity; and that his loyalest affection and his hope waits on your proceedings. His highest praising is not flattery, and his plainest advice is a kind of praising; for though I should affirm and hold by argument, that it would fare better with truth, with learning, and the commonwealth, if one of your published orders, which I should name, were called in; yet at the same time it could not but much redound to the lustre of your mild and equal government, whenas private persons are hereby animated to think ye better pleased with public advice than other statists have been delighted heretofore with public flattery. And men will then see what difference there is between the magnanimity of a triennial parliament, and that jealous haughtiness of prelates and cabin counsellors that usurped of late, whenas they shall observe ye in the midst of your victories and successes more gently brooking written exceptions against a voted order, than other courts, which had produced nothing worth memory but the weak ostentation of wealth, would have endured the least signified dislike at any sudden proclamation.

If I should thus far presume upon the meek demeanour of your civil and gentle greatness, lords and commons! as what your published order hath directly said, that to gainsay, I might defend myself with ease, if any should accuse me of being new or insolent, did they but know how much better I find ye esteem it to imitate the old and elegant humanity of Greece, than the barbaric pride of a Hunnish and Norwegian stateliness. And out of those ages, to whose polite wisdom and letters we owe that we are not yet Goths and Jutlanders, I could name him who from his private house wrote that discourse to the parliament of Athens, that persuades them to change the form of democracy which was then established. Such honour was done in those days to men who professed the study of wisdom and eloquence, not only in their own country, but in other lands, that cities and signiories heard them gladly, and with great respect, if they had aught in public to admonish the state. . . . But if from the industry of a life wholly dedicated to studious labours, and those natural endowments haply not the worst for two and fifty degrees of northern latitude, so much must be derogated, as to count me not equal to any of those who had this privilege, I would obtain to be thought not so inferior, as yourselves are superior to the most of them who received their counsel; and how far you excel them, be assured, lords and commons! there can no greater testimony appear, than when your prudent spirit acknowledges and obeys the voice of reason, from what quarter soever it be heard speaking; and renders ye as willing to repeal any act of your own setting forth, as any set forth by your predecessors.

If ye be thus resolved, as it were injury to think ye were not, I know not what should withhold me from presenting ye with a fit instance wherein to show both that love of truth which ye eminently profess, and that uprightness of your judgment which is not wont to be partial to yourselves; by judging over again that order which ye have ordained "to regulate printing: that no book, pamphlet, or paper shall be henceforth printed, unless the same be first approved and licensed by such, or at least one of such, as shall be thereto appointed." For that part which preserves justly every man's copy to himself, or provides for the poor, I touch not; only wish they be not made pretences to abuse and persecute honest and painful men, who offend not in either of these particulars. But that other clause of licensing books, which we thought had died with his brother quadragesimal and matrimonial when the prelates expired, I shall now attend with such a homily, as shall lay before ye, first, the inventors of it to be those whom ye will be loath to own; next, what is to be thought in general of reading, whatever sort the books be; and that this order avails nothing to the suppressing of scandalous, seditious, and libellous books, which were mainly intended to be suppressed. Last, that it will be primely to the discouragement of all learning, and the stop of truth, not only by disexercising and blunting our abilities, in what we know already, but by hindering and cropping the discovery that might be yet further made, both in religious and civil wisdom.

I deny not, but that it is of greatest concernment in the church and commonwealth, to have a vigilant eye how books demean themselves, as well as men; and thereafter to confine, imprison, and do sharpest justice on them as malefactors; for books are not absolutely dead things, but do contain a progeny of life in them to be as active as that soul was whose progeny they are; nay, they do preserve as in a vial the purest efficacy and extraction of that living intellect that bred them. I know they are as lively, and as vigorously productive, as those fabulous dragon's teeth: and being sown up and down, may chance to spring up armed men. And yet, on the other hand, unless wariness be used, as good almost kill a man as kill a good book: who kills a man kills a reasonable creature, God's image; but he who destroys a good book, kills reason itself, kills the image of God, as it were, in the eye. Many a man lives a burden to the earth; but a good book is the precious life-blood of a master-spirit, embalmed and treasured up on purpose to a life beyond life. It is true, no age can restore a life, whereof, perhaps, there is no great loss; and revolutions of ages do not oft recover the loss of a rejected truth, for the want of which whole nations fare the worse. We should be wary, therefore, what persecution we raise against the living labours of public men, how we spill that seasoned life of man, preserved and stored up in books; since we see a kind of homicide may be thus committed, sometimes a martyrdom; and if it extend to the whole impression, a kind of massacre, whereof the execution ends not in the slaying of an elemental life, but strikes at the ethereal and fifth essence, the breath of reason itself; slays an immortality rather than a life. But lest I should be con-

demned of introducing license, while I oppose licensing, I refuse not the pains to be so much historical, as will serve to
shew what hath been done by ancient and famous commonwealths, against this disorder, till the very time that this
project of licensing crept out of the inquisition, was catched up
by our prelates, and hath caught some of our presbyters.

In Athens, where books and wits were ever busier than in
any other part of Greece, I find but only two sorts of writings
which the magistrate cared to take notice of; those either blas-
phemous and atheistical, or libellous. Thus the books of Pro-
tagoras were by the judges of Areopagus, commanded to be
burnt, and himself banished the territory for a discourse,
begun with his confessing not to know "whether there were
gods, or whether not." And against defaming, it was agreed that
none should be traduced by name, as was the manner of Vetus
Comœdia, whereby we may guess how they censured libelling;
and this course was quick enough, as Cicero writes, to quell
both the desperate wits of other atheists, and the open way of
defaming, as the event showed. Of other sects and opinions,
though tending to voluptuousness, and the denying of divine
Providence, they took no heed. Therefore we do not read that
either Epicurus, or that libertine school of Cyrene, or what the
Cynic impudence uttered, was ever questioned by the laws.
Neither is it recorded that the writings of those old comedians
were suppressed, though the acting of them were forbid; and
that Plato commended the reading of Aristophanes, the loosest
of them all, to his royal scholar, Dionysius, is commonly
known, and may be excused, if holy Chrysostom, as is reported,
nightly studied so much the same author, and had the art to
cleanse a scurrilous vehemence into the style of a rousing
sermon. . . .

This much may give us light after what sort of books were
prohibited among the Greeks. The Romans also for many
ages trained up only to a military roughness, resembling most
the Lacedæmonian guise, knew of learning little but what their
twelve tables and the pontific college with their augurs and
flamens taught them in religion and law; so unacquainted with
other learning, that when Carneades and Critolaus, with the
stoic Diogenes, coming ambassadors to Rome, took thereby

occasion to give the city a taste of their philosophy, they were
suspected for seducers by no less a man than Cato the Censor,
who moved it in the senate to dismiss them speedily, and to
banish all such Attic babblers out of Italy. But Scipio and others
of the noblest senators withstood him and his old Sabine aus-
terity; honoured and admired the men; and the censor himself
at last, in his old age, fell to the study of that whereof before
he was so scrupulous. And yet, at the same time, Nævius and
Plautus, the first Latin comedians, had filled the city with all
the borrowed scenes of Menander and Philemon. Then began
to be considered there also what was to be done to libellous
books and authors; for Nævius was quickly cast into prison for
his unbridled pen, and released by the tribunes upon his recan-
tation: we read also that libels were burnt, and the makers
punished, by Augustus.

The like severity, no doubt, was used, if aught were impiously
written against their esteemed gods. Except in these two points,
how the world went in books, the magistrate kept no reckoning.
And therefore Lucretius, without impeachment, versifies his
Epicurism to Memmius, and had the honour to be set forth the
second time by Cicero, so great a father of the commonwealth;
although himself disputes against that opinion in his own writings. Nor was the satirical sharpness or naked plainness of
Lucilius, or Catullus, or Flaccus, by any order prohibited. And
for matters of state, the story of Titus Livius, though it extolled
that part which Pompey held, was not therefore suppressed by
Octavius Cæsar, of the other faction. But that Naso was by
him banished in his old age, for the wanton poems of his youth,
was but a mere covert of state over some secret cause; and
besides, the books were neither banished nor called in. From
hence we shall meet with little else but tyranny in the Roman
empire, that we may not marvel, if not so often bad as good
books were silenced. I shall therefore deem to have been large
enough, in producing what among the ancients was punishable to write, save only which, all other arguments were free to
treat on.

By this time the emperors were become Christians, whose
discipline in this point I do not find to have been more severe
than what was formerly in practice. The books of those whom

they took to be grand heretics were examined, refuted, and condemned in the general councils; and not till then were prohibited, or burnt, by authority of the emperor. As for the writings of heathen authors, unless they were plain invectives against Christianity, as those of Porphyrius and Proclus, they met with no interdict that can be cited, till about the year 400, in a Carthaginian council, wherein bishops themselves were forbid to read the books of Gentiles, but heresies they might read; while others long before them, on the contrary, scrupled more the books of heretics, than of Gentiles. And that the primitive councils and bishops were wont only to declare what books were not commendable, passing no further, but leaving it to each one's conscience to read or to lay by, till after the year 800, is observed already by Padre Paolo, the great unmasker of the Trentine council. After which time the popes of Rome, engrossing what they pleased of political rule into their own hands, extended their dominion over men's eyes, as they had before over their judgments, burning and prohibiting to be read what they fancied not; yet sparing in their censures, and the books not many which they so dealt with; till Martin the Fifth, by his bull, not only prohibited, but was the first that excommunicated the reading of heretical books; for about that time Wickliffe and Husse growing terrible, were they who first drove the papal court to a stricter policy of prohibiting. Which course Leo the Tenth and his successors followed, until the council of Trent and the Spanish inquisition, engendering together, brought forth or perfected those catalogues and expurging indexes, that rake through the entrails of many an old good author, with a violation worse than any could be offered to his tomb.

Nor did they stay in matters heretical, but any subject that was not to their palate, they either condemned in a prohibition, or had it straight into the new purgatory of an index. To fill up the measure of encroachment, their last invention was to ordain that no book, pamphlet, or paper should be printed (as if St. Peter had bequeathed them the keys of the press also as well as of Paradise) unless it were approved and licensed under the hands of two or three gluttonous friars. For example: —

"Let the chancellor Cini be pleased to see if in this present work be contained aught that may withstand the printing.

"Vincent Rabbata, Vicar of Florence."

"I have seen this present work, and find nothing athwart the catholic faith and good manners: in witness whereof I have given, &c.

"Nicolo Cini, Chancellor of Florence."

"Attending the precedent relation, it is allowed that this present work of Davanzati may be printed.

"Vincent Rabbata," &c.

"It may be printed, July 15.

"Friar Simon Mompei d'Amelia, Chancellor of the Holy Office in Florence."

Sure they have a conceit, if he of the bottomless pit had not long since broke prison, that this quadruple exorcism would bar him down. I fear their next design will be to get into their custody the licensing of that which they say Claudius intended,[1] but went not through with. Vouchsafe to see another of their forms, the Roman stamp:—

"Imprimatur, If it seem good to the reverend master of the Holy Palace.

"Belcastro, Vicegerent."

"Imprimatur,

"Friar Nicholo Rodolphi, Master of the Holy Palace."

Sometimes five imprimaturs are seen together, dialogue wise, in the piazza of one titlepage, complimenting and ducking each to other with their shaven reverences, whether the author, who stands by in perplexity at the foot of his epistle, shall to the press or to the spunge. These are the pretty responsories, these are the dear antiphonies, that so bewitched of late our prelates and their chaplains, with the goodly echo they made; and besotted us to the gay imitation of a lordly imprimatur, one from Lambeth-house, another from the west end of Paul's; so apishly romanizing, that the word of command still was set down in Latin; as if the learned grammati-

---

[1] Quo veniam daret flatum crepitumque ventris in convivio emittendi.— (Sueton. in Claudio.) [Milton's note.]

cal pen that wrote it would cast no ink without Latin; or perhaps, as they thought, because no vulgar tongue was worthy
to express the pure conceit of an imprimatur; but rather, as I
hope, for that our English, the language of men ever famous
and foremost in the achievements of liberty, will not easily
find servile letters enow to spell such a dictatory presumption
Englished.

And thus ye have the inventors and the original of book
licensing ripped up and drawn as lineally as any pedigree. We
have it not, that can be heard of, from any ancient state, or
polity, or church, nor by any statute left us by our ancestors
elder or later; nor from the modern custom of any reformed
city or church abroad; but from the most anti-christian council, and the most tyrannous inquisition that ever inquired.
. . . And this was the rare morsel so officiously snatched up,
and so illfavouredly imitated by our inquisiturient bishops,
and the attendant minorites, their chaplains. That ye like not
now these most certain authors of this licensing order, and
that all sinister intention was far distant from your thoughts,
when ye were importuned the passing it, all men who know
the integrity of your actions, and how ye honour truth, will
clear ye readily.

But some will say, what though the inventors were bad, the
thing for all that may be good. It may so; yet if that thing be
no such deep invention, but obvious and easy for any man to
light on, and yet best and wisest commonwealths through all
ages and occasions have forborne to use it, and falsest seducers
and oppressors of men were the first who took it up, and to no
other purpose but to obstruct and hinder the first approach of
reformation; I am of those who believe, it will be a harder
alchymy than Lullius ever knew, to sublimate any good use out
of such an invention. Yet this only is what I request to gain
from this reason, that it may be held a dangerous and suspicious fruit, as certainly it deserves, for the tree that bore it,
until I can dissect one by one the properties it has. But I have
first to finish, as was propounded, what is to be thought in general of reading books, whatever sort they be, and whether be
more the benefit or the harm that thence proceeds.

Not to insist upon the examples of Moses, Daniel, and Paul,

who were skilful in all the learning of the Egyptians, Chal-
deans, and Greeks, which could not probably be without reading their books of all sorts, in Paul especially, who thought it
no defilement to insert into holy scripture the sentences of
three Greek poets, and one of them a tragedian; the question
was notwithstanding sometimes controverted among the primitive doctors, but with great odds on that side which affirmed
it both lawful and profitable, as was then evidently perceived,
when Julian the Apostate, and subtlest enemy to our faith,
made a decree forbidding Christians the study of heathen
learning; for, said he, they wound us with our own weapons,
and with our own arts and sciences they overcome us. And indeed the Christians were put so to their shifts by this crafty
means, and so much in danger to decline into all ignorance,
that the two Appollinarii were fain, as a man may say, to coin
all the seven liberal sciences out of the Bible, reducing it into
divers forms of orations, poems, dialogues, even to the calculat-
ing of a new Christian grammar.

But, saith the historian, Socrates, the providence of God provided better than the industry of Appollinarius and his son, by
taking away that illiterate law with the life of him who devised
it. So great an injury they then held it to be deprived of Hel-
lenic learning; and thought it a persecution more undermining,
and secretly decaying the church, than the open cruelty of
Decius or Diocletian. And perhaps it was with the same politic
drift that the devil whipped St. Jerome in a lenten dream, for
reading Cicero; or else it was a phantasm, bred by the fever
which had then seized him. For had an angel been his disci-
pliner, unless it were for dwelling too much on Ciceronianisms,
and had chastised the reading, not the vanity, it had been
plainly partial, first, to correct him for grave Cicero, and not
for scurril Plautus, whom he confesses to have been reading
not long before; next to correct him only, and let so many
more ancient fathers wax old in those pleasant and florid
studies, without the lash of such a tutoring apparition. . . .

But if it be agreed we shall be tried by visions, there is a
vision recorded by Eusebius, far ancienter than this tale of
Jerome, to the nun Eustochium, and besides, has nothing of a
fever in it. Dionysius Alexandrinus was, about the year 240, a

person of great name in the church, for piety and learning, who had wont to avail himself much against heretics, by being conversant in their books; until a certain presbyter laid it scrupulously to his conscience, how he durst venture himself among those defiling volumes. The worthy man, loath to give offence, fell into a new debate with himself, what was to be thought; when suddenly a vision sent from God (it is his own epistle that so avers it) confirmed him in these words: "Read any books whatever come to thy hands, for thou art sufficient both to judge aright, and to examine each matter." To this revelation he assented the sooner, as he confesses, because it was answerable to that of the apostle to the Thessalonians: "Prove all things, hold fast that which is good."

And he might have added another remarkable saying of the same author: "To the pure, all things are pure;" not only meats and drinks, but all kind of knowledge, whether of good or evil: the knowledge cannot defile, nor consequently the books, if the will and conscience be not defiled. For books are as meats and viands are; some of good, some of evil substance; and yet God in that unapocryphal vision said without exception, "Rise, Peter, kill and eat;" leaving the choice to each man's discretion. Wholesome meats to a vitiated stomach differ little or nothing from unwholesome; and best books to a naughty mind are not unapplicable to occasions of evil. Bad meats will scarce breed good nourishment in the healthiest concoction; but herein the difference is of bad books, that they to a discreet and judicious reader serve in many respects to discover, to confute, to forewarn, and to illustrate. . . .

I conceive, therefore, that when God did enlarge the universal diet of man's body, (saving ever the rules of temperance,) he then also, as before, left arbitrary the dieting and repasting of our minds; as wherein every mature man might have to exercise his own leading capacity. How great a virtue is temperance, how much of moment through the whole life of man! Yet God commits the managing so great a trust, without particular law or prescription, wholly to the demeanour of every grown man. And therefore when he himself tabled the Jews from heaven, that omer, which was every man's daily portion of manna, is computed to have been more than might have well sufficed the heartiest feeder thrice as many meals. For those actions which enter into a man, rather than issue out of him, and therefore defile not, God uses not to captivate under a perpetual childhood of prescription, but trusts him with the gift of reason to be his own chooser; there were but little work left for preaching, if law and compulsion should grow so fast upon those things which heretofore were governed only by exhortation. Solomon informs us, that much reading is a weariness to the flesh; but neither he, nor other inspired author, tells us that such or such reading is unlawful; yet certainly had God thought good to limit us herein, it had been much more expedient to have told us what was unlawful, than what was wearisome.

As for the burning of those Ephesian books by St. Paul's converts; it is replied, the books were magic, the Syriac so renders them. It was a private act, a voluntary act, and leaves us to a voluntary imitation: the men in remorse burnt those books which were their own; the magistrate by this example is not appointed; these men practised the books, another might perhaps have read them in some sort usefully. Good and evil we know in the field of this world grow up together almost inseparably; and the knowledge of good is so involved and interwoven with the knowledge of evil, and in so many cunning resemblances hardly to be discerned, that those confused seeds which were imposed upon Psyche as an incessant labour to cull out, and sort asunder, were not more intermixed. It was from out the rind of one apple tasted, that the knowledge of good and evil, as two twins cleaving together, leaped forth into the world. And perhaps this is that doom which Adam fell into of knowing good and evil; that is to say, of knowing good by evil.

As therefore the state of man now is; what wisdom can there be to choose, what continence to forbear, without the knowledge of evil? He that can apprehend and consider vice with all her baits and seeming pleasures, and yet abstain, and yet distinguish, and yet prefer that which is truly better, he is the true warfaring Christian. I cannot praise a fugitive and cloistered virtue unexercised and unbreathed, that never sallies out and seeks her adversary, but slinks out of the race, where that immortal garland is to be run for, not without dust and heat. Assuredly we bring not innocence into the world, we bring impurity much rather; that which purifies us is trial, and trial is by what is contrary. That virtue therefore which is but a youngling in the contemplation of evil, and knows not the utmost that vice promises to her followers, and rejects it, is but a blank virtue, not a pure; her whiteness is but an excremental whiteness; which was the reason why our sage and serious poet Spenser, (whom I dare be known to think a better teacher than Scotus or Aquinas,) describing true temperance under the person of Guion, brings him in with his palmer through the cave of Mammon, and the bower of earthly bliss, that he might see and know, and yet abstain.

Since therefore the knowledge and survey of vice is in this world so necessary to the constituting of human virtue, and the scanning of error to the confirmation of truth, how can we more safely, and with less danger, scout into the regions of sin and falsity, than by reading all manner of tractates, and hearing all manner of reason? And this is the benefit which may be had of books promiscuously read. But of the harm that may result hence, three kinds are usually reckoned. First, is feared the infection that may spread; but then, all human learning and controversy in religious points must remove out of the world, yea, the Bible itself; for that ofttimes relates blasphemy not nicely, it describes the carnal sense of wicked men not unelegantly, it brings in holiest men passionately murmuring against Providence through all the arguments of Epicurus: in other great disputes it answers dubiously and darkly to the common reader. . . . For these causes we all know the Bible itself put by the papist into the first rank of prohibited books. The ancientest fathers must be next removed, as Clement of Alexandria, and that Eusebian book of evangelic preparation, transmitting our ears through a hoard of heathenish obscenities to receive the gospel. Who finds not that Irenæus, Epiphanius, Jerome, and others discover more heresies than they well confute, and that oft for heresy which is the truer opinion?

Nor boots it to say for these, and all the heathen writers of greatest infection, if it must be thought so, with whom is bound up the life of human learning, that they wrote in an unknown tongue, so long as we are sure those languages are known as well to the worst of men, who are both most able and most diligent to instil the poison they suck, first into the courts of princes, acquainting them with the choicest delights, and criticisms of sin. As perhaps did that Petronius, whom Nero called his arbiter, the master of his revels; and that notorious ribald of Arezzo, dreaded and yet dear to the Italian courtiers, I name not him, for posterity's sake, whom Henry the Eighth named in merriment his vicar of hell.[2] By which compendious way all the contagion that foreign books can infuse will find a passage to the people far easier and shorter than an Indian voyage, though it could be sailed either by the north of Cataio eastward, or of Canada westward, while our Spanish licensing gags the English press never so severely. . . .

Seeing therefore that those books, and those in great abundance, which are likeliest to taint both life and doctrine, cannot be suppressed without the fall of learning, and of all ability in disputation, and that these books of either sort are most and soonest catching to the learned, (from whom to the common people whatever is heretical or dissolute may quickly be conveyed,) and that evil manners are as perfectly learnt without books a thousand other ways which cannot be stopped, and evil doctrine not with books can propagate, except a teacher guide, which he might also do without writing, and so beyond prohibiting; I am not unable to unfold, how this cautelous enterprise of licensing can be exempted from the number of vain and impossible attempts. And he who were pleasantly disposed, could not well avoid to liken it to the exploit of that gallant man, who thought to pound up the crows by shutting his park gate.

Besides another inconvenience, if learned men be the first receivers out of books, and dispreaders both of vice and error, how shall the licensers themselves be confided in, unless we can confer upon them, or they assume to themselves, above all others in the land, the grace of infallibility and uncorruptedness? And again, if it be true, that a wise man, like a good refiner, can gather gold out of the drossiest volume, and that

[2] Sir Francis Bryan [*Editors' note*].

a fool will be a fool with the best book, yea, or without book; there is no reason that we should deprive a wise man of any advantage to his wisdom, while we seek to restrain from a fool that which being restrained will be no hinderance to his folly. For if there should be so much exactness always used to keep that from him which is unfit for his reading, we should in the judgment of Aristotle not only, but of Solomon, and of our Saviour, not vouchsafe him good precepts, and by consequence not willingly admit him to good books; as being certain that a wise man will make better use of an idle pamphlet, than a fool will do of sacred scripture.

It is next alleged, we must not expose ourselves to temptations without necessity, and next to that, not employ our time in vain things. To both these objections one answer will serve, out of the grounds already laid, that to all men such books are not temptations, nor vanities; but useful drugs and materials wherewith to temper and compose effective and strong medicines, which man's life cannot want. The rest, as children and childish men, who have not the art to qualify and prepare these working minerals, well may be exhorted to forbear; but hindered forcibly they cannot be, by all the licensing that sainted inquisition could ever yet contrive; which is what I promised to deliver next: that this order of licensing conduces nothing to the end for which it was framed; and hath almost prevented me by being clear already while thus much hath been explaining. See the ingenuity of truth, who, when she gets a free and willing hand, opens herself faster than the pace of method and discourse can overtake her. It was the task which I began with, to shew that no nation, or well instituted state, if they valued books at all, did ever use this way of licensing; and it might be answered, that this is a piece of prudence lately discovered.

To which I return, that as it was a thing slight and obvious to think on, so if it had been difficult to find out, there wanted not among them long since, who suggested such a course; which they not following, leave us a pattern of their judgment that it was not the not knowing, but the not approving, which was the cause of their not using it. Plato, a man of high authority indeed, but least of all for his Commonwealth, in the book of his laws, which no city ever yet received, fed his fancy with making many edicts to his airy burgomasters, which they who otherwise admire him, wish had been rather buried and excused in the genial cups of an academic night sitting. By which laws he seems to tolerate no kind of learning, but by unalterable decree, consisting most of practical traditions, to the attainment whereof a library of smaller bulk than his own dialogues would be abundant. And there also enacts, that no poet should so much as read to any private man what he had written, until the judges and law keepers had seen it, and allowed it; but that Plato meant this law peculiarly to that commonwealth which he had imagined, and to no other, is evident. Why was he not else a lawgiver to himself, but a transgressor, and to be expelled by his own magistrates, both for the wanton epigrams and dialogues which he made, and his perpetual reading of Sophron Mimus and Aristophanes, books of grossest infamy; and also for commending the latter of them, though he were the malicious libeller of his chief friends, to be read by the tyrant Dionysius, who had little need of such trash to spend his time on? But that he knew this licensing of poems had reference and dependence to many other provisoes there set down in his fancied republic, which in this world could have no place; and so neither he himself, nor any magistrate or city, ever imitated that course, which, taken apart from those other collateral injunctions, must needs be vain and fruitless.

For if they fell upon one kind of strictness, unless their care were equal to regulate all other things of like aptness to corrupt the mind, that single endeavour they knew would be but a fond labour; to shut and fortify one gate against corruption, and be necessitated to leave others round about wide open. If we think to regulate printing, thereby to rectify manners, we must regulate all recreations and pastimes, all that is delightful to man. No music must be heard, no song be set or sung, but what is grave and doric. There must be licensing dancers, that no gesture, motion, or deportment be taught our youth, but what by their allowance shall be thought honest; for such Plato was provided of. It will ask more than the work of twenty licensers to examine all the lutes, the violins, and the guitars in every house; they must not be suffered to prattle as they do, but must be licensed what they may say. And who shall silence all the airs and madrigals that whisper softness in chambers? The windows also, and the balconies, must be thought on; these are shrewd books, with dangerous frontispieces, set to sale: who shall prohibit them, shall twenty licensers? The villages also must have their visitors to inquire what lectures the bagpipe and the rebec reads, even to the ballatry and the gamut of every municipal fiddler; for these are the countryman's Arcadias, and his Monte Mayors.

Next, what more national corruption, for which England hears ill abroad, than household gluttony? Who shall be the rectors of our daily rioting? And what shall be done to inhibit the multitudes that frequent those houses where drunkenness is sold and harboured? Our garments also should be referred to the licensing of some more sober work-masters, to see them cut into a less wanton garb. Who shall regulate all the mixed conversation of our youth, male and female together, as is the fashion of this country? Who shall still appoint what shall be discoursed, what presumed, and no further? Lastly, who shall forbid and separate all idle resort, all evil company? These things will be, and must be; but how they shall be least hurtful, how least enticing, herein consists the grave and governing wisdom of a state.

To sequester out of the world into Atlantic and Utopian politics, which never can be drawn into use, will not mend our condition; but to ordain wisely as in this world of evil, in the midst whereof God hath placed us unavoidably. Nor is it Plato's licensing of books will do this, which necessarily pulls along with it so many other kinds of licensing, as will make us all both ridiculous and weary, and yet frustrate; but those unwritten, or at least unconstraining laws of virtuous education, religious and civil nurture, which Plato there mentions, as the bonds and ligaments of the commonwealth, the pillars and the sustainers of every written statute; these they be, which will bear chief sway in such matters as these, when all licensing will be easily eluded. Impunity and remissness for certain are the bane of a commonwealth; but here the great art lies, to discern in what the law is to bid restraint and punishment, and in what things persuasion only is to work. If every action which is good or evil in man at ripe years were to be under pittance, prescription, and compulsion, what were virtue but a name, what praise could be then due to well doing, what gramercy to be sober, just, or continent?

Many there be that complain of divine Providence for suffering Adam to transgress. Foolish tongues! when God gave him reason, he gave him freedom to choose, for reason is but choosing; he had been else a mere artificial Adam, such an Adam as he is in the motions. We ourselves esteem not of that obedience, or love, or gift, which is of force; God therefore left him free, set before him a provoking object ever almost in his eyes; herein consisted his merit, herein the right of his reward, the praise of his abstinence. Wherefore did he create passions within us, pleasures round about us, but that these rightly tempered are the very ingredients of virtue? They are not skilful considerers of human things, who imagine to remove sin, by removing the matter of sin; for, besides that it is a huge heap increasing under the very act of diminishing, though some part of it may for a time be withdrawn from some persons, it cannot from all, in such a universal thing as books are; and when this is done, yet the sin remains entire. Though ye take from a covetous man all his treasure, he has yet one jewel left, ye cannot bereave him of his covetousness. Banish all objects of lust, shut up all youth into the severest discipline that can be exercised in any hermitage, ye cannot make them chaste, that came not thither so: such great care and wisdom is required to the right managing of this point.

Suppose we could expel sin by this means; look how much we thus expel of sin, so much we expel of virtue: for the matter of them both is the same: remove that, and ye remove them both alike. This justifies the high providence of God, who, though he commands us temperance, justice, continence, yet pours out before us even to a profuseness all desirable things, and gives us minds that can wander beyond all limit and satiety. Why should we then affect a rigour contrary to the manner of God and of nature, by abridging or scanting those means, which books freely permitted, are both to the trial of virtue, and the exercise of truth?

It would be better done, to learn that the law must needs

be frivolous, which goes to restrain things, uncertainly and yet equally working to good and to evil. And were I the chooser, a dram of well-doing should be preferred before many times as much the forcible hinderance of evil doing. For God sure esteems the growth and completing of one virtuous person, more than the restraint of ten vicious. . . .

If then the order shall not be vain and frustrate, behold a new labour, lords and commons, ye must repeal and proscribe all scandalous and unlicensed books already printed and divulged; after ye have drawn them up into a list, that all may know which are condemned, and which not; and ordain that no foreign books be delivered out of custody, till they have been read over. This office will require the whole time of not a few overseers, and those no vulgar men. There be also books which are partly useful and excellent, partly culpable and pernicious; this work will ask as many more officials, to make expurgations and expunctions, that the commonwealth of learning be not damnified. In fine, when the multitude of books increase upon their hands, ye must be fain to catalogue all those printers who are found frequently offending, and forbid the importation of their whole suspected typography. In a word, that this your order may be exact, and not deficient, ye must reform it perfectly, according to the model of Trent and Sevil, which I know ye abhor to do.

Yet though ye should condescend to this, which God forbid, the order still would be but fruitless and defective to that end whereto ye meant it. If to prevent sects and schisms, who is so unread or uncathechised in story, that hath not heard of many sects refusing books as a hinderance, and preserving their doctrine unmixed for many ages, only by unwritten traditions? The Christian faith (for that was once a schism!) is not unknown to have spread all over Asia, ere any gospel or epistle was seen in writing. If the amendment of manners be aimed at, look into Italy and Spain, whether those places be one scruple the better, the honester, the wiser, the chaster, since all the inquisitional rigour that hath been executed upon books.

Another reason, whereby to make it plain that this order will miss the end it seeks, consider by the quality which ought to be in every licenser. It cannot be denied, but that he who is made judge to sit upon the birth or death of books, whether they may be wafted into this world or not, had need to be a man above the common measure, both studious, learned, and judicious; there may be else no mean mistakes in the censure of what is passable or not; which is also no mean injury. If he be of such worth as behoves him, there cannot be a more tedious and unpleasing journeywork, a greater loss of time levied upon his head, than to be made the perpetual reader of unchosen books and pamphlets, ofttimes huge volumes. There is no book that is acceptable, unless at certain seasons; but to be enjoined the reading of that at all times, and in a hand scarce legible, whereof three pages would not down at any time in the fairest print, is an imposition I cannot believe how he that values time, and his own studies, or is but of a sensible nostril, should be able to endure. In this one thing I crave leave of the present licensers to be pardoned for so thinking: who doubtless took this office up, looking on it through their obedience to the parliament, whose command perhaps made all things seem easy and unlaborious to them; but that this short trial hath wearied them out already, their own expressions and excuses to them who make so many journeys to solicit their licence, are testimony enough. Seeing therefore those, who now possess the employment, by all evident signs wish themselves well rid of it, and that no man of worth, none that is not a plain unthrift of his own hours, is ever likely to succeed them, except he mean to put himself to the salary of a press corrector, we may easily foresee what kind of licensers we are to expect hereafter, either ignorant, imperious, and remiss, or basely pecuniary. This is what I had to show, wherein this order cannot conduce to that end whereof it bears the intention.

I lastly proceed from the no good it can do, to the manifest hurt it causes, in being first the greatest discouragement and affront that can be offered to learning and to learned men. It was the complaint and lamentation of prelates, upon every least of a motion to remove pluralities, and distribute more equally church revenues, that then all learning would be for ever dashed and discouraged. But as for that opinion, I never found cause to think that the tenth part of learning stood or fell with the clergy: nor could I ever but hold it for a sordid and unworthy speech of any churchman, who had a competency left him. If therefore ye be loath to dishearten utterly and discontent, not the mercenary crew of false pretenders to learning, but the free and ingenuous sort of such as evidently were born to study and love learning for itself, not for lucre, or any other end, but the service of God and of truth, and perhaps that lasting fame and perpetuity of praise, which God and good men have consented shall be the reward of those whose published labours advance the good of mankind: then know, that so far to distrust the judgment and the honesty of one who hath but a common repute in learning, and never yet offended, as not to count him fit to print his mind without a tutor and examiner, lest he should drop a schism, or something of corruption, is the greatest displeasure and indignity to a free and knowing spirit that can be put upon him.

What advantage is it to be a man, over it is to be a boy at school, if we have only escaped the ferula, to come under the fescue of an imprimatur? if serious and elaborate writings, as if they were no more than the theme of a grammar-lad under his pedagogue, must not be uttered without the cursory eyes of a temporizing and extemporizing licenser? He who is not trusted with his own actions, his drift not being known to be evil, and standing to the hazard of law and penalty, has no great argument to think himself reputed in the commonwealth wherein he was born for other than a fool or a foreigner. When a man writes to the world, he summons up all his reason and deliberation to assist him; he searches, meditates, is industrious, and likely consults and confers with his judicious friends; after all which done, he takes himself to be informed in what he writes, as well as any that wrote before him; if in this, the most consummate act of his fidelity and ripeness, no years, no industry, no former proof of his abilities, can bring him to that state of maturity, as not to be still mistrusted and suspected, unless he carry all his considerate diligence, all his midnight watchings, and expense of Palladian oil, to the hasty view of an unleisured licenser, perhaps much his younger, perhaps far his inferior in judgment, perhaps one who never knew the labour of bookwriting; and if he be not repulsed, or slighted, must appear in print like a puny with his guardian, and his censor's hand on the back of his title to be his bail and surety, that he is no idiot or seducer; it cannot be but a dishonour and derogation to the author, to the book, to the privilege and dignity of learning.

And what if the author shall be one so copious of fancy, as to have many things well worth the adding, come into his mind after licensing, while the book is yet under the press, which not seldom happens to the best and diligentest writers; and that perhaps a dozen times in one book. The printer dares not go beyond his licensed copy; so often then must the author trudge to his leave-giver, that those his new insertions may be viewed; and many a jaunt will be made, ere that licenser, for it must be the same man, can either be found, or found at leisure; meanwhile either the press must stand still, which is no small damage, or the author lose his accuratest thoughts, and send the book forth worse than he had made it, which to a diligent writer is the greatest melancholy and vexation that can befall.

And how can a man teach with authority, which is the life of teaching; how can he be a doctor in his book, as he ought to be, or else had better be silent, whenas all he teaches, all he delivers, is but under the tuition, under the correction of his patriarchal licenser, to blot or alter what precisely accords not with the hide-bound humour which he calls his judgment? When every acute reader, upon the first sight of a pedantic licence, will be ready with these like words to ding the book a quoit's distance from him: —"I hate a pupil teacher; I endure not an instructor that comes to me under the wardship of an overseeing fist. I know nothing of the licenser, but that I have his own hand here for his arrogance; who shall warrant me his judgment?" "The state, sir," replies, the stationer: but has a quick return:—"The state shall be my governors, but not my critics; they may be mistaken in the choice of a licenser, as easily as this licenser may be mistaken in an author. This is some common stuff:" and he might add from Sir Francis Bacon, that "such authorized books are but the language of the times." For though a licenser should happen to be judicious more than ordinary, which will be a great jeopardy of

the next succession, yet his very office and his commission
enjoins him to let pass nothing but what is vulgarly received
already.

Nay, which is more lamentable, if the work of any deceased
author, though never so famous in his lifetime, and even to
this day, comes to their hands for licence to be printed, or
reprinted, if there be found in his book one sentence of a ven-
turous edge, uttered in the height of zeal, (and who knows
whether it might not be the dictate of a divine spirit?) yet,
not suiting with every low decrepit humour of their own,
though it were Knox himself, the reformer of a kingdom, that
spake it, they will not pardon him their dash; the sense of
that great man shall to all posterity be lost, for the fearfulness,
or the presumptuous rashness of a perfunctory licenser. And
to what an author this violence hath been lately done, and in
what book, of greatest consequence to be faithfully published,
I could now instance, but shall forbear till a more convenient
season. Yet if these things be not resented seriously and timely
by them who have the remedy in their power, but that such
ironmoulds as these shall have authority to gnaw out the
choicest periods of exquisitest books, and to commit such a
treacherous fraud against the orphan remainders of worthiest
men after death, the more sorrow will belong to that hapless
race of men, whose misfortune it is to have understanding.
Henceforth let no man care to learn, or care to be more than
worldly wise; for certainly in higher matters to be ignorant
and slothful, to be a common steadfast dunce, will be the only
pleasant life, and only in request.

And as it is a particular disesteem of every knowing person
alive, and most injurious to the written labours and monuments of the dead, so to me it seems an undervaluing and
vilifying of the whole nation. I cannot set so light by all the
invention, the art, the wit, the grave and solid judgment which
is in England, as that it can be comprehended in any twenty
capacities, how good soever; much less that it should not pass
except their superintendence be over it, except it be sifted and
strained with their strainers, that it should be uncurrent without their manual stamp. Truth and understanding are not
such wares as to be monopolized and traded in by tickets, and

statutes, and standards. We must not think to make a staple commodity of all the knowledge in the land, to mark and license it like our broad-cloth and our woolpacks. What is it but a servitude like that imposed by the Philistines, not to be allowed the sharpening of our own axes and coulters, but we must repair from all quarters to twenty licensing forges?

Had any one written and divulged erroneous things and scandalous to honest life, misusing and forfeiting the esteem had of his reason among men, if after conviction this only censure were adjudged him, that he should never henceforth write, but what were first examined by an appointed officer, whose hand should be annexed to pass his credit for him, that now he might be safely read; it could not be apprehended less than a disgraceful punishment. Whence to include the whole nation, and those that never yet thus offended, under such a diffident and suspectful prohibition, may plainly be understood what a disparagement it is. So much the more whenas debtors and delinquents may walk abroad without a keeper, but unoffensive books must not stir forth without a visible jailor in their title. Nor is it to the common people less than a reproach; for if we be so jealous over them, as that we dare not trust them with an English pamphlet, what do we but censure them for a giddy, vicious, and ungrounded people; in such a sick and weak state of faith and discretion, as to be able to take nothing down but through the pipe of a licenser? That this is care or love of them, we cannot pretend, whenas in those popish places, where the laity are most hated and despised, the same strictness is used over them. Wisdom we cannot call it, because it stops but one breach of licence, nor that neither: whenas those corruptions, which it seeks to prevent, break in faster at other doors, which cannot be shut.

And in conclusion it reflects to the disrepute of our ministers also, of whose labours we should hope better, and of their proficiency which their flock reaps by them, than that after all this light of the gospel which is, and is to be, and all this continual preaching, they should be still frequented with such an unprincipled, unedified, and laic rabble, as that the whiff of every new pamphlet should stagger them out of their catechism and Christian walking. This may have much reason to discourage the ministers, when such a low conceit is had of all their exhortations, and the benefiting of their hearers, as that they are not thought fit to be turned loose to three sheets of paper without a licenser; that all the sermons, all the lectures preached, printed, vended in such numbers, and such volumes, as have now well-nigh made all other books unsaleable, should not be armour enough against one single Enchiridion, without the castle of St. Angelo of an imprimatur.

And least some should persuade ye, lords and commons, that these arguments of learned men's discouragement at this your order are mere flourishes, and not real, I could recount what I have seen and heard in other countries, where this kind of inquisition tyrannizes; when I have sat among their learned men, (for that honour I had,) and been counted happy to be born in such a place of philosophic freedom, as they supposed England was, while themselves did nothing but bemoan the servile condition into which learning amongst them was brought; that this was it which had damped the glory of Italian wits; that nothing had been there written now these many years but flattery and fustian. There it was that I found and visited the famous Galileo, grown old, a prisoner to the inquisition, for thinking in astronomy otherwise then the Franciscan and Dominican licensers thought. And though I knew that England then was groaning loudest under the prelatical yoke, nevertheless I took it as a pledge of future happiness, that other nations were so persuaded of her liberty.

Yet was it beyond my hope, that those worthies were then breathing in her air, who should be her leaders to such a deliverance, as shall never be forgotten by any revolution of time that this world hath to finish. When that was once begun, it was as little in my fear, that what words of complaint I heard among learned men of other parts uttered against the inquisition, the same I should hear, by as learned men at home, uttered in time of parliament against an order of licensing; and that so generally, that when I had disclosed myself a companion of their discontent, I might say, if without envy, that he whom an honest quæstorship had endeared to the Sicilians, was not more by them importuned against Verres, than the favourable opinion which I had among many who honour ye, and are known and respected by ye, loaded me with entreaties and persuasions, that I would not despair to lay together that which just reason should bring into my mind, towards the removal of an undeserved thraldom upon learning.

That this is not therefore the disburdening of a particular fancy, but the common grievance of all those who had prepared their minds and studies above the vulgar pitch, to advance truth in others, and from others to entertain it, thus much may satisfy. And in their name I shall for neither friend nor foe conceal what the general murmur is; that if it come to inquisitioning again, and licensing, and that we are so timorous of ourselves, and suspicious of all men, as to fear each book, and the shaking of each leaf, before we know what the contents are; if some who but of late were little better than silenced from preaching, shall come now to silence us from reading, except what they please, it cannot be guessed what is intended by some but a second tyranny over learning: and will soon put it out of controversy, that bishops and presbyters are the same to us, both name and thing. . . .

Lords and commons of England! consider what nation it is whereof ye are, and whereof ye are the governors: a nation not slow and dull, but of a quick, ingenious, and piercing spirit; acute to invent, subtile and sinewy to discourse, not beneath the reach of any point the highest that human capacity can soar to. Therefore the studies of learning in her deepest sciences have been so ancient, and so eminent among us, that writers of good antiquity and able judgment have been persuaded, that even the school of Pythagoras, and the Persian wisdom, took beginning from the old philosophy of this island. And that wise and civil Roman, Julius Agricola, who governed once here for Cæsar, preferred the natural wits of Britain before the laboured studies of the French.

Nor is it for nothing that the grave and frugal Transylvanian sends out yearly from as far as the mountainous borders of Russia, and beyond the Hercynian wilderness, not their youth, but their staid men, to learn our language and our theological arts. Yet that which is above all this, the favour and the love of Heaven, we have great argument to think in a peculiar manner propitious and propending towards us. Why else was this nation chosen before any other, that out of her, as out of Sion, should be proclaimed and sounded forth the first tidings and trumpet of reformation to all Europe? And had it not been the obstinate perverseness of our prelates against the divine and admirable spirit of Wickliffe, to suppress him as a schismatic and innovator, perhaps neither the Bohemian Husse and Jerome, no, nor the name of Luther or of Calvin, had been ever known: the glory of reforming all our neighbours had been completely ours. But now, as our obdurate clergy have with violence demeaned the matter, we are become hitherto the latest and the backwardest scholars, of whom God offered to have made us the teachers.

Now once again by all concurrence of signs, and by the general instinct of holy and devout men, as they daily and solemnly express their thoughts, God is decreeing to begin some new and great period in his church, even to the reforming of reformation itself; what does he then but reveal himself to his servants, and as his manner is, first to his Englishmen? I say, as his manner is, first to us, though we mark not the method of his counsels, and are unworthy. Behold now this vast city, a city of refuge, the mansion-house of liberty, encompassed and surrounded with his protection; the shop of war hath not there more anvils and hammers working, to fashion out the plates and instruments of armed justice in defence of beleaguered truth, than there be pens and heads there, sitting by their studious lamps, musing, searching, revolving new notions and ideas wherewith to present, as with their homage and their fealty, the approaching reformation: others as fast reading, trying all things, assenting to the force of reason and convincement.

What could a man require more from a nation so pliant and so prone to seek after knowledge? What wants there to such a towardly and pregnant soil, but wise and faithful labourers, to make a knowing people, a nation of prophets, of sages, and of worthies? We reckon more than five months yet to harvest; there need not be five weeks, had we but eyes to lift up, the fields are white already. Where there is much desire to learn, there of necessity will be much arguing, much writing, many opinions; for opinion in good men is but knowledge in the making. Under these fantastic terrors of sect and schism, we wrong the earnest and zealous thirst after knowledge and understanding, which God hath stirred up in this city. What some lament of, we rather should rejoice at, should rather praise this pious forwardness among men, to reassume the ill-deputed care of their religion into their own hands again. A little generous prudence, a little forbearance of one another, and some grain of charity might win all these diligencies to join and unite into one general and brotherly search after truth; could we but forego this prelatical tradition of crowding free consciences and Christian liberties into canons and precepts of men. I doubt not, if some great and worthy stranger should come among us, wise to discern the mould and temper of a people, and how to govern it, observing the high hopes and aims, the diligent alacrity of our extended thoughts and reasonings in the pursuance of truth and freedom, but that he would cry out as Pyrrhus did, admiring the Roman docility and courage, "If such were my Epirots, I would not despair the greatest design that could be attempted to make a church or kingdom happy." . . .

What should ye do then, should ye suppress all this flowery crop of knowledge and new light sprung up and yet springing daily in this city? Should ye set an oligarchy of twenty engrossers over it, to bring a famine upon our minds again, when we shall know nothing but what is measured to us by their bushel? Believe it, lords and commons! they who counsel ye to such a suppressing, do as good as bid ye suppress yourselves; and I will soon show how. If it be desired to know the immediate cause of all this free writing and free speaking, there cannot be assigned a truer than your own mild, and free, and humane government; it is the liberty, lords and commons, which your own valorous and happy counsels have purchased us; liberty which is the nurse of all great wits: this is that which hath rarified and enlightened our spirits like the influence of heaven: this is that which hath enfranchised, enlarged, and lifted up our apprehensions degrees above themselves. Ye cannot make us now less capable, less knowing, less eagerly pursuing of the truth, unless ye first make yourselves, that made us so, less the lovers, less the founders of our true liberty. We can grow ignorant again, brutish, formal, and slavish, as ye found us; but you then must first become that which ye cannot be, oppressive, arbitrary, and tyrannous, as they were from whom ye have freed us. That our hearts are now more capacious, our thoughts more erected to the search and expectation of greatest and exactest things, is the issue of your own virtue propagated in us; ye cannot suppress that unless ye reinforce an abrogated and merciless law, that fathers may dispatch at will their own children. And who shall then stick closest to ye and excite others? Not he who takes up arms for coat and conduct, and his four nobles of Danegelt. Although I dispraise not the defence of just immunities, yet love my peace better, if that were all. Give me the liberty to know, to utter, and to argue freely according to conscience, above all liberties. . . .

QUESTIONS

1. Who was it "who from his private house wrote that discourse to the parliament of Athens"?
2. To what in the licensing act does Milton refer when he speaks of "that part which preserves justly every man's copy to himself"? What modern provision is made for this preservation?
3. Where in the essay does Milton first lay before his audience the principle on which his speech is organized? Make an outline of the essay.
4. Find in Burchard's essay a corollary to Milton's statement that "books are not absolutely dead things."
5. Study Milton's punctuation, and determine how his use of the colon and semicolon differs from that employed today. Note also any peculiarities of grammatical construction and explain them.
6. Where in *Areopagitica* do you find Milton expressing the doctrine *Quis custodiet ipsos custodes*?
7. On what grounds does Milton excuse Plato for advocating licensing in his *Republic*? (For an attack on Plato's illiberalism, see K. R. Popper's *The Open Society and Its Enemies*.)
8. Can you account for the use of a singular verb with a compound subject, as in "his very office and his commission enjoins him . . ."?
9. The rhythm of the prose undergoes a subtle change near the end of the essay. Describe the change and account for it.

LIBERTY OF THE PRESS
IN THE UNITED STATES
✓ Alexis de Tocqueville

The influence of the liberty of the press does not affect
political opinions alone, but it extends to all the opinions of
men, and it modifies customs as well as laws. In another part
of this work I shall attempt to determinate the degree of influence which the liberty of the press has exercised upon civil
society in the United States, and to point out the direction
which it has given to the ideas, as well as the tone which it
has imparted to the character and the feelings, of the Anglo-
Americans, but at present I purpose simply to examine the
effects produced by the liberty of the press in the political
world. . . .

In the countries in which the doctrine of the sovereignty of
the people ostensibly prevails, the censorship of the press is
not only dangerous, but it is absurd. When the right of every
citizen to co-operate in the government of society is acknowledged, every citizen must be presumed to possess the power
of discriminating between the different opinions of his con-
temporaries, and of appreciating the different facts from
which inferences may be drawn. The sovereignty of the people
and the liberty of the press may therefore be looked upon as
correlative institutions; just as the censorship of the press and
universal suffrage are two things which are irreconcilably
opposed, and which cannot long be retained among the insti-

From *Democracy in America* (1835; the Henry Reeve translation).

tutions of the same people. Not a single individual of the twelve millions who inhabit the territory of the United States has as yet dared to propose any restrictions to the liberty of the press. . . .

America is perhaps, at this moment, the country of the whole world which contains the fewest germs of revolution; but the press is not less destructive in its principles than in France, and it displays the same violence without the same reasons for indignation. In America, as in France, it constitutes a singular power, so strangely composed of mingled good and evil that it is at the same time indispensable to the existence of freedom, and nearly incompatible with the maintenance of public order. Its power is certainly much greater in France than in the United States; though nothing is more rare in the latter country than to hear of a prosecution having been instituted against it. The reason of this is perfectly simple: the Americans, having once admitted the doctrine of the sovereignty of the people, apply it with perfect consistency. It was never their intention to found a permanent state of things with elements which undergo daily modifications; and there is consequently nothing criminal in an attack upon the existing laws, provided it be not attended with a violent infraction of them. They are moreover of opinion that courts of justice are unable to check the abuses of the press; and that as the subtlety of human language perpetually eludes the severity of judicial analysis, offenses of this nature are apt to escape the hand which attempts to apprehend them. They hold that to act with efficacy upon the press it would be necessary to find a tribunal, not only devoted to the existing order of things, but capable of surmounting the influence of public opinion; a tribunal which should conduct its proceedings without publicity, which should pronounce its decrees without assigning its motives, and punish the intentions even more than the language of an author. Whosoever should have the power of creating and maintaining a tribunal of this kind would waste his time in prosecuting the liberty of the press; for he would be the supreme master of the whole community, and he would be as free to rid himself of the authors as of their writings. In this question, therefore, there is no medium between servitude and extreme license; in order to enjoy the inestimable benefits which the liberty of the press ensures, it is necessary to submit to the inevitable evils which it engenders. To expect to acquire the former and to escape the latter is to cherish one of those illusions which commonly mislead nations in their times of sickness, when, tired with faction and exhausted by effort, they attempt to combine hostile opinions and contrary principles upon the same soil.

The small influence of the American journals is attributable to several reasons, amongst which are the following:

The liberty of writing, like all other liberty, is most formidable when it is a novelty; for a people which has never been accustomed to co-operate in the conduct of State affairs places implicit confidence in the first tribune who arouses its attention. The Anglo-Americans have enjoyed this liberty ever since the foundation of the settlements; moreover, the press cannot create human passions by its own power, however skilfully it may kindle them where they exist. In America politics are discussed with animation and a varied activity, but they rarely touch those deep passions which are excited whenever the positive interest of a part of the community is impaired: but in the United States the interests of the community are in a most prosperous condition. A single glance upon a French and an American newspaper is sufficient to show the difference which exists between the two nations on this head. In France the space allotted to commercial advertisements is very limited, and the intelligence is not considerable, but the most essential part of the journal is that which contains the discussion of the politics of the day. In America three-quarters of the enormous sheet which is set before the reader are filled with advertisements, and the remainder is frequently occupied by political intelligence or trivial anecdotes: it is only from time to time that one finds a corner devoted to passionate discussions like those with which the journalists of France are wont to indulge their readers.

It has been demonstrated by observation, and discovered by the innate sagacity of the pettiest as well as the greatest of despots, that the influence of a power is increased in proportion as its direction is rendered more central. In France the press combines a twofold centralization; almost all its power is centered in the same spot, and vested in the same hands, for its organs are far from numerous. . . .

Neither of these kinds of centralization exists in America. The United States have no metropolis; the intelligence as well as the power of the country are dispersed abroad, and instead of radiating from a point, they cross each other in every direction; the Americans have established no central control over the expression of opinion, any more than over the conduct of business. These are circumstances which do not depend on human foresight; but it is owing to the laws of the Union that there are no licenses to be granted to printers, no securities demanded from editors as in France, and no stamp duty as in France and formerly in England. The consequence of this is that nothing is easier than to set up a newspaper, and a small number of readers suffices to defray the expenses of the editor.

The number of periodical and occasional publications which appear in the United States actually surpasses belief. The most enlightened Americans attribute the subordinate influence of the press to this excessive dissemination; and it is adopted as an axiom of political science in that country that the only way to neutralize the effect of public journals is to multiply them indefinitely. . . .

In America there is scarcely a hamlet which has not its own newspaper. It may readily be imagined that neither discipline nor unity of design can be communicated to so multifarious a host, and each one is consequently led to fight under his own standard. All the political journals of the United States are indeed arrayed on the side of the administration or against it; but they attack and defend in a thousand different ways. They cannot succeed in forming those great currents of opinion which overwhelm the most solid obstacles. This division of the influence of the press produces a variety of other consequences which are scarcely less remarkable. The facility with which journals can be established induces a multitude of individuals to take a part in them; but as the extent of competition precludes the possibility of considerable profit, the most distinguished classes of society are rarely led to engage in these undertakings. But such is the number of the public prints that, even if they were a source of wealth, writers of ability could not be found to direct them all. . . . The characteristics of the American journalist consist in an open and coarse appeal to the passions of the populace; and he habitually abandons the principles of political science to assail the characters of individuals, to track them into private life, and disclose all their weaknesses and errors. . . .

It cannot be denied that the effects of this extreme license of the press tend indirectly to the maintenance of public order. The individuals who are already in the possession of a high station in the esteem of their fellow-citizens are afraid to write in the newspapers, and they are thus deprived of the most powerful instrument which they can use to excite the passions of the multitude to their own advantage. . . .

But although the press is limited to these resources, its influence in America is immense. It is the power which impels the circulation of political life through all the districts of that vast territory. Its eye is constantly open to detect the secret springs of political designs, and to summon the leaders of all parties to the bar of public opinion. It rallies the interests of the community round certain principles, and it draws up the creed which factions adopt; for it affords a means of intercourse between parties which hear, and which address each other without ever having been in immediate contact. When a great number of the organs of the press adopt the same line of conduct, their influence becomes irresistible; and public opinion, when it is perpetually assailed from the same side, eventually yields to the attack. In the United States each separate journal exercises but little authority, but the power of the periodical press is only second to that of the people. . . .

In the United States the democracy perpetually raises fresh individuals to the conduct of public affairs; and the measures of the administration are consequently seldom regulated by the strict rules of consistency or of order. But the general principles of the Government are more stable, and the opinions most prevalent in society are generally more durable than in many other countries. When once the Americans have taken up an idea, whether it be well or ill founded, nothing is more difficult than to eradicate it from their minds. The same tenacity of opinion has been observed in England where, for the last century, greater freedom of conscience and more invincible prejudices have existed than in all the other countries of Europe. I attribute this consequence to a cause which may at first sight appear to have a very opposite tendency, namely, to the liberty of the press. The nations amongst which this liberty exists are as apt to cling to their opinions from pride as from conviction. They cherish them because they hold them to be just, and because they exercised their own free-will in choosing them; and they maintain them not only because they are true, but because they are their own. Several other reasons conduce to the same end. . . .

It has been remarked that in times of great religious fervor men sometimes change their religious opinions; whereas in times of general scepticism every one clings to his own persuasion. The same thing takes place in politics under the liberty of the press. In countries where all the theories of social science have been contested in their turn, the citizens who have adopted one of them stick to it, not so much because they are assured of its excellence, as because they are not convinced of the superiority of any other. In the present age men are not very ready to die in defence of their opinions, but they are rarely inclined to change them; and there are fewer martyrs as well as fewer apostates.

Another still more valid reason may yet be adduced: when no abstract opinions are looked upon as certain, men cling to the mere propensities and external interests of their position, which are naturally more tangible and more permanent than any opinions in the world.

It is not a question of easy solution whether aristocracy or democracy is most fit to govern a country. But it is certain that democracy annoys one part of the community, and that aristocracy oppresses another part. When the question is reduced to the simple expression of the struggle between poverty and wealth, the tendency of each side of the dispute becomes perfectly evident without further controversy.

QUESTIONS

1. Discuss the extent to which Tocqueville's early nineteenth-century observations of America are true (or untrue) today.
2. Is the contrast between liberty of the press in France and in the United States central to the organization of the essay?

QUESTIONS ON PART II

1. How would a really national press, such as that in France in Tocqueville's time, modify Davis's arguments about the responsibility of a free press?
2. Compare Davis's idea of nonobjectivity of the individual reporter with Franklin's explanation of the objectivity of the printer.
3. Relate in detail Milton's principal arguments to the ideals of diversity expressed in Part I.
4. Write an essay criticizing a local newspaper and its coverage of the news in the light of the essays in Part II.

III ✍ Freedom of Speech

THE METAPHYSICAL BASIS
OF TOLERATION
Walter Bagehot

One of the most marked peculiarities of recent times in England is the increased liberty in the expression of opinion. Things are now said constantly and without remark, which even ten years ago would have caused a hubbub, and have drawn upon those who said them much obloquy. But already I think there are signs of a reaction. In many quarters of orthodox opinion I observe a disposition to say, "Surely this is going too far; really we cannot allow such things to be said." And what is more curious, some writers, whose pens are just set at liberty, and who would, not at all long ago, have been turned out of society for the things that they say, are setting themselves to explain the "weakness" of liberty, and to extol the advantages of persecution. As it appears to me that the new practice of this country is a great improvement on its old one, and as I conceive that the doctrine of Toleration rests on what may be called a metaphysical basis, I wish shortly to describe what that basis is.

I should say that, except where it is explained to the contrary, I use the word "Toleration" to mean toleration by law. Toleration by Society of matters not subject to legal penalty is a kindred subject on which, if I have room, I will add a few words, but in the main I propose to deal with the simpler subject,—toleration by law. And by toleration, too, I mean, when

From *Literary Studies*.

it is not otherwise said, toleration in the public expression of opinions. Toleration of acts and practices is another allied subject on which I can, in a paper like this, but barely hope to indicate what seems to me to be the truth. And I should add, that I deal only with the discussion of impersonal doctrines. The law of libel, which deals with accusations of living persons, is a topic requiring consideration by itself.

Meaning this by "toleration," I do not think we ought to be surprised at a reaction against it. What was said long ago of slavery seems to be equally true of persecution,—it "exists by the law of nature." It is so congenial to human nature, that it has arisen everywhere in past times, as history shows; that the cessation of it is a matter of recent times in England; that even now, taking the world as a whole, the practice and the theory of it are in a triumphant majority. Most men have always much preferred persecution, and do so still; and it is therefore only natural that it should continually reappear in discussion and argument.

One mode in which it tempts human nature is very obvious. Persons of strong opinions wish, above all things, to propagate those opinions. They find close at hand what seems an immense engine for that propagation; they find the *State*, which has often in history interfered for and against opinions,—which has had a great and undeniable influence in helping some and hindering others,—and in their eagerness they can hardly understand why they should not make use of this great engine to crush the errors which they hate, and to replace them with the tenets they approve. So long as there are earnest believers in the world, they will always wish to punish opinions, even if their judgment tells them it is unwise, and their conscience that it is wrong. They may not gratify their inclination, but the inclination will not be the less real.

Since the time of Carlyle, "earnestness" has been a favourite virtue in literature, and it is customary to treat this wish to twist other people's belief into ours as if it were a part of the love of truth. And in the highest minds so it may be. But the mass of mankind have, as I hold, no such fine motive. Independently of truth or falsehood, the spectacle of a different belief from ours is disagreeable to us, in the same way that the spectacle of a different form of dress and manners is disagreeable. A set of schoolboys will persecute a new boy with a new sort of jacket; they will hardly let him have a new-shaped penknife. Grown-up people are just as bad, except when culture has softened them. A mob will hoot a foreigner who looks very unlike themselves. Much of the feeling of "earnest believers" is, I believe, altogether the same. They wish others to think as they do, not only because they wish to diffuse doctrinal truth, but also and much more because they cannot bear to hear the words of a creed different from their own. At any rate, without further analysing the origin of the persecuting impulse, its deep root in human nature, and its great power over most men, are evident.

But this natural impulse was not the only motive—perhaps was not the principal one—of historical persecutions. The main one, or a main one, was a most ancient political idea which once ruled the world, and of which deep vestiges are still to be traced on many sides. The most ancient conception of a State is that of a "religious partnership," in which any member may by his acts bring down the wrath of the gods on the other members, and, so to speak, on the whole company. This danger was, in the conception of the time, at once unlimited and inherited; in any generation, partners A, C, D, etc., might suffer loss of life, or health, or goods—the whole association even might perish, because in a past generation the ancestors of Z had somehow offended the gods. Thus the historian of Athens tells us that after a particular act of sacrilege —a breach of the local privileges of sanctuary—the perpetrators were compelled "to retire into banishment"; and that those who had died before the date he is speaking of were "disinterred and cast beyond the borders." "Yet," he adds, "their exile continuing, as it did, only for a time, was not held sufficient to expiate the impiety for which they have been condemned. The Alkmoônids, one of the most powerful families in Attica, long continued to be looked upon as a tainted race, and in cases of public calamity were liable to be singled out as having by their sacrilege drawn down the judgment of the gods upon their countrymen."[1] And as false opinions about the gods have almost always been thought to be peculiarly odious to them, the misbeliever, the "miscreant," has been almost always thought to be likely not only to impair hereafter the salvation of himself and others in a future world, but also to bring on his neighbours and his nation grievous calamities immediately in this. He has been persecuted to stop political danger more than to arrest intellectual error.

But it will be said: Put history aside, and come to things now. Why should not those who are convinced that certain doctrines are errors, that they are most dangerous, that they may ruin man's welfare here and his salvation hereafter, use the power of the State to extirpate those errors? Experience seems to show that the power of the State can be put forth in that way effectually. Why, then, should it not be put forth? If I had room, I should like for a moment to criticise the word "effectually." I should say that the State, in the cases where it is most wanted, is not of the use which is thought. I admit that it extirpates error, but I doubt if it creates belief—at least, if it does so in cases where the persecuted error is suitable to the place and time. In such cases, I think the effect has often been to eradicate a heresy among the few, at the cost of creating a scepticism among the many; to kill the error no doubt, but also to ruin the general belief. And this is the cardinal point, for the propagation of the "truth" is the end of persecution; all else is only a means. But I have not space to discuss this, and will come to the main point.

I say that the State power should not be used to arrest discussion, because the State power may be used equally for truth or error, for Mohammedanism or Christianity, for belief or no-belief, but in discussion truth has an advantage. Arguments always tell for truth as such, and against error as such; if you let the human mind alone, it has a preference for good argument over bad; it oftener takes truth than not. But if you do not let it alone, you give truth no advantage at all; you substitute a game of force, where all doctrines are equal, for a game of logic, where the truer have the better chance.

The process by which truth wins in discussion is this,—cer-

[1] Grote's *History of Greece*, part ii., chap. x. [Bagehot's note.]

tain strong and eager minds embrace original opinions, seldom all wrong, never quite true, but of a mixed sort, part truth,
part error. These they inculcate on all occasions, and on every
side, and gradually bring the cooler sort of men to a hearing
of them. These cooler people serve as quasi-judges, while the
more eager ones are a sort of advocates; a Court of Inquisition
is sitting perpetually, investigating, informally and silently,
but not ineffectually, what, on all great subjects of human interest, is truth and error. There is no sort of infallibility about
the court; often it makes great mistakes, most of its decisions
are incomplete in thought and imperfect in expression. Still, on
the whole, the force of evidence keeps it right. The truth has
the best of the proof, and therefore wins most of the judgments. The process is slow, far more tedious than the worst
Chancery suit. Time in it is reckoned not by days, but by
years, or rather by centuries. Yet, on the whole, it creeps along,
if you do not stop it. But all is arrested, if persecution begins
—if you have a *coup d'état*, and let loose soldiers on the court;
for it is perfect chance which litigant turns them in, or what
creed they are used to compel men to believe.

This argument, however, assumes two things. In the first
place, it presupposes that we are speaking of a state of society
in which discussion is possible. And such societies are not very
common. Uncivilised man is not capable of discussion: savages have been justly described as having "the intellect of children with the passions and strength of men."[2] Before anything
like speculative argument can be used with them, their intellect must be strengthened and their passions restrained. There
was, as it seems to me, a long preliminary period before human
nature, as we now see it, existed, and while it was being
formed. During that preliminary period, persecution, like
slavery, played a most considerable part. Nations mostly became nations by having a common religion. It was a necessary condition of the passage from a loose aggregate of savages
to a united polity, that they should believe in the same gods
and worship these gods in the same way. What was necessary
was, that they should for a long period—for centuries, perhaps

[2] Sir John Lubbock's *Prehistoric Times*, p. 465. [Bagehot's note.]

—lead the same life and conform to the same usages. They believed that the "gods of their fathers" had commanded these usages. Early law is hardly to be separated from religious ritual: it is more like the tradition of a Church than the enactments of a statute-book. It is a thing essentially immemorial and sacred. It is not conceived of as capable either of addition or diminution; it is a body of holy customs which no one is allowed either to break or to impugn. The use of these is to aid in creating a common national character, which in after-times may be tame enough to bear discussion, and which may suggest common axioms upon which discussion can be founded. Till that common character has been formed, discussion is impossible; it cannot be used to find out truth, for it cannot exist; it is not that we have to forego its efficacy on purpose, we have not the choice of it, for its prerequisities cannot be found. The case of civil liberty is, as I conceive, much the same. Early ages need a coercive despotism more than they need anything else. The age of debate comes later. An omnipotent power to enforce the sacred law is that which is then most required. A constitutional opposition would be born before its time. It would be dragging the wheel before the horses were harnessed. The strongest advocates both of Liberty and Toleration may consistently hold that there were unhappy ages before either became possible, and when attempts at either would have been pernicious.

The case is analogous to that of education. Every parent wisely teaches his child his own creed, and till the child has attained a certain age, it is better that he should not hear too much of any other. His mind will in the end be better able to weigh arguments, because it does not begin to weigh them so early. He will hardly comprehend any creed unless he has been taught some creed. But the restrictions of childhood must be relaxed in youth, and abandoned in manhood. One object of education is to train us for discussion, and as that training gradually approaches to completeness, we should gradually begin to enter into and to take part in discussion. The restrictions that are useful at nine years old are pernicious at nineteen.

This analogy would have seemed to me obvious, but there

are many most able persons who turn the matter just the other way. They regard the discipline of education as a precedent for persecution. They say, "I would no sooner let the nation at large read that bad book than I would let my children read it." They refuse to admit that the age of the children makes any difference. At heart they think that they are wiser than the mass of mankind, just as they are wiser than their children, and would regulate the studies of both unhesitatingly. But experience shows that no man is on all points so wise as the mass of men are after a good discussion, and that if the ideas of the very wisest were by miracle to be fixed on the race, the certain result would be to stereotype monstrous error. If we fixed the belief of Bacon, we should believe that the earth went round the sun; if we fixed that of Newton, we should believe "that the Argonautic expedition was a real event, and occurred B.C. 937; that Hercules was a real person, and delivered Theseus, another real person, B.C. 936; that in the year 1036 Ceres, a woman of Sicily, in seeking her daughter who was stolen, came into Attica, and there taught the Greeks to sow corn." And the worst is, that the minds of most would-be persecutors are themselves unfixed: their opinions are in a perpetual flux; they would persecute all others for tenets which yesterday they had not heard of and which they will not believe to-morrow.

But it will be said, the theory of Toleration is not so easy as that of education. We know by a certain fact when a young man is grown up and can bear discussion. We judge by his age, as to which every one is agreed. But we cannot tell by any similar patent fact when a State is mature enough to bear discussion. There may be two opinions about it. And I quite agree that the matter of fact is more difficult to discover in one case than in the other; still it is a matter of fact which the rulers of the State must decide upon their responsibility, and as best they can. And the highest sort of rulers will decide it like the English in India—with no reference to their own belief. For years the English prohibited the preaching of Christianity in India, though it was their own religion, because they thought that it could not be tranquilly listened to. They now permit it, because they find that the population can bear the discussion.

Of course, most Governments are wholly unequal to so high a morality and so severe a self-command. The Governments of most countries are composed of persons who wish everybody to believe as they do, merely because they do. Some here and there, from a higher motive, so eagerly wish to propagate their opinions, that they are unequal to consider the problem of toleration impartially. They persecute till the persecuted become strong enough to make them desist. But the delicacy of a rule and the unwillingness of Governments to adopt it, do not prove that it is not the best and the right one. There are already in inevitable jurisprudence many lines of vital importance just as difficult to draw. The line between sanity and insanity has necessarily to be drawn, and it is as nice as anything can be. The competency of people to bear discussion is not intrinsically more difficult than their competency to manage their own affairs, though perhaps a Government is less likely to be impartial and more likely to be biassed in questions of discussion than in pecuniary ones.

Secondly, the doctrine that rulers are to permit discussion, assumes not only, as we have seen, that discussion is possible, but also that discussion will not destroy the Government. No Government is bound to permit a controversy which will annihilate itself. It is a trustee for many duties, and if possible, it must retain the power to perform those duties. The controversies which may ruin it are very different in different countries. The Government of the day must determine in each case what those questions are. If the Roman Emperors who persecuted Christianity really did so because they imagined that Christianity would destroy the Roman Empire, I think they are to be blamed not for their misconception of duty, but for their mistake of fact. The existence of Christianity was not really more inconsistent with the existence of the Empire in the time of Diocletian than in that of Constantine; but if Diocletian thought that it was inconsistent, it was his duty to preserve the Empire.

It will be asked, "What do you mean by preserving a society? All societies are in a state of incipient change; the best of them are often the most changing; what is meant, then, by saying you will 'preserve' any? You admit that you cannot keep them

unaltered, what then do you propose to do?" I answer that, in
this respect, the life of societies is like the life of the individuals
composing them. You cannot interfere so as to keep a man's
body unaltered; you can interfere so as to keep him alive. What
changes in such cases will be fatal, is a question of fact. The
Government must determine what will, so to say, "break up
the whole thing" and what will not. No doubt it may decide
wrong. In France, the country of experiments, General
Cavaignac said, "A Government which allows its principle to
be discussed, is a lost Government," and therefore he persecuted on behalf of the Republic, thinking it was essential to
society. Louis Napoleon similarly persecuted on behalf of the
Second Empire; M. Thiers on behalf of the Republic again; the
Duc de Broglie now persecutes on behalf of the existing non-
descript. All these may be mistakes, or some of them, or none.
Here, as before, the practical difficulties in the application of
a rule do not disprove its being the true and the only one.

It will be objected that this principle is applicable only to
truths which are gained by discussion. "We admit," such
objectors say, "that where discussion is the best or the only
means of proving truth, it is unadvisable to prohibit that discussion, but there are other means besides discussion of arriving at truth, which are sometimes better than discussion even
where discussion is applicable, and sometimes go beyond it
and attain regions in which it is inapplicable; and where those
more efficient means are applicable, it may be wise to prohibit
discussion, for in these instances discussion may confuse the
human mind and impede it in the use of those higher means.
The case is analogous to that of the eyes. For the most part it
is a sound rule to tell persons who want to see things, that they
must necessarily use *both* their eyes, and rely on them. But
there are cases in which that rule is wrong. If a man wants to
see things too distant for the eyes, as the satellites of Jupiter
and the ring of Saturn, you must tell him, on the contrary,
to shut one eye and look through a telescope with the other.
The ordinary mode of using the common instruments may, in
exceptional cases, interfere with the right use of the supple-
mentary instruments." And I quite admit that there are such
exceptional cases and such additional means; but I say that

their existence introduces no new difficulty into the subject, and that it is no reason for prohibiting discussion except in the cases in which we have seen already that it was advisable to prohibit it.

Putting the matter in the most favourable way for these objectors, and making all possible concessions to them, I believe the exceptions which they contend for must come at last to three.

First, there are certain necessary propositions which the human mind *will* think, must think, and cannot help thinking. For example, we must believe that things which are equal to the same thing are equal to each other,—that a thing cannot *both* be and not be,—that it must *either* be or not be. These truths are not gained by discussion; on the contrary, discussion presupposes at least some of them, for you cannot argue without first principles any more than you can use a lever without a fulcrum. The prerequisites of reasoning must somehow be recognised by the human mind before we begin to reason. So much is obvious, but then it is obvious also that in such cases attempts at discussion cannot do any harm. If the human mind has in it certain first principles which it cannot help seeing, and which it accepts of itself, there is no harm in arguing against those first principles. You may contend as long as you like, that things which are equal to the same thing are *not* equal to each other, or that a thing *can* both exist and not exist at the same time, but you will not convince any one. If you could convince any one you would do him irreparable harm, for you would hurt the basis of his mind and destroy the use of his reason. But happily you cannot convince him. That which the human mind cannot help thinking, it cannot help thinking, and discussion can no more remove the primary perceptions than it can produce them. The multiplication table will remain the multiplication table, neither more nor less, however much we may argue either for it or against it.

But, though the denial of the real necessary perceptions of the human mind cannot possibly do any harm, the denial of alleged necessary perceptions is often essential to the discovery of truth. The human mind, as experience shows, is apt to manufacture sham self-evidences. The most obvious case is, that men perpetually "do sums" wrong. If we dwell long enough and intently enough on the truths of arithmetic they are in each case self-evident; but, if we are too quick, or let our minds get dull, we may make any number of mistakes. A certain deliberation and a certain intensity are both essential to correctness in the matter. Fictitious necessities of thought will be imposed on us without end unless we are careful. The greatest minds are not exempt from the risk of such mistakes even in matters most familiar to them. On the contrary, the history of science is full of cases in which the ablest men and the most experienced assumed that it was impossible to think things which are in matter of fact true, and which it has since been found possible to think quite easily. The mode in which these sham self-evidences are distinguished from the real ones is by setting as many minds as possible to try as often as possible whether they can help thinking the thing or not. But such trials will never exist without discussion. So far, therefore, the existence of self-evidences in the human mind is not a reason for discouraging discussion, but a reason for encouraging it.

Next, it is certainly true that many conclusions which are by no means self-evident and which are gradually obtained, nevertheless, are not the result of discussion. For example, the opinion of a man as to the characters of his friends and acquaintances is not the result of distinct argument, but the aggregate of distinct impressions: it is not the result of an investigation consciously pursued, but the effect of a multiplicity of facts involuntarily presented; it is a definite thing and has a most definite influence on the mind, but its origin is indefinite and not to be traced; it is like a great fund raised in very small subscriptions and of which the subscribers' names are lost. But here again, though these opinions too were not gained by discussion, their existence is a reason for promoting discussion, not for preventing it. Every-day experience shows that these opinions as to character are often mistaken in the last degree. Human character is a most complex thing, and the impressions which different people form of it are as various as the impressions which the inhabitants of an impassable mountain have of its shape and size. Each observer has an aggregate idea derived from certain actions and certain sayings, but the real man has always or almost always said a thousand sayings of a kind quite different and in a connection quite different; he has done a vast variety of actions among "other men" and "other minds"; a mobile person will often seem hardly the same if you meet him in very different societies. And how, except by discussion, is the true character of such a person to be decided? Each observer must bring his contingent to the list of *data*; those data must be arranged and made use of. The certain and positive facts as to which every one is agreed must have their due weight; they must be combined and compared with the various impressions as to which no two people exactly coincide. A rough summary must be made of the whole. In no other way is it possible to arrive at the truth of the matter. Without discussion each mind is dependent on its own partial observation. A great man is one image—one thing, so to speak—to his valet, another to his son, another to his wife, another to his greatest friend. None of these must be stereotyped; all must be compared. To prohibit discussion is to prohibit the corrective process.

Lastly, I hold that there are first principles or first perceptions which are neither the result of constant though forgotten trials like those last spoken of, nor common to all the race like the first. The most obvious seem to me to be the principles of taste. The primary perceptions of beauty vary much in different persons, and for different persons at different times, but no one can say that they are not most real and most influential parts of human nature. There is hardly a thing made by human hands which is not affected more or less by the conception of beauty felt by the maker; and there is hardly a human life which would not have been different if the idea of beauty in the mind of the man who lived it had been different.

But certainly it would not answer to exclude subjects of taste from discussion, and to allow one school of taste-teachers to reign alone, and to prohibit the teaching of all rival schools. The effect would be to fix on all ages the particular ideas of one age on a matter which is beyond most others obscure and difficult to reduce to a satisfactory theory. The human mind evidently differs at various times immensely in its conclusions upon it, and there is nothing to show that the era of the persecutor is wiser than any other era, or that his opinion is better than any one else's.

The case of these variable first principles is much like that of the "personal equation," as it is called in the theory of observations. Some observers, it is found, habitually see a given phenomenon, say the star coming to the meridian, a little sooner than most others; some later; no two persons exactly coincide. The first thing done when a new man comes into an observatory for practical work is to determine whether he sees quick or slow; and this is called the "personal equation." But, according to the theory of persecution, the national astronomer in each country would set up his own mind as the standard; in one country he would be a quick man, and would not let the slow people contest what he said; in another he would be a slow man, and would not tolerate the quick people, or let men speak their minds; and so the astronomical observations—the astronomical *creeds* if I may say so—of different countries would radically differ. But as toleration and discussion are allowed, no such absurd result follows. The observations of different minds are compared with those of others, and truth is assumed to lie in the mean between the errors of the quick people and the errors of the slow ones.

No such accurate result can be expected in more complex matters. The phenomena of astronomical observation relate only to very simple events, and to a very simple fact about these events. But perceptions of beauty have an infinite complexity: they are all subtle aggregates of countless details, and about each of these details probably every mind in some degree differs from every other one. But in a rough way the same sort of agreement is possible. Discussion is only an organised mode by which various minds compare their conclusions with those of various others. Bold and strong minds describe graphic and definite impressions: at first sight these impressions seem wholly different. Writers of the last century thought classical architecture altogether superior to Gothic; many writers now put it just the other way, and maintain a mediæval cathedral to be a thing altogether superior in kind and nature to anything classical. For years the world thought Claude's landscapes perfect. Then came Mr. Ruskin, and by his ability and

eloquence he has made a whole generation depreciate them,
and think Turner's altogether superior. The extrication of truth
by such discussions is very slow; it is often retarded; it is often
thrown back; it often seems to pause for ages. But upon the
whole it makes progress, and the principle of that progress is
this: Each mind which is true to itself, and which draws its
own impressions carefully, and which compares those impressions with the impressions of others, arrives at certain conclusions, which as far as that mind is concerned are ultimate,
and are its highest conclusions. These it sets down as expres-
sively as it can on paper, or communicates by word of mouth,
and these again form data which other minds can contrast with
their own. In this incessant comparison eccentric minds fall
off on every side; some like Milton, some Wordsworth, some
can see nothing in Dryden, some find Racine intolerably dull,
some think Shakespeare barbarous, others consider the contents of the Iliad "battles and schoolboy stuff." With history it
is the same; some despise one great epoch, some another.
Each epoch has its violent partisans, who will listen to nothing else, and who think every other epoch in comparison mean
and wretched. These violent minds are always faulty and sometimes absurd, but they are almost always useful to mankind.
They compel men to hear neglected truth. They uniformly ex-
aggerate their gospel; but it generally *is* a gospel. Carlyle said
many years since of the old Poor-law in England: "It being
admitted then that outdoor relief should at once cease, what
means did great Nature take to make it cease? She created
various men who thought the cessation of outdoor relief the
one thing needful." In the same way, it being desirable that
the taste of men should be improved on some point, Nature's
instrument on that point is some man of genius, of attractive
voice and limited mind, who declaims and insists, not only
that the special improvement is a good thing in itself, but the
best of all things, and the root of all other good things. Most
useful, too, are others less apparent; shrinking, sensitive, testing minds, of whom often the world knows nothing, but each
of whom is in the circle just near him an authority on taste,
and communicates by personal influence the opinions he has
formed. The human mind of a certain maturity, if left alone,

prefers real beauty to sham beauty, and prefers it the sooner if original men suggest new charms, and quiet men criticise and judge of them.

But an æsthetical persecution would derange all this, for generally the compulsive power would be in the hands of the believers in some tradition. The State represents "the rough force of society," and is little likely to be amenable to new charms or new ideas; and therefore the first victim of the persecution would be the original man who was proposing that which in the end would most improve mankind; and the next would be the testing and discerning critic who was examining these ideas and separating the chaff from the wheat in them. Neither would conform to the old tradition. The inventor would be too eager; the critics too scrupulous; and so a heavy code of ancient errors would be chained upon mankind. Nor would the case be at all the better if by some freak of events the propounder of the new doctrine were to gain full control, and were to prohibit all he did not like. He would try, and try in vain, to make the inert mass of men accept or care for his new theory, and his particular enemy would be the careful critic who went with him a little way and then refused to go any further. If you allow persecution, the partisans of the new sort of beauty will, if they can, attack those of the old sort; and the partisans of the old sort will attack those of the new sort; while both will turn on the quiet and discriminating person who is trying to select what is good from each. Some chance taste will be fixed for ages.

But it will be said, "Whoever heard of such nonsense as an æsthetical persecution? Everybody knows such matters of taste must be left to take care of themselves; as far as they are concerned, nobody wants to persecute or prohibit." But I have spoken of matters of taste because it is sometimes best to speak in parables. The case of morals and religion, in which people have always persecuted and still wish to persecute, is the very same. If there are (as I myself think there are) ultimate truths of morals and religion which more or less vary for each mind, some sort of standard and some kind of agreement can only be arrived at about it in the very same way. The same comparison of one mind with another is necessary; the same discussion; the same use of criticising minds; the same use of original ones. The mode of arriving at truth is the same, and also the mode of stopping it.

We now see the reason why, as I said before, religious persecution often extirpates new doctrines, but commonly fails to maintain the belief in old tenets. You can prevent whole classes of men from hearing of the religion which is congenial to them, but you cannot make men believe a religion which is uncongenial. You can prevent the natural admirers of Gothic architecture from hearing anything of it, or from seeing it; but you cannot make them admire classical architecture. You may prevent the admirers of Claude from seeing his pictures, or from praising them; but you cannot make them admirers of Turner. Just so, you may by persecution prevent minds prone to be Protestant from being Protestant; but you will not make men real Catholics: you may prevent naturally Catholic minds from being Catholic; but you will not make them genuine Protestants. You will not make those believe your religion who are predisposed by nature in favour of a different kind of religion; you will make of them, instead, more or less conscious sceptics. Being denied the sort of religion of which the roots are in their minds and which they could believe, they will for ever be conscious of an indefinite want. They will constantly feel after something which they are never able to attain; they will never be able to settle upon anything; they will feel an instinctive repulsion from everything; they will be sceptics at heart, because they were denied the creed for which their heart craves; they will live as indifferentists, because they were withheld by force from the only creed to which they would not be indifferent. Persecution in intellectual countries produces a superficial conformity, but also underneath an intense, incessant, implacable doubt.

Upon examination, therefore, the admission that certain truths are not gained by discussion introduces no new element into the subject. The discussion of such truths is as necessary as of all other truths. The only limitations are that men's minds shall in the particular society be mature enough to bear the discussion, and that the discussion shall not destroy the society.

I acknowledge these two limitations to the doctrine that discussion should be free, but I do not admit another which is often urged. It is said that those who write against toleration should not be tolerated; that discussion should not aid the enemies of discussion. But why not? If there is a strong Government and a people fit for discussion, why should not the cause be heard? We must not assume that the liberty of discussion has no case of exception. We have just seen that there are, in fact, several such. In each instance, let the people decide whether the particular discussion shall go on or not. Very likely, in some cases, they may decide wrong; but it is better that they should so decide, than that we should venture to anticipate all experience, and to make sure that they cannot possibly be right.

It is plain, too, that the argument here applied to the toleration of opinion has no application to that of actions. The human mind in the cases supposed, learns by freely hearing all arguments, but in no case does it learn by trying freely all practices. Society, as we now have it, cannot exist at all unless certain acts are prohibited. It goes on much better because many other acts are prohibited also. The Government must take the responsibility of saying what actions it will allow; that is its first business, and the allowance of all would be the end of civilisation. But it must, under the conditions specified, hear all opinions, for the tranquil discussion of all more than anything else promotes the progressive knowledge of truth, which is the mainspring of civilisation.

Nor does the argument that the law should not impose a penalty on the expression of any opinion equally prove that society should not in many cases apply a penalty to that expression. Society can deal much more severely than the law with many kinds of acts, because it need be far less strict in the evidence it requires. It can take cognisance of matters of common repute and of things of which every one is sure, but which nobody can prove. Particularly, it can fairly well compare the character of the doctrine with the character of the agent, which law can do but imperfectly, if at all. And it is certain that opinions are evidence of the character of those who hold them—not conclusive evidence, but still presumptive. Experience shows that every opinion is compatible with what every one would admit to be a life fairly approvable, a life far higher than that of the mass of men. Great scepticism and great belief have both been found in characters whom both sceptics and believers must admire. Still, on the whole, there is a certain kinship between belief and character; those who disagree with a man's fundamental creed will generally disapprove of his habitual character. If, therefore, society sees a man maintaining opinions which by experience it has been led to connect with actions such as it discountenances, it is justified in provisionally discountenancing the man who holds those opinions. Such a man should be put to the proof to show by his life that the opinions which he holds are not connected with really pernicious actions, as society thinks they are. If he is visibly leading a high life, society should discountenance him no longer; it is then clear that he did not lead a bad life, and the idea that he did or might lead such a life was the only reason for so doing. A doubt was suggested, but it also has been removed. This habit of suspicion does not, on the whole, impair free discussion; perhaps even it improves it. It keeps out the worst disputants, men of really bad character, whose opinions are the results of that character, and who refrain from publishing them, because they fear what society may say. If the law could similarly distinguish between good disputants and bad, it might usefully impose penalties on the bad. But, of course, this is impossible. Law cannot distinguish between the niceties of character; it must punish the publication of an opinion, if it punishes at all, no matter whether the publisher is a good man or whether he is a bad one. In such a matter, society is a discriminating agent: the law is but a blind one.

To most people I may seem to be slaying the slain, and proving what no one doubts. People, it will be said, no longer wish to persecute. But I say, they *do* wish to persecute. In fact, from their writings, and still better from their conversation, it is easy to see that very many believers would persecute sceptics, and that very many sceptics would persecute believers. Society may be wiser; but most earnest believers and most earnest unbelievers are not at all wiser.

QUESTIONS

1. Explain the manner in which Bagehot introduces his subject. Is the reader made aware in the first and second paragraphs of the manner in which the essay is to be developed? Note the means of transition from definition to development. Outline the essay to determine its whole pattern of organization.
2. Discuss Bagehot's implied theory of social evolution, and account for it in terms of nineteenth-century scientific theory.
3. On what grounds does Bagehot conclude that the human mind prefers truth to error? What ancient philosopher promulgated the same view?
4. Why does Bagehot assert the need of a "coercive despotism"? How does he differentiate the state of mankind in which it was necessary from the state of contemporary man?
5. Do you know any groups or organizations that would disagree with Bagehot that "no man is . . . so wise as the mass of men are after a good discussion"?
6. Compare Bagehot's statement that "if the ideas of the very wisest were . . . to be fixed on the race, the certain result would be to stereotype monstrous error" with Mill's position in the essay "On the Liberty of Thought and Discussion."
7. What justification is there for Bagehot's use of the word "metaphysical" in his title?

FREEDOM OF SPEECH
AND PRESS
✍ Zechariah Chafee, Jr.

Human beings do not instinctively desire to live in a community where freedom of speech prevails. Instead, they long for a unified society. Even sophisticated men feel a strong exhilaration when they march in a procession which keeps perfect step with everybody singing in unison. Distaste is a common initial reaction to anybody who is very different from the general run, whether a deformed person or a foreigner. A century ago in Massachusetts, one of Bronson Alcott's fellow-Utopians at "Fruitlands" was imprisoned because he persisted in wearing such a long beard that people kept mobbing him, until law and order were maintained by shutting him up. It is natural for us to feel a similar hostility toward anybody who expresses unfamiliar opinions or views which we intensely dislike.

Through many centuries of bitter experience of the effects of intolerance and after much thinking, men convinced themselves that they ought to master such impulses and adopt the opposite policy of giving a very wide latitude for the expression of diverse statements of fact and belief. In this way human beings would lead happier, richer lives, and the society which they composed would follow wiser and more fruitful courses and possess the capacity of reshaping itself in order to meet new needs.

A *Freedom Agenda* pamphlet published by the Carrie Chapman Catt Memorial Fund, Inc. (New York, 1955).

Knowledge about the growth of the idea of free speech is very helpful to American citizens when they have to decide how a problem of objectionable talk or writing may best be solved. In the first place, awareness of past mistakes lessens the risk of our repeating them. Hardly any such problem arises today for the first time in history. Some similar danger has confronted men before. If persecution and suppression then failed to change the minority or produce consequences worse than the danger, we may be led to try some milder remedy and get more satisfactory results. The arguments for toleration used by wise men of earlier days often apply with much force to current situations. The old emotional impulses toward an artificial unity of opinion are always present in a community. Awareness of history makes them less liable to surge up and sweep us into suppressions which we shall later regret.

Furthermore, since the solution we adopt for any problem about restricting discussion ought to preserve our constitutional guarantees of freedom, it is important for us to understand what the men who wrote the First Amendment intended it to accomplish. We ought to shrink from betraying their high hopes of safeguarding our freedom down the years. Yet, if we ignore the historical background of the Amendment, we shall be baffled in our search for what its framers wished it to prevent and to obtain.

During the years between 1787 and 1791 when ratifying conventions, the First Congress, and state legislatures were putting "the freedom of speech and of the press" into the Constitution, nobody I know of said anything precise to show what this phrase meant to him. Since everybody wanted it to be part of our fundamental law, there was no need to make elaborate arguments in its favor. So we have no contemporary source for the First Amendment comparable to the *Federalist,* which told a great deal about the original Constitution while trying to win supporters for it.

However, we know that the long struggle for open discussion was very familiar to Americans of the generation which won the Revolution, that they had expressed detestation for actual past suppressions of speech at home or in England, and that they admired authors who strongly urged open discussion. The thinking which went into the First Amendment is revealed by what our ancestors read as well as by what they wrote.

The chief aim of the ensuing sketch is to state some of the events and sayings which were known to Americans who brought about the First Amendment and probably influenced them. In addition it should be helpful to our own understanding of the desirability of open discussion. . . .

Before American Independence . . . freedom of speech and the press was a principle of political wisdom. When it was embodied in the First Amendment and, earlier or later, in the constitutions of all our states, it became in addition a principle of law—a barrier against governmental action.

Consequently, a new set of problems arose about the meaning of freedom of speech. The vague admiration with which men had spoken about this right was not enough, now that it was a boundary around discussion which legislators and officials must not cross. This boundary had to be fixed with considerable precision—no easy task.

Difficulties would be avoided if the words "Congress shall pass *no law* . . ." meant just what they said. Then every Act which restricts thinking, talking, and printing would be unconstitutional. My old friend Alexander Meiklejohn goes far in this direction in his *Free Speech And Its Relation to Self-Government*:

> When men govern themselves, it is they—and no one else who must pass judgment upon unwisdom and unfairness and danger. . . . Just so far as, at any point, the citizens who are to decide an issue are denied acquaintance with information or opinion or doubt or disbelief or criticism which is relevant to that issue, just so far the result must be ill-considered, ill-balanced planning for the general good. *It is that mutilation of the thinking process of the community against which the First Amendment to the Constitution is directed.*

This to me is not law but wise policy. It is not a correct statement of the constitutional boundary, but it is sound advice as to what Congresses and Presidents should do outside the boundary. Nevertheless, if they choose to disregard this wise policy, they will not in all cases be stopped by the Supreme

Court. The Court has repeatedly rejected an absolutist interpretation of the First Amendment. Thus the late Chief Justice
Vinson recently said:

[Both] the majority of the Court and the dissenters in particular
cases have recognized that this is not an unlimited, qualified right,
but that the societal value of speech must, on occasion, be *sub-
ordinated to other values and considerations.*

Although the framers had no very clear idea as to what they
meant by "the freedom of speech or of the press," we can be
reasonably sure that the freedom which Congress was forbidden to abridge was, for them, the freedom which they believed
they already had—what they had wanted before the Revolution and had acquired through Independence. In thinking
about it, they took for granted the limitations which had been
customarily applied in the day-to-day work of colonial courts.
For instance, they could hardly have intended to wipe out
suits for slander and libel. Now, they were setting up a new
federal government of great potential strength, and (as in the
rest of the Bill of Rights) they were determined that it should
not take away the freedoms which they then enjoyed in their
thirteen sovereign states.

Not that the intention of the framers is conclusive as to the
meaning of the First Amendment. The idea . . . had been
gradually molded in men's minds by centuries of conflict. It
was the product of a people, of whom the framers were merely
the mouthpiece and its significance was not fixed by their per-
sonalities. Nor did the meaning of the amendment crystallize
in 1791. Men at that time would probably have been horrified
at the thought of protecting books by Darwin or Bernard
Shaw. Even so "commerce" for them did not include airplanes
and radio, but it does now. In John Marshall's words, "we must
never forget, that it is a *constitution* we are expounding."

The true meaning of freedom of speech seems to be this:
One of the most cherished desires of many a human being is to
think and express his thoughts to others—to speak out the
truth that is in him. And one of the most important purposes
of society and government is the discovery and spread of truth
as to facts and sound judgments as to subjects of general con-

cern. Therefore, no problem about objectionable talk and books can be satisfactorily solved by men who think only of the risks from open discussion. It is indispensable for them to remember that every restraint on speaking and printing hampers the two important interests of individuals and society in open discussion, especially when the views sought to be suppressed are unpopular and may be easily overlooked unless heard.

True, some sacrifice of discussion is occasionally required. After careful balancing, the scales may tip in favor of other purposes of society than the spread of truth; for example, protection from internal disorder or foreign conquest. Nevertheless, it is essential that such careful balancing shall take place in the minds of the men who wield power and in the minds of private citizens, and that the great human and social values of open speech and an untrammeled press shall weigh very heavily in the scale. The First Amendment gives binding force to this principle of political wisdom.

It is profitable to look at events in the United States since the First Amendment as illustrative of the varying ways in which the process of balancing was conducted in Washington and among citizens at large whenever it was proposed to stifle objectionable opinions by law. The extent of freedom of speech at any given time has depended on the size of the weights at the two ends of the scales. At one end, the current estimate of the values proclaimed by the First Amendment. At the other end, the current estimate of dangers from the particular sort of ideas to which a substantial portion of the community then objects.

Accordingly, for each of the periods in our history I am going to review, two questions should be kept in mind:

First, is there at this time a strong faith in the American tradition of open discussion? When we read contemporary newspapers and pamphlets or the debates in Congress on a restrictive law or the arguments of prosecutors and judges, do we find them expressing any confidence in the substantial capacity of the American people to sift good ideas from bad ideas through their own intelligence and common sense? And do they show awareness of the harmful consequences of suppression, for instance, the possibility that when peaceable talk is made punishable the silenced minority will resort to violence instead of talk? I am not denying that despite these reasons for toleration some situations may require repressive measures. Our question is whether those reasons are thoroughly canvassed before such measures are enacted and during their enforcement. Or is very little said about the dangers from suppression and a great deal said about the dangers from talk?

The second question concerns the other end of the scales. Is the need for punishing discussion by law estimated satisfactorily? It is foolish to shut our eyes against national perils, and a commoner harm is to see them enlarged by delirium. An adequate estimate of the need for suppression requires from citizens, legislators, judges, a determination to size up calmly and wisely the real dangers from talk. It requires a willingness to consider the effectiveness of weapons other than force for fighting bad ideas, such as skillful presentation of good ideas and remedying serious grievances. Are these qualities exhibited during the particular crisis? Or do we find denunciations, lurid predictions of disaster, and a panic-stricken zeal to nip detested doctrines in the bud?

For a century and a quarter after the First Amendment, the Supreme Court had little opportunity to clarify its meaning and few attempts were made to restrict discussion by law.

The most notable strain on the First Amendment before World War I came seven years after its adoption. The possibility of war with France, the spread of its revolutionary doctrines in our midst, and the disastrous operation of those doctrines abroad—facts that have a familiar sound today—led the Federalists to enact the Sedition Act of 1798. It punished with a fine of $2,000 and two years in prison false, scandalous, and malicious writings against the government, either House of Congress, or the President, if intended to excite the hatred of the people against them or to stir up sedition, etc.

Thus the act closely resembled the crime of seditious libel in the detested English prosecutions and the Zenger case. It punished writers merely because their opinions were disliked by the current wielders of power. It ignored the fact that "freedom of animadversion" (as Madison argued) is an essential part of the political process when men elect the government.

The act was bitterly resented as invading the liberty of the press.

Although the act provided for liberal reforms of making truth a defense and letting the jury pass on criminality, convictions were easily obtained. One expert had observed that party newspapers and speakers today make statements as a matter of course in every political campaign much more violent than those for which editors and publishers were fined and imprisoned in 1799–1800. The administration did its best to suppress the four leading Jeffersonian newspapers as well [as] many smaller journals.

We regard the Sedition Act of 1798 as wholly unneeded. Yet most Federalists were then firmly convinced that they were stamping out a foreign menace from France and Napoleon fully as dangerous as the foreign menace which confronts the United States today. A committee of the House told how successful France had been in infiltrating other countries with her spies. Her conquest of Switzerland was used (like the fate of Czechoslovakia in our time) as a fearful warning that our nation would be a similar victim if we did not save ourselves by putting American citizens in prison. Washington declared the Sedition Act necessary to protect us from men "who acknowledge no allegiance to this country, and are poisoning the minds of our people, thus endeavoring to dissolve the Union."

The Act of 1798 did have one good provision. Like the last English censorship statutes, it expired by its own terms after two years. Unfortunately, recent American sedition laws do not copy this provision, which prevents legislation passed in an emergency from staying on the statute-book after the emergency has passed. Many legislators are too timid to support the repeal of a sedition law which has worked badly, but they are too sensible to vote for its re-enactment.

Before the Sedition Act thus died, it ruined the Federalist Party and made Thomas Jefferson President in 1801. His First Inaugural brought the nation back to the First Amendment:

If there be any among us who wish to dissolve this union, or to change its republican form, let them stand undisturbed, as monuments of the safety with which error of opinion may be tolerated where reason is left free to combat it.

For the next sixty years the issue of suppressing objectionable utterances arose only once. President Jackson in 1836 urged Congress to prohibit the transmission of Abolitionist publications through the mail, because they might cause slave insurrections. The firm hold which freedom of speech and press had on men's hearts during the nineteenth century is shown by the fact that the suggested measure was opposed and killed by John C. Calhoun, the chief spokesman of the slaveowners.

Calhoun denied that because the government operates the mails, it can refuse to carry anything it dislikes regardless of the First Amendment. "The object of publication is circulation; and to prohibit circulation is, in effect to prohibit publication. If Congress has the right to discriminate [as to] the mail, [this] would subject the freedom of the press on all subjects completely to its will and pleasure."

Some private citizens were less tolerant. In 1837 mobs in Alton, Illinois, four times threw the press of an Abolitionist newspaper into the Mississippi and finally shot the editor, Elijah P. Lovejoy. Afterwards his friend, Edward Beecher Stowe, emphasized an aspect of freedom of speech which is often overlooked:

We are more especially called upon to maintain the principles of free discussion in case of unpopular sentiments or persons, *as in no other case will any effort to maintain them be needed.*

The Civil War caused the only widespread suppression of speech in this country during the nineteenth century. From the time hostilities began, Lincoln was seriously disturbed by Northerners who were plotting to bring about acts interfering with the conduct of the war, e.g., desertions, mob attacks on Union soldiers, and, later, resistance to the draft. Soon after Congress met, it created (July 21, 1861) the new crime of conspiracy "to overthrow . . . by force the government of the United States . . . or to oppose by force the authority thereof, or by force to prevent, hinder, or delay the execution of any

[federal] law. . . ." This statute is now in the United States
Code, as Title 18, section 2384. In my opinion, it adequately
protects the nation against any real dangers of revolution and
other conspiracies for the actual use of force and violence to
impede our government. The Conspiracy Act of 1861 makes
unnecessary all our recent peacetime sedition laws.

During the months between the attack on Fort Sumter and
the enactment of this statute, there were undoubtedly substantial dangers to the Union from active disloyalists, especially in Maryland and other border states. Lincoln was too
busy to deal with this problem himself, so he gave a free hand
to military officers. They began arresting civilians all over the
North as they pleased and locked them up in forts and military prisons. Unfortunately, Lincoln allowed these arbitrary
arrests to continue for years. Most prisoners were not tried at
all. A few got convicted by a tribunal of soldiers.

Although this policy was aimed at active disloyalists, it did
not stop there. Zealous subordinates undertook to silence mere
sympathizers with the Confederacy and sincere advocates of
ending the bloodshed by a negotiated peace. General Burnside,
while in charge of Ohio, Indiana, and Illinois, announced in
April 1863, "The habit of declaring sympathy for the enemy
will not be allowed." In June, he declared it unlawful to publish or circulate books and newspapers containing sentiments
of a disloyal tendency, and at once suppressed the *Chicago
Times*. Calling a man a "suspect" required no proof; it was as
easy as calling him a "subversive" today and equally injurious.

James Ford Rhodes, a strong admirer of Lincoln, declares
that all of these arbitrary arrests and interferences with freedom of the press in states outside the theatre of war were
"inexpedient, unnecessary and wrong."

Lincoln's hope that the right of public discussion would be
fully restored after victory was realized. Faith in the Bill of
Rights was strengthened by the extension of liberty to all
human beings in our midst through the abolition of slavery.

Also the idea of free speech was enriched for many Americans when they read *On Liberty* by John Stuart Mill, published
in England in 1859. I wish I could quote from this great book
. . . freely . . . but Mill's final reflection must suffice:

[A] State which dwarfs its men, in order that they may be more docile instruments in its hands even for beneficial purposes, will find that with small men no great thing can really be accomplished. . . .

Unfortunately, Mill's arguments did not become deeply ingrained in popular consciousness in this country. Freedom of speech was a cherished tradition, but remained without specific content. Perhaps the very absence of interference allowed the philosophical and political principles which underlay the constitutional guarantees to be forgotten for lack of constant assertion and examination of them. Consequently, these guarantees proved of slight use against the growing tendency to resort to governmental action for the limitation of individual liberty in the field of discussion, as well as in other departments of life.

The Haymarket bomb in 1886 marks the turning-point away from toleration for extremists. After the assassination of McKinley the new spirit entered into legislation with the New York Criminal Anarchy Act of 1902 and the Act of Congress in 1903 excluding even peaceable anarchists from our shores. More serious suppressions were forecast in industrial disputes —for instance, the prohibition of street meetings in San Diego in 1912. The sedition laws during and after World War I did not come out of a clear sky.

One hundred and twenty-five years after the First Amendment, the scope of freedom of speech suddenly became a burning issue. It has stayed so ever since. Since recent events are too complex to consider profitably in this brief sketch, I shall review only the next quarter-century, from our entry into World War I on April 6, 1917, to our entry into World War II on December 7, 1941. This period falls naturally into three stages. The first comprises three years, 1917–1920.

Misfortunes never come singly. Problems of war are bad enough. It is very hard, in the agony of fighting, to keep working toward wise solutions of such unmilitary questions as peace aims through the fruitful formation of public opinion. Yet on top of all these problems of war in 1917 were heaped almost immediately the problems of the Russian Revolution. Thus the traditions of free speech which had come down to us from Milton and Jefferson were subjected to a double strain.

Without reviewing the statutes enacted during this war, I shall merely show what happened. By June 30, 1919, 877 persons had been convicted for speaking and publishing. At least 35 were sentenced to prison for twenty years, and 58 for ten up to fifteen years. It became criminal to advocate heavier taxation instead of bond issues, to state that conscription was unconstitutional though the Supreme Court had not yet held it valid, to say that the sinking of merchant vessels was legal, to urge that a referendum should have preceded our declaration of war, to say that war was contrary to the teachings of Christ. Men were punished for criticizing the Red Cross and the Y.M.C.A. A state court in Minnesota held it a crime to discourage women from knitting by the remark, "No soldier ever sees these socks." One judge sentenced a woman to ten years in prison for writing, in a letter to the editor of the *Kansas City Star*, "I am for the people and the government is for the profiteers," because what was said to mothers, sisters, and sweethearts might lessen their enthusiasm for the war.

All through the fighting these prosecutions and convictions were stifling discussion of war policies and peace aims when it was most needed. Nobody could know then that after the Armistice some speakers would be let out by appellate courts and others gradually pardoned before serving their full time in a cell. Meanwhile, Woodrow Wilson's acquiescence in these imprisonments was alienating many of "the forward-looking men and women" who had hitherto been his warmest supporters.

When the fighting was over and the Germans were out of the way, the Russians and their numerous sympathizers in this country still remained. The flames of intolerance had soared too high for the Armistice to extinguish them. Eagerness for restrictions spread from Congress to state legislatures. Statutes punishing "criminal syndicalism" multiplied as fast as the victims of Spanish influenza. The old New York law of 1902 enacted against anarchists and never used was suddenly revived and directed against Socialists, who are at the opposite pole of political thought. The federal deportation statutes were amended to include Communists, and Attorney General Palmer seized thousands of peaceable aliens without warrants. The tide of suppression reached its height on January 7, 1920, when the New York Assembly refused to seat five duly elected Socialist members.

The careful balancing between the values of open discussion and the risks of it which I have presented as essential rarely took place between 1917 and 1920. The First Amendment had no hold on men's minds because it was not associated with live facts or concrete images. Like an empty box with beautiful words on it, the Amendment collapsed under the impact of terror of Prussian battalions and terror of Bolshevik mobs.

It is the fashion nowadays to say that in 1917–1920 the nation was in little danger from heterodox discussion, and hence the eventual condemnation of the suppressions during those years has no application to restrictions which will save us from the "real dangers" created by domestic Communists in our own time. Thus a lawyer who has done much to bring about recent sedition laws wrote in 1948: "It is true that the dangers from subversive organizations at the time of World War I were much exaggerated [but] we are no longer in the days of T-model socialism." Chief Justice Vinson suggested in 1951 that the constitutionality of the Smith Act is not affected by what Holmes and Brandeis said about the desirability of freedom of speech for left-wing Socialists in 1920, because those agitators were not "any substantial threat to the safety of the community."

But that was not the way the authorities during the First World War and the Red Menace looked at the people they were suppressing. It was then almost a hopeless task to try to convince any solid citizen that the danger was small. A bomb exploded under the window of the Attorney General of the United States. Another bomb exploded at the corner of Wall Street between the New York Stock Exchange and J. P. Morgan's office. The newspapers were filled with discoveries of great caches of arms and ammunition in cellars. A score of sedition bills were introduced in the Senate and House and supported by lurid descriptions of the national peril if they were not passed. In the New York Assembly, the men who expelled the five Socialist members described their party as "having the single purpose of destroying our institutions and government."

Reading what everybody now agrees about the panic-stricken alarmists of 1920, I wonder what will be said thirty years from now about the alarmists of 1955.

Fortunately, many old-fashioned Americans were still alive in 1917–1920 who liked the kind of country in which they grew up in the nineteenth century. Their vigorous protests kept the idea of free speech from withering away. Indeed, it got toughened by the struggle. The ablest among these men gave the idea the concrete expression which it badly needed. Most notable in this work were Justice Oliver Wendell Holmes, former Justice Charles Evans Hughes, Judge Learned Hand, and Roger Baldwin, the founder of the American Civil Liberties Union. I regret that I cannot describe here what the last two men accomplished.

Holmes, in the spring of 1919 when the first war cases reached the Supreme Court, succeeded in getting his colleagues to support unanimously his location of the boundary between speech which the Constitution protects and speech which can be punished under sedition laws:

> The question in every case is whether the words used are used in such circumstances and are of such a nature as to create a clear and present danger that they will bring about the substantive evils that Congress has a right to prevent. It is a question of proximity and degree.

Although this test does not take care of all speech problems, it is a big advance. Bad acts are the main crime. Words may be infected when they are closely connected with bad acts. But words can no longer be punished because they have a remote tendency to bring about bad acts somehow, sometime.

On November 10, 1919, Holmes and Brandeis broke away from the other Justices who upheld sentences of 20 years upon a group of young men and 15 years for a girl, because, after our troops had landed in Russian ports when we were not at war with Russia, they had thrown out of a window handbills urging workers not to make munitions which might be used to crush the Russian Revolution. In his famous dissent in the Abrams case, Holmes said in part:

But when men have realized that time has upset many fighting faiths, they may come to believe even more than they believe the very foundations of their own conduct that the ultimate good desired is better reached by free trade in ideas—that the best test of truth is the power of the thought to get itself accepted in the competition of the market, and that truth is the only ground upon which their wishes safely can be carried out. That at any rate is the theory of our Constitution. It is an experiment, as all life is an experiment. Every year if not every day we have to wager our salvation upon some prophecy based upon imperfect knowledge. While that experiment is part of our system I think that we should be eternally vigilant against attempts to check the expression of opinions that we loathe and believe to be fraught with death, unless they so imminently threaten immediate interference with the lawful and pressing purposes of the law that an immediate check is required to save the country.

Hughes spoke out two months later against the exclusion of the five Socialists from the New York Assembly, and left for our use in the present crisis these wise words:

If there was anything against these men as individuals, if they were deemed to be guilty of criminal offenses, they should have been charged accordingly. But I understand that the action is not directed against these five elected members as individuals but that the proceeding is virtually an attempt to indict a political party. This is not, in my judgment, American government.

This courageous action by Hughes made Americans realize how foolish their suppressions had been. They began to laugh. The tide turned.

The second stage of the quarter-century, between 1920 and 1930, was a time of hope. Congress rejected every peacetime sedition bill. Aside from deportations and an absurd censorship in the customs, there was little more federal suppression. A few states still ran rampant, notably New York and California. Some of the Industrial Workers of the World did create serious dangers of sabotage and crop-destruction, but the organization was a symptom of the evil of homeless migratory laborers. Instead of trying to cure the evil, California increased

it by imprisoning its victims. Nevertheless, the forces of toleration were growing. California juries began refusing to convict
I.W.W.'s. Oregon actually repealed a sedition law. State governors began to check the excesses of their legislatures.

Outstanding among these was Alfred Emanuel Smith of New
York. His messages in vetoing or repealing sedition legislation
are full of shrewd advice for our own days:

> The traditional abhorrence of a free people of all kinds of spies
> and secret police is justified.
> The test established is not what the teacher teaches, but what
> the teacher believes. No man is so omniscient or wise as to have
> entrusted to him such arbitrary and complete power not only to
> condemn any individual teacher, but to decree what belief is
> opposed to the institutions of the country.

The greatest victory for freedom of speech in my lifetime
was won in 1925 by Walter Heilprin Pollak in the Gitlow case.
Hitherto the Constitution had not prevented state legislatures
from suppressing discussion as much as they pleased. The
Supreme Court could not stop them because the First Amendment applied only to Congress. True, the Fourteenth Amendment in 1868 did say, "nor shall any State deprive any person
of . . . *liberty* . . . without due process of law. . . ." Still,
for the next fifty-seven years it was doubtful whether "liberty"
included liberty of speech and press.

The opportunity to get the question settled arose when Benjamin Gitlow, a left-wing Socialist, was convicted under the
New York Criminal Anarchy Act of 1902 for publishing a som-
niferous pamphlet of variations on Marx's Communist Mani-
festo of 1848. The conviction was sustained by the highest
New York court, but Judge Cuthbert Pound dissented with
Chief Judge Cardozo and said:

> Although the defendant may be the worst of men, the rights of
> the best of men are secure only as the rights of the vilest and most
> abhorrent are protected.

Pollak took the case to the United States Supreme Court
and persuaded the Justices to hold unanimously:

Freedom of speech and of the press are among the fundamental personal right and "liberties" protected from impairment by the states.

This decision made freedom of speech henceforth as safe from state governments under the Fourteenth Amendment as it is from the national government under the First.

The third and last stage of this period began on February 3, 1930, when President Hoover appointed Charles Evans Hughes as Chief Justice of the United States. Under his leadership Holmes and Brandeis, who had again and again gone down fighting for free speech, found themselves in the majority along with their younger colleagues, Stone and Roberts, and later with Justices appointed by Franklin Roosevelt. Now the Supreme Court struck down one state suppression after another. These included a conviction for hoisting a red flag with a hammer and sickle at a children's camp; an injunction against the further publication of a scandal-sheet; a tax on the gross receipts of large newspapers; city ordinances designed to stifle the peculiar activities of Jehovah's Witnesses; and the expulsion of children from school for refusal to engage in a daily flag-worshipping ceremony, if they considered it idolatrous or meaningless. In such cases, the judicial opinions of Hughes and his associates gave increasing clearness and richness to the idea of free speech.

However, along with the forces of freedom, the forces of suppression were also growing. In 1938, the national House of Representatives established a Committee on Un-American Activities, which has been imitated twice over by the Senate and many times by state legislatures. In 1940 Congress passed by overwhelming votes the Smith Act, the first peacetime sedition law since the detested Act of 1798. It contains practically everything which Attorney General Palmer wanted at the height of the Red Menace.

Then the quarter-century closed with Pearl Harbor. As in the First World War, we were faced with two staggering sets of problems. Again we had to defend ourselves against German military might, and the Japanese too; again we were perplexed by the revolutionary rulers of Russia.

In 1920, Hughes, in a speech at Harvard Law School, wondered "whether constitutional government as heretofore maintained in this republic could survive another great war even victoriously waged." Yet his prediction was to prove utterly false in World War II. This, I believe, was because the nation was facing calmly and courageously the greatest dangers it had confronted since General Lee marched south from Gettysburg. Freedom of speech belongs to a people which is free from fear.

QUESTIONS

1. Discuss the distinction between the positive concern of government for the spread of truth and the negative concern about the risks from open discussion.
2. Account for the considerable difference in sentence length between this essay and that by Burchard.
3. Recast the sentence beginning "Lincoln's hope . . ." so that its meaning is more immediately obvious.
4. Consider various cases in your own knowledge in which action is urged against unlimited freedom of speech. Apply the test contained in Justice Holmes's opinion of 1919. Do you think all "disloyal" speeches or writings ought to be censored or punished by law?
5. What is the connotation of the term "flag-worshipping ceremony"? Is Chafee justified in using this type of language?

THE ABOLITIONISTS
✍ William Ellery Channing

. . . It is not my purpose to speak of the Abolitionists as Abolitionists. They now stand before the world in another character, and to this I shall give my present attention. Of their merits and demerits as Abolitionists, I have formerly spoken. In my short work on Slavery, I have expressed my fervent attachment to the great end to which they are pledged, and at the same time my disapprobation, to a certain extent, of their spirit and measures. I have no disposition to travel over this ground again. Had the Abolitionists been left to pursue their object with the freedom which is guaranteed to them by our civil institutions; had they been resisted only by those weapons of reason, rebuke, reprobation, which the laws allow, I should have no inducement to speak of them again either in praise or censure. But the violence of their adversaries has driven them to a new position. Abolitionism forms an era in our history, if we consider the means by which it has been opposed. Deliberate, systematic efforts have been made, not here or there, but far and wide, to wrest from its adherents that liberty of speech and the press, which our fathers asserted unto blood, and which our national and state governments are pledged to protect as our most sacred right. Its most conspicuous advocates have been hunted and stoned, its meetings scattered, its presses broken up, and nothing but the patience, constancy, and intrepidity of its members, has saved it from extinction.

Written in 1836. From *The Works of William E. Channing, D.D.*, Vol. II (Boston, 1841).

The Abolitionists then not only appear in the character of champions of the colored race. In their persons the most sacred rights of the white man and the free man have been assailed. They are sufferers for the liberty of thought, speech, and the press; and, in maintaining this liberty amidst insult and violence, they deserve a place among its most honored defenders. In this character I shall now speak of them.

In regard to the methods adopted by the Abolitionists of promoting emancipation, I might find much to censure; but when I regard their firm, fearless assertion of the rights of free discussion, of speech and the press, I look on them with unmixed respect. I see nothing to blame, and much to admire. To them has been committed the most important bulwark of liberty, and they have acquitted themselves of the trust like men and Christians. No violence has driven them from their post. Whilst, in obedience to conscience, they have refrained from opposing force to force, they have still persevered amidst menace and insult, in bearing their testimony against wrong, in giving utterance to their deep convictions. Of such men, I do not hesitate to say, that they have rendered to freedom a more essential service, than any body of men among us. The defenders of freedom are not those, who claim and exercise rights which no one assails, or who win shouts of applause by well turned compliments to liberty in the days of her triumph. They are those, who stand up for rights which mobs, conspiracies, or single tyrants put in jeopardy; who contend for liberty in that particular form, which is threatened at the moment by the many or the few. To the Abolitionists this honor belongs. The first systematic effort to strip the citizen of freedom of speech they have met with invincible resolution. From my heart I thank them. I am myself their debtor. I am not sure, that I should this moment write in safety, had they shrunk from the conflict, had they shut their lips, imposed silence on their presses, and hid themselves before their ferocious assailants. I know not where these outrages would have stopped, had they not met resistance from their first destined victims. The newspaper press, with a few exceptions, uttered no genuine indignant rebuke of the wrong-doers, but rather countenanced, by its gentle censures, the reign of Force. The mass of the people looked supinely on this new tyranny, under which a portion of their fellow-citizens seemed to be sinking. A tone of denunciation was beginning to proscribe *all* discussion of slavery; and had the spirit of violence, which selected associations as its first objects, succeeded in this preparatory enterprise, it might have been easily turned against any and every individual, who might presume to agitate the unwelcome subject. It is hard to say, to what outrage the fettered press of the country might not have been reconciled. I thank the Abolitionists, that in this evil day, they were true to the rights which the multitude were ready to betray. Their purpose to suffer, to die, rather than surrender their dearest liberties, taught the lawless, that they had a foe to contend with, whom it was not safe to press, whilst, like all manly appeals, it called forth reflection and sympathy in the better portion of the community. In the name of freedom and humanity, I thank them. Through their courage, the violence, which might have furnished a precedent fatal to freedom, is to become, I trust, a warning to the lawless, of the folly as well as crime of attempting to crush opinion by Force.

Of all powers, the last to be intrusted to the multitude of men, is that of determining what questions shall be discussed. The greatest truths are often the most unpopular and exasperating; and were they to be denied discussion, till the many should be ready to accept them, they would never establish themselves in the general mind. The progress of society depends on nothing more, than on the exposure of time-sanctioned abuses, which cannot be touched without offending multitudes, than on the promulgation of principles, which are in advance of public sentiment and practice, and which are consequently at war with the habits, prejudices, and immediate interests of large classes of the community. Of consequence, the multitude, if once allowed to dictate or proscribe subjects of discussion, would strike society with spiritual blindness, and death. The world is to be carried forward by truth, which at first offends, which wins its way by degrees, which the many hate and would rejoice to crush. The right of free discussion is therefore to be guarded by the friends of mankind, with peculiar jealousy. It is at once the most sacred, and most endangered of all our rights. He who would rob his neighbour of it, should have a mark set on him as the worst enemy of freedom.

I do not know that our history contains a page, more disgraceful to us as freemen, than that which records the violences against the Abolitionists. As a people, we are chargeable with other and worse misdeeds, but none so flagrantly opposed to the spirit of liberty, the very spirit of our institutions, and of which we make our chief boast. Who, let me ask, are the men, whose offences are so aggravated, that they must be denied the protection of the laws, and be given up to the worst passions of the multitude? Are they profligate in principle and life, teachers of impious or servile doctrines, the enemies of God and their race? I speak not from vague rumor, but from better means of knowledge, when I say, that a body of men and women, more blameless than the Abolitionists in their various relations, or more disposed to adopt a rigid construction of the Christian precepts, cannot be found among us. Of their judiciousness and wisdom, I do not speak; but I believe they yield to no party in moral worth. Their great crime, and one, which in this land of liberty is to be punished above all crimes, is this, that they carry the doctrine of human equality to its full extent, that they plead vehemently for the oppressed, that they assail wrong-doing however sanctioned by opinion or intrenched behind wealth and power, that their zeal for human rights is without measure, that they associate themselves fervently with the Christians and philanthropists of other countries against the worst relic of barbarous times. Such is the offence, against which mobs are arrayed, and which is counted so flagrant, that a summary justice, too indignant to wait for the tardy progress of tribunals, must take the punishment into its own hands.

How strange in a free country, that the men, from whom the liberty of speech is to be torn, are those who use it in pleading for freedom, who devote themselves to the vindication of human rights! What a spectacle is presented to the world by a republic, in which sentence of proscription is passed on citizens, who labor, by addressing men's consciences, to enforce the truth, that slavery is the greatest of wrongs! Through the civilized world, the best and greatest men are bearing joint witness against slavery. Christians of all denominations and conditions, rich and poor, learned and ignorant, are bound in a holy league against this most degrading form of oppression. But in free America, the language which despots tolerate, must not be heard. One would think, that freemen might be pardoned, if the view of fellow-creatures stripped of all human rights should move them to vehemence of speech. But, whilst, on all other subjects, the deeply stirred feelings may overflow in earnest remonstrance, on slavery the freemen must speak in whispers, or pay the penalty of persecution for the natural utterance of strong emotion.

I am aware, that the outrages on the Abolitionists are justified or palliated by various considerations; nor is this suprising; for when did violence ever want excuse? It is said, that Abolitionism tends to stir up insurrection at the South, and to dissolve the Union. Of all pretences for resorting to lawless force, the most dangerous is the *tendency* of measures or opinions. Almost all men see ruinous tendencies in whatever opposes their particular interests or views. All the political parties, which have convulsed our country, have seen tendencies to national destruction in the principles of their opponents. So infinite are the connexions and consequences of human affairs, that nothing can be done in which some dangerous tendency may not be detected. There is a tendency in arguments against any old establishment to unsettle all institutions, because all hang together. There is a tendency in the laying bare of deep-rooted abuses to throw a community into a storm. Liberty tends to licentiousness, government to despotism. Exclude all enterprises which *may* have evil results, and human life will stagnate. Wise men are not easily deterred by difficulties and perils from a course of action, which promises great good. Especially when justice and humanity cry aloud for the removal of an enormous social evil, it is unworthy of men and Christians to let the imagination run riot among possible dangers, instead of rousing every energy of mind to study how the evil may be taken away, and the perils, which accompany beneficial changes, may be escaped. . . .

In these remarks you learn my abhorrence of the violence

offered to the Abolitionists, and my admiration of the spirit
they have opposed to it. May they vindicate to the end the
rights which in their persons have been outraged. Allow me
now to express my earnest desire and hope, that the Abolitionists will maintain the liberty of speech and the press, not
only by asserting it firmly, but by using it wisely, deliberately,
generously, and under the control of the severest moral principle. It is my earnest desire, that they will exercise it in the
spirit of Christians and philanthropists, with a supreme love
of truth, without passion or bitterness, and without that fanaticism which cannot discern the true proportions of things,
which exaggerates or distorts whatever favors or conflicts with
its end, which sees no goodness except in its own ranks, which
shuts itself up in one object and is blind to all besides. Liberty
suffers from nothing more, than from licentiousness, and I
fear that Abolitionists are not to be absolved from this abuse
of it. It seems to me that they are particularly open to one
reproach. Their writings have been blemished by a spirit of
intolerance, sweeping censure, and rash, injurious judgment.
I do not mean to bring this charge against all their publications. . . . But Abolitionism, in the main, has spoken in an
intolerant tone, and in this way has repelled many good minds,
given great advantage to its opponents, and diminished the
energy and effect of its appeals. I should rejoice to see it puri-
fied from this stain. . . .

I have said that I have no desire to shield the unworthy
among ourselves. We have those, whose opposition to Abolitionism has been wicked, and merits reprobation. Such are to
be found in all classes, forming indeed a minority in each, yet
numerous enough to deserve attention and to do much harm.
Such are to be found in what is called the highest class of society, that is, among the rich and fashionable; and the cause is
obvious. The rich and fashionable belong to the same caste
with the slave-holder; and men are apt to sympathize with their
own caste more readily than with those beneath them. The
slave is too low, too vulgar, to awaken interest in those, who
abhor vulgarity more than oppression and crime, and who
found all their self-admiration on the rank they occupy in the
social scale. Far be it from me to charge on the rich or fash-

ionable, as a class, this moral degradation; but among them are the worshippers of high degree, who would think their dignity soiled, by touching the cause of a menial, degraded race, and who load its advocates with ridicule and scorn.

Then, in the commercial class, there are unworthy opposers of Abolitionism. There are those, whose interests rouse them to withstand every movement, which may offend the South. They have profitable connexions with the slave-holder, which must not be endangered by expressions of sympathy with the slave. Gain is their god, and they sacrifice on this altar without compunction the rights and happiness of their fellow-creatures. To such, the philanthropy, which would break every chain, is fanaticism, or a pretence. Nothing in their own souls helps them to comprehend the fervor of men, who feel for the wronged, and who hazard property and life in exposing the wrong. . . . Our present civilization is characterized and tainted by a devouring greediness of wealth; and a cause, which asserts right against wealth, must stir up bitter opposition, especially in cities where this divinity is most adored. Every large city will furnish those, who would sooner rivet the chain on the slave than lose a commission, or retrench an expenditure. I would on no account intimate, that such men constitute the majority of the commercial class. I rejoice to know that a more honorable spirit prevails in the community which falls more immediately under my notice. Still, the passion for gain is everywhere sapping pure and generous feeling, and everywhere raises up bitter foes against any reform which may threaten to turn aside a stream of wealth. I sometimes feel as if a great social revolution were necessary to break up our present mercenary civilization, in order that Christianity, now repelled by the almost universal worldliness, may come into new contact with the soul, and may reconstruct society after its own pure and disinterested principles.

In another class, which contains many excellent people, may also be found unworthy opposers of all anti-slavery movements. I refer to the Conservative class, to those who are tremblingly alive to the spirit of innovation now abroad in the world, who have little or no faith in human progress, who are anxious to secure what is now gained rather than to gain more, to whom that watchword of the times, Reform, sounds like a knell. Among these are to be found individuals, who, from no benevolent interest in society, but simply because they have drawn high prizes in the lottery of life, are unwilling that the most enormous abuses should be touched, lest the established order of things, so propitious to themselves, should be disturbed. A palsying, petrifying order, keeping things as they are, seems to them the Ideal of a perfect community, and they have no patience with the rude cry of reformers for the restoration of human beings to their long-lost rights.

I will only add the politicians, as another class, which has furnished selfish assailants of Abolitionism. Among our politicians are men, who regard public life as a charmed circle into which moral principle must not enter, who know no law but expediency, who are prepared to kiss the feet of the South for southern votes, and who stand ready to echo all the vituperations of the slave-holder against the active enemies of slavery in the Free States.

For these various descriptions of selfish opponents of Abolitionism, I make no apology. Let them be visited with just rebuke. But they, after all, form but a small part of that great body in the Free States, who look on the present anti-slavery movement with distrust and disapprobation. The vast majority in the Free States, who refuse communion with [the Abolitionists], are not actuated by base considerations. The fear of a servile war, the fear of political convulsions, a perception of the difficulties of great social changes, self-distrust, a dread of rashness, these, and the like motives, have great influence in deterring multitudes from giving their countenance to what seem to them violent movements for the abolition of slavery. That a culpable insensibility to the evils and wrongs of this nefarious institution is too common in the class of which I now speak, I do not mean to deny. Still, how vast a proportion of the intelligence, virtue, and piety of the country is to be found in their ranks! To speak of them slightly, contemptuously, bitterly, is to do great wrong, and such speaking, I fear, has brought much reproach on Abolitionism. . . .

QUESTIONS

1. Define the following words as they are used in Channing's essay: "profligate," "flagrant," "enormous." In the last paragraph, near the end, what word would we use today instead of "slightly"?
2. Channing seems to change the subject from freedom of speech to abolitionism itself. Does he really?
3. Discuss instances at the present time in which people try to stifle discussion on the grounds of the *tendency* of the programs discussed.

QUESTIONS ON PART III

1. Do you know anyone who actively advocates suppression (directly or indirectly) of the right to speak with absolute freedom? What arguments in this Part seem to you most apt for refutation of such a position now?
2. Collect and analyze the passages from all three essays in this Part that state or imply that freedom of speech entails concomitant responsibilities.
3. Write an essay showing how one or all of the writers in this Part would justify Jefferson's statement that he who wishes to dissolve this union or change its republican form should "stand undisturbed. . . ."

IV ✌ Due Process of Law

JUDICIAL POWER
IN THE UNITED STATES
✐ Alexis de Tocqueville

I have thought it essential to devote a separate chapter to the judicial authorities of the United States, lest their great political importance should be lessened in the reader's eyes by a merely incidental mention of them. Confederations have existed in other countries beside America, and republics have not been established upon the shores of the New World alone; the representative system of government has been adopted in several States of Europe, but I am not aware that any nation of the globe has hitherto organized a judicial power on the principle now adopted by the Americans. The judicial organization of the United States is the institution which a stranger has the greatest difficulty in understanding. He hears the authority of a judge invoked in the political occurrences of every day, and he naturally concludes that in the United States the judges are important political functionaries; nevertheless, when he examines the nature of the tribunals, they offer nothing which is contrary to the usual habits and privileges of those bodies, and the magistrates seem to him to interfere in public affairs of chance, but by a chance which recurs every day.

When the Parliament of Paris remonstrated, or refused to enregister an edict, or when it summoned a functionary accused of malversation to its bar, its political influence as a

From *Democracy in America* (1835; the Henry Reeve translation).

judicial body was clearly visible; but nothing of the kind is to be seen in the United States. The Americans have retained all the ordinary characteristics of judicial authority, and have carefully restricted its action to the ordinary circle of its functions.

The first characteristic of judicial power in all nations is the duty of arbitration. But rights must be contested in order to warrant the interference of a tribunal; and an action must be brought to obtain the decision of a judge. As long, therefore, as the law is uncontested, the judicial authority is not called upon to discuss it, and it may exist without being perceived. When a judge in a given case attacks a law relating to that case, he extends the circle of his customary duties, without however stepping beyond it; since he is in some measure obliged to decide upon the law in order to decide the case. But if he pronounces upon a law without resting upon a case, he clearly steps beyond his sphere, and invades that of the legislative authority.

The second characteristic of judicial power is that it pronounces on special cases, and not upon general principles. If a judge in deciding a particular point destroys a general principle, by passing a judgment which tends to reject all the inferences from that principle, and consequently to annul it, he remains within the ordinary limits of his functions. But if he directly attacks a general principle without having a particular case in view, he leaves the circle in which all nations have agreed to confine his authority, he assumes a more important, and perhaps a more useful, influence than that of the magistrate, but he ceases to be a representative of the judicial power.

The third characteristic of the judicial power is its inability to act unless it is appealed to, or until it has taken cognizance of an affair. This characteristic is less general than the other two; but, notwithstanding the exceptions, I think it may be regarded as essential. The judicial power is by its nature devoid of action; it must be put in motion in order to produce a result. When it is called upon to repress a crime, it punishes the criminal; when a wrong is to be redressed, it is ready to redress it; when an act requires interpretation, it is prepared to interpret it; but it does not pursue criminals, hunt out wrongs, or examine into evidence of its own accord. A judicial functionary who should open proceedings, and usurp the censorship of the laws, would in some measure do violence to the passive nature of his authority.

The Americans have retained these three distinguishing characteristics of the judicial power; an American judge can only pronounce a decision when litigation has arisen, he is only conversant with special cases, and he cannot act until the cause has been duly brought before the court. His position is therefore perfectly similar to that of the magistrate of other nations; and he is nevertheless invested with immense political power. If the sphere of his authority and his means of action are the same as those of other judges, it may be asked whence he derives a power which they do not possess. The cause of this difference lies in the simple fact that the Americans have acknowledged the right of the judges to found their decisions on the constitution rather than on the laws. In other words, they have left them at liberty not to apply such laws as may appear to them to be unconstitutional.

I am aware that a similar right has been claimed—but claimed in vain—by courts of justice in other countries; but in America it is recognized by all the authorities; and not a party, nor so much as an individual, is found to contest it. This fact can only be explained by the principles of the American constitution. In France the constitution is (or at least is supposed to be) immutable; and the received theory is that no power has the right of changing any part of it. In England the Parliament has an acknowledged right to modify the constitution; as, therefore, the constitution may undergo perpetual changes, it does not in reality exist; the Parliament is at once a legislative and a constituent assembly. The political theories of America are more simple and more rational. An American constitution is not supposed to be immutable as in France, nor is it susceptible of modification by the ordinary powers of society as in England. It constitutes a detached whole, which, as it represents the determination of the whole people, is no less binding on the legislator than on the private citizen, but which may be altered by the will of the people in predetermined cases, according to established rules. In America the constitution may therefore vary, but as long as it exists it is the origin of all authority, and the sole vehicle of the predominating force. . . .

In the United States the constitution governs the legislator as much as the private citizen; as it is the first of laws it cannot be modified by a law, and it is therefore just that the tribunals should obey the constitution in preference to any law. This condition is essential to the power of the judicature, for to select that legal obligation by which he is most strictly bound is the natural right of every magistrate.

In France the constitution is also the first of laws, and the judges have the same right to take it as the ground of their decisions, but were they to exercise this right they must perforce encroach on rights more sacred than their own, namely, on those of society, in whose name they are acting. In this case the State-motive clearly prevails over the motives of an individual. In America, where the nation can always reduce its magistrates to obedience by changing its constitution, no danger of this kind is to be feared. Upon this point, therefore, the political and the logical reasons agree, and the people as well as the judges preserve their privileges.

Whenever a law which the judge holds to be unconstitutional is argued in a tribunal of the United States he may refuse to admit it as a rule; this power is the only one which is peculiar to the American magistrate, but it gives rise to immense political influence. Few laws can escape the searching analysis of the judicial power for any length of time, for there are few which are not prejudicial to some private interest or other, and none which may not be brought before a court of justice by the choice of parties, or by the necessity of the case. But from the time that a judge has refused to apply any given law in a case, that law loses a portion of its moral cogency. The persons to whose interests it is prejudicial learn that means exist of evading its authority, and similar suits are multiplied, until it becomes powerless. One of two alternatives must then be resorted to: the people must alter the constitution, or the legislature must repeal the law. The political power which the Americans have entrusted to their courts of justice is therefore immense, but the evils of this power are considerably diminished by the obligation which has been imposed of attacking the laws through the courts of justice alone. If the judge had been empowered to contest the laws on the ground of theoretical generalities, if he had been enabled to open an attack or to pass a censure on the legislator, he would have played a prominent part in the political sphere; and as the champion or the antagonist of a party, he would have arrayed the hostile passions of the nation in the conflict. But when a judge contests a law applied to some particular case in an obscure proceeding, the importance of his attack is concealed from the public gaze, his decision bears upon the interest of an individual, and if the law is slighted it is only collaterally. Moreover, although it is censured, it is not abolished; its moral force may be diminished, but its cogency is by no means suspended, and its final destruction can only be accomplished by the reiterated attacks of judicial functionaries. It will readily be understood that by connecting the censorship of the laws with the private interests of members of the community, and by intimately uniting the prosecution of the law with the prosecution of an individual, legislation is protected from wanton assailants, and from the daily aggressions of party spirit. The errors of the legislator are exposed whenever their evil consequences are most felt, and it is always a positive and appreciable fact which serves as the basis of a prosecution.

I am inclined to believe this practice of the American courts to be at once the most favorable to liberty as well as to public order. If the judge could only attack the legislator openly and directly, he would sometimes be afraid to oppose any resistance to his will; and at other moments party spirit might encourage him to brave it at every turn. The laws would consequently be attacked when the power from which they emanate is weak, and obeyed when it is strong. That is to say, when it would be useful to respect them they would be contested, and when it would be easy to convert them into an instrument of oppression they would be respected. But the American judge is brought into the political arena independently of his own will. He only judges the law because he is obliged to judge a case. The political question which he is called upon to resolve is connected with the interest of the suitors, and he cannot refuse to decide it without abdicating the duties of his post. He performs his functions as a citizen by fulfilling the precise duties which belong to his profession as a magistrate. It is true that upon this system the judicial censorship which is exercised by the courts of justice over the legislation cannot extend to all laws indiscriminately, inasmuch as some of them can never give rise to that exact species of contestation which is termed a lawsuit; and even when such a contestation is possible, it may happen that no one cares to bring it before a court of justice. The Americans have often felt this disadvantage, but they have left the remedy incomplete, lest they should give it an efficacy which might in some cases prove dangerous. Within these limits the power vested in the American courts of justice of pronouncing a statute to be unconstitutional forms one of the most powerful barriers which has ever been devised against the tyranny of political assemblies. . . .

It is perfectly natural that in a free country like America all the citizens should have the right of indicting public functionaries before the ordinary tribunals, and that all the judges should have the power of punishing public offenses. The right granted to the courts of justice of judging the agents of the executive government, when they have violated the laws, is so natural a one that it cannot be looked upon as an extraordinary privilege. Nor do the springs of government appear to me to be weakened in the United States by the custom which renders all public officers responsible to the judges of the land. The Americans seem, on the contrary, to have increased by this means that respect which is due to the authorities, and at the same time to have rendered those who are in power more scrupulous of offending public opinion. I was struck by the small number of political trials which occur in the United States, but I had no difficulty in accounting for this circumstance. A lawsuit, of whatever nature it may be, is always a difficult and expensive undertaking. It is easy to attack a public man in a journal, but the motives which can warrant an action at law must be serious. A solid ground of complaint must therefore exist to induce an individual to prosecute a public officer, and public officers are careful not to furnish these grounds of complaint when they are afraid of being prosecuted.

This does not depend upon the republican form of American

institutions, for the same facts present themselves in England. These two nations do not regard the impeachment of the principal officers of State as a sufficient guarantee of their independence. But they hold that the right of minor prosecutions, which are within the reach of the whole community, is a better pledge of freedom than those great judicial actions which are rarely employed until it is too late. . . .

QUESTIONS

1. What does Tocqueville mean by "the passive nature" of judicial authority?
2. In what particulars of his essay does Tocqueville discuss and analyze the system of checks and balances?
3. How is the political power of judges in America curtailed? How is this fact related to the organization of the essay?

THE SUPREME COURT AND THE FLAG SALUTE

✐ Justice Felix Frankfurter

A grave responsibility confronts this Court whenever in course of litigation it must reconcile the conflicting claims of liberty and authority. But when the liberty invoked is liberty of conscience, and the authority is authority to safeguard the nation's fellowship, judicial conscience is put to its severest test. Of such a nature is the present controversy.

Lillian Gobitis, aged twelve, and her brother William, aged ten, were expelled from the public schools of Minersville, Pennsylvania, for refusing to salute the national flag as part of a daily school exercise. The local Board of Education required both teachers and pupils to participate in this ceremony. The ceremony is a familiar one. The right hand is placed on the breast and the following pledge recited in unison: "I pledge allegiance to my flag, and to the Republic for which it stands; one nation indivisible, with liberty and justice for all." While the words are spoken, teachers and pupils extend their right hands in salute to the flag. The Gobitis family are affiliated with "Jehovah's Witnesses," for whom the Bible as the Word of God is the supreme authority. The children had been brought up conscientiously to believe that such a gesture of respect for the flag was forbidden by command of Scripture.[1]

310 U.S. 586, *United States Reports* (1939).

[1] Reliance is especially placed on the following verses from Chapter 20 of Exodus:
"3. Thou shalt have no other gods before me.
"4. Thou shalt not make unto thee any graven image, or any likeness of any thing that is in heaven above, or that is in the earth beneath, or that is in the water under the earth:
"5. Thou shalt not bow down thyself to them, nor serve them: . . ."

176

The Gobitis children were of an age for which Pennsylvania makes school attendance compulsory. Thus they were denied a free education, and their parents had to put them into private schools. To be relieved of the financial burden thereby entailed, their father, on behalf of the children and in his own behalf, brought this suit. He sought to enjoin the authorities from continuing to exact participation in the flag-salute ceremony as a condition of his children's attendance at the Minersville school. After trial of the issues, Judge Maris gave relief in the District Court, 24 F. Supp. 271, on the basis of a thoughtful opinion at a preliminary stage of the litigation, 21 F. Supp. 581; his decree was affirmed by the Circuit Court of Appeals, 108 F. 2d 683. Since this decision ran counter to several *per curiam* dispositions of this Court, we granted *certiorari* to give the matter full reconsideration. 309 U.S. 645. By their able submissions, the Committee on the Bill of Rights of the American Bar Association and the American Civil Liberties Union, as friends of the Court, have helped us to our conclusion.

We must decide whether the requirement of participation in such a ceremony, exacted from a child who refuses upon sincere religious grounds, infringes without due process of law the liberty guaranteed by the Fourteenth Amendment.

Centuries of strife over the erection of particular dogmas as exclusive or all-comprehending faiths led to the inclusion of a guarantee for religious freedom in the Bill of Rights. The First Amendment, and the Fourteenth through its absorption of the First, sought to guard against repetition of those bitter religious struggles by prohibiting the establishment of a state religion and by securing to every sect the free exercise of its faith. So pervasive is the acceptance of this precious right that its scope is brought into question, as here, only when the conscience of individuals collides with the felt necessities of society.

Certainly the affirmative pursuit of one's convictions about the ultimate mystery of the universe and man's relation to it is placed beyond the reach of law. Government may not interfere with organized or individual expression of belief or disbelief. Propagation of belief—or even of disbelief—in the supernatural is protected, whether in church or chapel, mosque or synagogue, tabernacle or meeting-house. Likewise the Constitution assures generous immunity to the individual from imposition of penalties for offending, in the course of his own religious activities, the religious views of others, be they a minority or those who are dominant in government. *Cantwell* v. *Connecticut, ante,* p. 296.

But the manifold character of man's relations may bring his conception of religious duty into conflict with the secular interests of his fellow-men. When does the constitutional guarantee compel exemption from doing what society thinks necessary for the promotion of some great common end, or from a penalty for conduct which appears dangerous to the general good? To state the problem is to recall the truth that no single principle can answer all of life's complexities. The right to freedom of religious belief, however dissident and however obnoxious to the cherished beliefs of others—even of a majority—is itself the denial of an absolute. But to affirm that the freedom to follow conscience has itself no limits in the life of a society would deny that very plurality of principles which, as a matter of history, underlies protection of religious toleration. Compare Mr. Justice Holmes in *Hudson Water Co.* v. *McCarter,* 209 U.S. 349, 355. Our present task, then, as so often the case with courts, is to reconcile two rights in order to prevent either from destroying the other. But, because in safeguarding conscience we are dealing with interests so subtle and so dear, every possible leeway should be given to the claims of religious faith.

In the judicial enforcement of religious freedom we are concerned with a historic concept. See Mr. Justice Cardozo in *Hamilton* v. *Regents,* 293 U.S. at 265. The religious liberty which the Constitution protects has never excluded legislation of general scope not directed against doctrinal loyalties of particular sects. Judicial nullification of legislation cannot be justified by attributing to the framers of the Bill of Rights views for which there is no historic warrant. Conscientious scruples have not, in the course of the long struggle for religious toleration, relieved the individual from obedience to a general law not aimed at the promotion or restriction of religious beliefs. The mere possession of religious convictions which contradict the relevant concerns of a political society does not relieve the citizen from the discharge of political responsibilities. The necessity for this adjustment has again and again been recognized. In a number of situations the exertion of political authority has been sustained, while basic considerations of religious freedom have been left inviolate. *Reynolds* v. *United States*, 98 U.S. 145; *Davis* v. *Beason*, 133 U.S. 333; *Selective Draft Law Cases*, 245 U.S. 366; *Hamilton* v. *Regents*, 293 U.S. 245. In all these cases the general laws in question, upheld in their application to those who refused obedience from religious conviction, were manifestations of specific powers of government deemed by the legislature essential to secure and maintain that orderly, tranquil, and free society without which religious toleration itself is unattainable. Nor does the freedom of speech assured by Due Process move in a more absolute circle of immunity than that enjoyed by religious freedom. Even if it were assumed that freedom of speech goes beyond the historic concept of full opportunity to utter and to disseminate views, however heretical or offensive to dominant opinion, and includes freedom from conveying what may be deemed an implied but rejected affirmation, the question remains whether school children, like the Gobitis children, must be excused from conduct required of all the other children in the promotion of national cohesion. We are dealing with an interest inferior to none in the hierarchy of legal values. National unity is the basis of national security. To deny the legislature the right to select appropriate means for its attainment presents a totally different order of problem from that of the propriety of subordinating the possible ugliness of littered streets to the free expression of opinion through distribution of handbills. Compare *Schneider* v. *State*, 308 U.S. 147.

Situations like the present are phases of the profoundest problem confronting a democracy—the problem which Lincoln cast in memorable dilemma: "Must a government of necessity be too *strong* for the liberties of its people, or too *weak* to maintain its own existence?" No mere textual reading or logical talisman can solve the dilemma. And when the issue demands judicial determination, it is not the personal notion of judges of what wise adjustment requires which must prevail.

Unlike the instances we have cited, the case before us is not concerned with an exertion of legislative power for the promotion of some specific need or interest of secular society—the protection of the family, the promotion of health, the common defense, the raising of public revenues to defray the cost of government. But all these specific activities of government presuppose the existence of an organized political society. The ultimate foundation of a free society is the binding tie of cohesive sentiment. Such a sentiment is fostered by all those agencies of the mind and spirit which may serve to gather up the traditions of a people, transmit them from generation to generation, and thereby create that continuity of a treasured common life which constitutes a civilization. "We live by symbols." The flag is the symbol of our national unity, transcending all internal differences, however large, within the framework of the Constitution. This Court has had occasion to say that ". . . the flag is the symbol of the Nation's power, the emblem of freedom in its truest, best sense. . . . It signifies government resting on the consent of the governed; liberty regulated by law; the protection of the weak against the strong; security against the exercise of arbitrary power; and absolute safety for free institutions against foreign aggression." *Halter* v. *Nebraska*, 205 U. S. 34, 43. And see *United States* v. *Gettysburg Electric Ry. Co.*, 160 U. S. 668.

The case before us must be viewed as though the legislature of Pennsylvania had itself formally directed the flag-salute for the children of Minersville; had made no exemption for children whose parents were possessed of conscientious scruples like those of the Gobitis family; and had indicated its belief in the desirable ends to be secured by having its public school children share a common experience at those periods of development when their minds are supposedly receptive to its assimilation, by an exercise appropriate in time and place and setting, and one designed to evoke in them appreciation of the nation's hopes and dreams, its sufferings and sacrifices. The precise issue, then, for us to decide is whether the legislatures of the various states and the authorities in a thousand counties and school districts of this country are barred from determining the appropriateness of various means to evoke that unifying sentiment without which there can ultimately be no liberties, civil or religious. To stigmatize legislative judgment in providing for this universal gesture of respect for the symbol of our national life in the setting of the common school as a lawless inroad on that freedom of conscience which the Constitution protects, would amount to no less than the pronouncement of pedagogical and psychological dogma in a field where courts possess no marked and certainly no controlling competence. The influences which help toward a common feeling for the common country are manifold. Some may seem harsh and others no doubt are foolish. Surely, however, the end is legitimate. And the effective means for its attainment are still so uncertain and so unauthenticated by science as to preclude us from putting the widely prevalent belief in flag-saluting beyond the pale of legislative power. It mocks reason and denies our whole history to find in the allowance of a requirement to salute our flag on fitting occasions the seeds of sanction for obeisance to a leader.

The wisdom of training children in patriotic impulses by those compulsions which necessarily pervade so much of the educational process is not for our independent judgment. Even were we convinced of the folly of such a measure, such belief would be no proof of its unconstitutionality. For ourselves, we might be tempted to say that the deepest patriotism is best engendered by giving unfettered scope to the most crochety beliefs. Perhaps it is best, even from the standpoint of those interests which ordinances like the one under review seek to promote, to give to the least popular sect leave from conformities like those here in issue. But the courtroom is not the arena for debating issues of educational policy. It is not our province to choose among competing considerations in the subtle process of securing effective loyalty to the traditional ideals of democracy, while respecting at the same time individual idiosyncrasies among a people so diversified in racial origins and religious allegiances. So to hold would in effect make us the school board for the country. That authority has not been given to this Court, nor should we assume it.

We are dealing here with the formative period in the development of citizenship. Great diversity of psychological and ethical opinion exists among us concerning the best way to train children for their place in society. Because of these differences and because of reluctance to permit a single, iron-cast system of education to be imposed upon a nation compounded of so many strains, we have held that, even though public education is one of our most cherished democratic institutions, the Bill of Rights bars a state from compelling all children to attend the public schools. *Pierce* v. *Society of Sisters*, 268 U.S. 510. But it is a very different thing for this Court to exercise censorship over the conviction of legislatures that a particular program or exercise will best promote in the minds of children who attend the common schools an attachment to the institutions of their country.

What the school authorities are really asserting is the right to awaken in the child's mind considerations as to the significance of the flag contrary to those implanted by the parent. In such an attempt the state is normally at a disadvantage in competing with the parent's authority, so long—and this is the vital aspect of religious toleration—as parents are unmolested in their right to counteract by their own persuasiveness the wisdom and rightness of those loyalties which the state's educational system is seeking to promote. Except where the transgression of constitutional liberty is too plain for argument, personal freedom is best maintained—so long as the remedial channels of the democratic process remain open and unobstructed—when it is ingrained in a people's habits and not enforced against popular policy by the coercion of adjudicated law. That the flag-salute is an allowable portion of a school program for those who do not invoke conscientious scruples is surely not debatable. But for us to insist that, though the ceremony may be required, exceptional immunity must be given to dissidents, is to maintain that there is no basis for a legislative judgment that such an exemption might introduce elements of difficulty into the school discipline, might cast doubts in the minds of the other children which would themselves weaken the effect of the exercise.

The preciousness of the family relation, the authority and

independence which give dignity to parenthood, indeed the enjoyment of all freedom, presuppose the kind of ordered society which is summarized by our flag. A society which is dedicated to the preservation of these ultimate values of civilization may in self-protection utilize the educational process for inculcating those almost unconscious feelings which bind men together in a comprehending loyalty, whatever may be their lesser differences and difficulties. That is to say, the process may be utilized so long as men's right to believe as they please, to win others to their way of belief, and their right to assemble in their chosen places of worship for the devotional ceremonies of their faith, are all fully respected.

Judicial review, itself a limitation on popular government, is a fundamental part of our constitutional scheme. But to the legislature no less than to courts is committed the guardianship of deeply-cherished liberties. See *Missouri, K. & T. Ry. Co. v. May,* 194 U. S. 267, 270. Where all the effective means of inducing political changes are left free from interference, education in the abandonment of foolish legislation is itself a training in liberty. To fight out the wise use of legislative authority in the forum of public opinion and before legislative assemblies rather than to transfer such a contest to the judicial arena, serves to vindicate the self-confidence of a free people.

QUESTIONS

1. Compare the tone of Mr. Justice Frankfurter's description of the flag-salute ceremony with that of Chafee. Are there significant reasons for the difference?
2. What is the jurisdiction of the Supreme Court in educational matters, according to Frankfurter? Is there any conflict between this position and that taken by the Court in *Brown* v. *Topeka* (1954)?

QUESTIONS ON PART IV

1. How does Mr. Justice Frankfurter's opinion in this case illustrate Tocqueville's concept of judicial power in the United States?

2. Read the Fourteenth Amendment to the Constitution, and relate the idea of "due process" therein expressed to both these essays.

3. Considering Tocqueville's concept of "the passive nature" of judicial authority, comment on the purpose and objective, and the legal nature, of a Supreme Court decision such as this.

V ∿ Intellectual Freedom

"OUT OF OLD FIELDS"
John Ely Burchard

Seven months ago the Massachusetts Institute of Technology inaugurated a new president. Like today, it was an occasion for greetings and felicitations. Referring to the fact that our new president had served us long in other capacities, and thus had proved himself in advance, James Bryant Conant said, "In short, you are to be envied for doing what most of us Americans spend our lives wishing for and aiming at, namely betting on a sure thing!" We do not assemble here today to dedicate an unused and untried building; we, too, are not laying wagers on an unknown horse. Here also, I suggest, we have a sure thing. My instructions are to help you to guess what this sure thing may mean for the Rice Institute, for the City of Houston, for the State of Texas, and for the other half of the nation. . . .

We live in a complicated age. Each educated man hangs on a dilemma. To be individually *useful* he must become, according to his bent, more and more specialized in what he knows how to do. But to be among the collectively *good* he needs to be better informed about more complex general problems than any previous man has ever had to be. These two requirements often seem to conflict or at least to compete. Adequate specialization clamors for all of the student's attention and for most of the adult's. Yet we sense that if each educated man attends

An address at the dedication of the Fondren Library of the Rice Institute, November 4, 1949. Reprinted from *The Rice Institute Pamphlet*, Vol. XXXVII, by permission of Rice University.

only to his own specialized knitting, the main patterns of our culture will suffer. The most important affairs of the world will then be managed either by less-educated non-specialists or, more dangerously, by specialists in governing men. We have seen one such group at work in the Reichschancellory. We did not like it overmuch.

Educators are steadily talking about this problem of how to develop depth and breadth at the same time. They want to know how to cultivate an intense understanding of a relatively little area, together with an intense interest in and a reasonable competence about a very much larger area. Educators make experiments in this direction. They call their programs core curricula, or new courses in general education, or integrated education. The proposals have a basic similarity although the name of the program changes from time to time. Fundamentally they are seeking the marriage of the general and the specific, to develop the student's capacity so that professional skill and able citizenship may march forward hand in hand. It is an extremely difficult assignment.

Specialization is possible in every field and common today in most fields. It is by no means unique to science and engineering, nor indeed does it take its most constricted forms in these studies. Nonetheless science has become, for many, symbolic of specialized education, and the liberal arts have become symbolic of general education. I could spend all the time you have allowed me debating the validity of these totems. But I won't. Let us, rather, take them at their face value. Let us agree that the whole man must have an understanding of both. What is important here is that if these two fields stand as symbols, so does the Fondren Library. There was something very significant in the decision taken here—a not very usual decision, you know—to house the libraries of both hemispheres of knowledge in this single building on this campus. It goes without saying that the integration we all seek will proceed more smoothly at the Rice Institute because of this single physical fact. Incidentally, it is also true that this unification would scarcely have been possible had not your faculty shown unity, had they not already been thinking in the direction of integration. I congratulate you on both of these circumstances.

My text is drawn from a fairly obscure verse by Geoffrey Chaucer. When Anne of Bohemia was getting herself betrothed to Richard II of England, so the tale says, Chaucer wrote his charming seven-hundred-line *Parlement of Foules*. In it the other birds come on St. Valentine's Day to advise the eagle on her choice of a mate. The full quatrain runs:

> For out of olde feldes, as men seyth,
> Cometh al this newe corn from yer to yere,
> And out of olde bokes, in good feyth,
> Cometh al this newe science that men lere.

I am not unmindful of the risks I run in using this quotation. I am familiar with the vernacular meaning of "corn"; I know that Texans do not look too kindly on old fields and think there must always be new ones, if not above, at least below the surface of the earth; I know that any conscientious scientist who is listening has already condemned the apparent meaning of the quotation. These are risks I must run.

I did not select it to display my Middle English; nor to intimidate you with a flash of erudition. I came on it looking for another quotation I could not remember accurately; it seemed apt; I adopted it. This is a very common way of finding erudite references!

I want to set against it, at once, another quotation which appeared a little less than two hundred years later in *Proposition Touching Amendment of Laws*. This was by Francis Bacon, and he said: "Books must follow sciences, and not sciences books."

These two sayings are not at all contradictory. "Science" meant something different to Chaucer than it did to Bacon; but Chaucer would have agreed that you should create by observation and then record, rather than record first. His whole literary life demonstrated that. And Bacon in turn, if he were living today, would have to agree that if one chose the right books he would find in them all that was to be learned at the moment, but would add that the knowledge in books can be increased only by further experiment.

A university library is, it seems to me, a perfect reconciliation of these two ideas.

We might, however, spend a moment seeing how we are going to define "old." It is, of course, a relative term.

The natural scientist, by and large, finds the greatest part of his useful references (though not all) in work published in the most recent decade. Something ten years past is likely to be old. The writings of Becquerel, J. J. Thomson, Planck, Rutherford, Bohr, and Meitner are in this sense old—in this sense, indeed, as old as the writings of Plato, St. Thomas Aquinas, or Shakespeare. All have already moved to an age where they are timeless.

It is an interesting if uncomfortable speculation to try to understand why the young in natural science ages so rapidly while the old in politics and ethics and philosophy remains so perpetually young. Great ideas from long, long ago have full force and vigor in some fields, notably in many of the liberal arts; great ideas from comparable thinkers in the sciences have either passed into disrepute or have been modified almost past recognition. Acceptance of major contradictory theories in the liberal arts is somewhat cyclical; major theories in science usually, though not always, are developed progressively and do not turn up again in full value in their older form. Why is this?

One might argue that it simply means that students in the liberal arts have not achieved the same asceticism and concentration and competence as students in the natural sciences, the corollary being that if they had, these old statements from the humanities would then be seen to have no validity or at least not full validity. But it could equally well be argued that the difficulty in the two kinds of study is of a different order and that the scientist works on vastly easier problems.

Or it could be said that the great and important situations in which human beings find themselves, the great hopes and fears which in perilous times are so emphatic, all these have been experienced long ago and many times since. "There is no new thing under the sun." Since we also have to admit, as the poet reminded the Greeks, that "there were brave men before Agamemnon," it is only natural that, by now, almost everything important which a man is likely to think up to say has been said. But this could be contradicted, too. Someone might remind us that the writings of Plato and Machiavelli do not tell us how to solve the traffic problem.

I do not propose to level a lance for any of these positions today. I simply want to rest the case on the fact that the university library has in it some very old old things and some very new old things and that these together constitute the stately "old fields" whence comes all the "new corn."

And what a remarkable thing a scholarly library is! How many different needs it serves! Behind its walls we may find all the most important things that man has known or learned or guessed since he seriously began to record his observations. Moreover, these will be remarkably current. Most important things recorded six months ago will be there in periodicals right alongside the important things which were recorded two thousand years ago. Usually the last crop will seem more exciting—but it may not always be the more significant, even for immediate situations.

Moreover, the size of this scholarly library will not place proportional limits upon its wealth of resource. For a very large percentage of the most important things will be found in the small, carefully husbanded library; and only peripheral scholarship will be found to be served better in the great repositories.

How amazing this really is, that in Houston, Texas, and Berkeley, California, and Cambridge, Massachusetts, and Oxford, England, and Paris, France, and in so many other places in the free world, there will be found the identical fundamental great store of knowledge! How important it is that the university library continue to be able to offer this harvest year after year for new generations of free men to glean! If these fields are to furnish an ever-recurring golden crop, how important it is that nothing happen which will turn the crop to weeds!

For there is risk as well as pleasure in farming.

When Samuel Johnson was sixty-nine years old, he was coming back from church one fine April day. Down Butcher-Row he walked with James Boswell tagging along behind. He was accosted by a man whom he had known at Pembroke College forty-nine years earlier and had not seen since, but whom he shortly identified as a Mr. Edwards. The ways of the two men had forked sharply. Edwards had trained for the bar and had finally retired to the country, which he lauded. Boswell, who preferred a cobblestone to a blade of grass every day in the week, objected to Edwards' eulogy of the glories of the country, and said, "What you have to entertain you, is, I think, exhausted in half an hour." Edwards protested at this, and said, "What! Don't you live to have hope realized? I see my grass, and my corn and my trees growing." Then as an afterthought he added, "Now, for instance, I am curious to see if this frost has not nipped my fruit trees." Johnson broke in at once and said, "You find, Sir, you have fears as well as hopes."

There are fears we, too, may have and they are by no means trivial fears. Since we are here dedicating a new set of old fields which we want to see bearing good crops for many years, we would be less than prudent if we did not ponder these dangers.

The scholarly library faces three such dangers today. One is a threat to its clientele, for books which are not read will not furnish new knowledge. The other two are threats to its freedom. I think the latter are the greater threats. So, if you will excuse me, I will speak first of the former.

We pride ourselves on the degree of literacy we have secured for the people of this country but we do not bother often to look beneath the cover and see if literacy is a word which may have quality as well as quantity. It is not enough that a democratic public shall know how to read and write; it is also of some significance that it shall have a high standard of what it chooses to read and write.

For there is more than one kind of literacy. For the most part we are satisfied to define it in its lowest terms, that is, as the simple ability to read and write. But even matter-of-fact dictionaries do not assign the preferred meaning to such a simple definition. There are higher meanings to literacy.

I am by no means sure that a society fares well simply because all its members read some kind of words every day at breakfast or listen to some kind of words emerging from a loud-speaker into the living room every night. Dictators know that standards matter. They do not want their people to be illiterate in the lowest sense. They want the people to be able to read and to listen; the only price they exact is the ability to determine what the people shall read and to what they shall listen.

So one of the clear dangers to the Fondren Library is born in indifference. It may be described as a decline in our sense of the first-rate. It has ironically been made possible by advances in technology but we can hardly blame it directly on the scientists or engineers. Big beaters and rapidly moving Fourdrinier wires whip a tree into a sheet of paper in a matter of minutes and the paper rolls on to the drums at a trivial cost a sheet; this paper passes through great presses recording words endlessly, day and night, indifferent to what the words say, for the machine is amoral; the press is as ready to print gibberish as sense, trash as sound coin, evil as good; it never rebels, it simply prints and prints and prints, so that Sunday newspapers are measured in pounds; and the same processes can be observed in the constantly flowing river of motion picture film or in the endless chatter of the air waves based upon the hypothesis that a moment of silence, ever, would presage the end of the earth and that if a speaker is not continuously out of breath he is probably boring his audience.

We might easily drown in this welter of words and sound, too easily seen, too easily heard. There has never been a time in the history of man when there has been so much literary provender or when such a colossal proportion of it was sawdust. The horse that was fed on sawdust died, as you may recall. The same thing could happen to the mind of a democracy.

Since we are being literary here today, let us turn to another quotation:

An intellectual man, as the world now conceives of him, is one who is full of "views" on all subjects of philosophy, on all matters of the day. It is almost thought a disgrace not to have a view at a moment's notice on any question from the Personal Advent to Cholera or Mesmerism. This is owing in great measure to the necessities of periodical literature, now so much in request. Every quarter of a year, every month, every day, there must be a supply for the gratification of the public, of new and luminous theories on the subjects of religion, foreign politics, home politics, civil economy, finance, trade, agriculture, emigration, and the colonies. . . . As the great man's guest must produce his good stories or songs at the evening banquet, as the platform orator exhibits his telling facts at mid-day, so the journalist lies under the stern obligation of extemporizing his lucid views, leading ideas, and nutshell truths for the breakfast table. The very nature of periodical literature, broken into small wholes, and demanded punctually to an hour, involves the habit of this extempore philosophy. "Almost all the Ramblers," says Boswell of Johnson, "were written just as they were wanted for the press; he sent a certain portion of the copy of an essay, and wrote the remainder while the former part of it was printing." Few men have the gifts of Johnson, who to great vigour and resource of intellect, when it was fairly roused, united a rare common-sense and a conscientious regard for veracity, which preserved him from flippancy or extravagance in writing. Few men are Johnsons; yet how many men at this day are assailed by incessant demands on their mental powers, which only a productiveness like his could suitably supply! There is a demand for a reckless originality of thought, and a sparkling plausibility of argument, which he would have despised, even if he could have displayed; a demand for crude theory and unsound philosophy, rather than none at all.

John Henry Newman said this in one of his Dublin lectures, later recorded in *The Idea of a University,* nearly a hundred years ago. Paper and type and ink were still not cheap in those days; the continuous alarm of the announcer or the bleat of the crooner did not invade his house; children were not tempted away from their few books by a televised picture of two overweight females going through a second-rate prepared comedy called wrestling; every statesman did not have a hundred interpreters of what he said and a hundred others to give the low-down on why he had not said something different. And there were no comics.

This flood of mediocrity or worse, this affront to the intelligence, might not be effective save through repetition. But if you say often enough that a cigarette is smoked by a good many doctors, you may trap the listener into drawing a conclusion which has no basis in logic. You have never lied, really. But you have softened his mind, and perhaps you have sold a package of cigarettes.

I am not fooling here. I think man is naturally easy-going. He has had to force himself to his present position. He can drop off a high position pretty rapidly, as history has shown over and over. The sons of the great Romans were not themselves great Romans. Something softened them up, too. I am not proposing any solution to this problem today, but I do mean to say that this constant low-level stimulation of words is likely to destroy incentives towards a higher literacy.

Such a lack of incentive towards the higher literacy impresses me as a threat to our democracy. I am not one of those who, because they find Shakespeare more impressive and more provocative and more beautiful than Maxwell Anderson, also believe that Elizabethan England was a better place than the United States of Harry Truman. I am certain it was a worse place.

I know that most Athenians were quite satisfied to tolerate slavery even though some of them attended lofty plays and discourses and erected noble cities; that there were many more starving swineherds in the Middle Ages than there were Abelards; and that the dignity of human life has probably never been held so high as it is held right now on this day in this country of ours.

But I cannot escape the notion that we may become satisfied to teach our citizens to run their eyes past lines of type rather than to think of what the type says, and to be content if what it does say is false or cheap or second-hand; and that at the same time we may manage to endow this print with a spurious and frightening sanctity. Any tendency of this sort constitutes a clear threat to everything for which the Fondren Library stands.

If the first danger stems from indifference, the other two stem from fear—from the same fear. But they manifest themselves quite differently. One relates to what sorts of new material the Fondren Library shall be permitted to offer its users; the second relates to censorship of the old material.

I doubt if anyone in this audience except perhaps a few of

the scientists knows the extent to which the secrecy policy of
the government of the United States has led us in limiting the
circulation of new information in some fields of science. The
story of secrecy is a long and complicated one and not to be
developed here. However, I know of no first-class scientist who
believes that this policy is anything but deleterious to the
progress of science in the United States or that it does not on
the whole create more insecurity than it does security. No
nation will survive if, in hiding things from a suspected enemy,
it also hides them from its friends so that they limp towards
their goals instead of running. No science will continually
endure if the corpus of scientists is divided into those who
elect to work for a government and hence can be let into the
know and those who cannot. Yet there are important contributions to science and engineering, important facts for the general public to know as well, which cannot be placed on the
open shelves of the Fondren Library today. There is nothing
in the logic of secrecy which confines this kind of censorship
to scientific material; there could equally well be economic
facts and political facts which it might seem to some people
in authority ought to be concealed from the American public.
The extension is perfectly logical. The argument would go that
our potential enemy is assumed not to know these things; that
it will hurt us if he learns them; that we should not help him
to learn them; that it is better that many of us should not learn
them if that is necessary to keep him from learning them. Then
the vicious circle closes and we end with an uninformed public in, of all places, a democracy. Gone are our open covenants
openly arrived at. We shall have to guess at everything which
is important in our national behavior—and then every few
years vote in blinders. This danger is real and can be averted
only by eternal vigilance.

The third danger stems at the moment, as I have said, from
the same apprehension. Let me start with a question, a nasty
question. Is there a fellow-traveler on this faculty? If there is,
what are you going to do with him? I know that fifty years
ago on these wide expanses your vigilantes would have had an
answer. But we have gone farther in our understanding of free-

dom since then and we look with horror on the purges of others. Most of all we fear the nice tight-rope we have to walk in determining what kinds of freedom shall be free and what kinds shall not. The universities of this country are still groping with this question. It would be much easier for them to find a solution if they had better support from the general public—if they could believe that the public meant business about freedom 365 days in the year.

Now what has a fellow-traveler on your campus got to do with the Fondren Library? Well, simply that there are far more brilliant fellow-travelers in your Fondren Library than you are ever likely to find on your campus. There are people who are brilliantly amoral and even immoral; there are radicals and tories; there are communists, and fascists. Specifically there are, I am sure, Karl Marx and Friedrich Engels and I hope there are also Nikolai Lenin and Joseph Stalin; I hope there are Plato and Adolf Hitler; and if you fear sex more than politics, there are surely Freud and Jung and James Joyce and all sorts of other troublesome people. Now this building is full of every kind of temptation to subversion, the most plausible and brilliant subversion, because it has been prepared by the most brilliant minds and because the texts are known to have influenced many men of action whose work we are worried about right now. It is essential that this be so. We are convinced that the mind arrives at mature convictions, convictions which are worth working for and dying for, only by the tough process of considering matters from all angles. One does not cherish freedom simply by reading eulogies of it; rather, this power is gained by close analysis of what the people who would destroy it say about it. And this is to be found best in their own words and not in those of an interpreter. The studies of a university are not to be deduced from a list of the textbooks it uses, or even a list of its assigned readings, but rather from its card catalogue. And the more catholic this catalogue is, the more complete, the greater will be the stature of the university, the greater its force for freedom. We must maintain Plato and Lenin in our libraries—and everybody else who has anything to say.

Alexander Meiklejohn asks us in his little book *Free Speech*:

Shall we give a hearing to those who hate and despise freedom, to those who, if they had the power, would destroy our institutions? Certainly, yes! Our action must be guided, not by their principles, but by ours. We listen, not because they desire to speak, but because we need to hear. . . .

Yet how insidious these writers are. One of your young men or young women can march in and take one of their books off the shelves and sit himself down in an easy chair in an air-conditioned atmosphere while it is hot as Tophet outside, and you will never know what he is absorbing. And all of a sudden he may come alive and something will happen. What are you going to do about that?

Now I expect there would be a great deal of different opinion in this gathering as to what to do about the fellow-traveler; but I expect that very few of us here would presume to name what books to root out, or even to suggest that any books should be rooted out. But that need not leave us much comfort. Everybody does not think that way. Some of you here have presumably heard of Congressman Wood of Georgia. Do you remember him?

Last June Congressman Wood called on all the universities to send him lists of the books they used in teaching. He is probably a naïve man and believes that university education relies on a few textbooks and that if he extirpated the "un-American" textbooks he would have solved a problem. Someone indeed suggested that he might want a microfilm of the card catalogue of the university library. This Wood foray was started by the suggestion of some Sons of the American Revolution. A mighty howl went up and Congressman Wood beat a hasty retreat. He said his inquiry was just "a routine check-up." Later he had even the greater effrontery to suggest that the Committee "does not desire to interfere in any manner with academic freedom nor does it intend to censor textbooks" —as though it had any right to, whatsoever.

But the implications of Mr. Wood's abortive try are very serious. If they were given in to at all, they could lead to all kinds of restrictions—and to a rapid decay in the educational power of a library. The best analysis of the implications I have come across was made by Bernard DeVoto in the September, 1949, issue of *Harper's Magazine*.

Mr. DeVoto says the colleges must make their stand right now, and continues:

If they abandon as much as one book to Mr. Wood they may as well throw in their hand. They will defy any government control of inquiry whatsoever, or they will be forced to submit to any political dictation, any limitation of academic freedom, and any coercion of academic procedure that a committee majority may care or may be induced to impose. There is no such thing as a partial virgin. There is no such thing as academic freedom that is just a mite restricted. The colleges are entirely free or they are not free at all. Mr. Wood's absent-minded asininity was no more innocent than a tidal wave. It means the colleges have got to make the fight. It can be won—but not unless it is made.

Here, then, are three dangers to the Fondren Library and its brethren which I think are real and present. They will not disappear simply because we elect not to think about them. There are no very easy remedies. But that there are no remedies must be categorically denied.

The treatment in each case probably demands a multitude of little steps which would be tedious to rehearse here in detail; the crusade against the dangers born of fear may need to be fairly aggressive, more aggressive than the colleges and universities have yet been prepared to be; if they are so aggressive they run some risk of defeat and in defeat some forms of disaster. But if there ever was a gage which the colleges should take up, and now, it is the persistent attack on their freedom, of which the witch hunt is but the most spectacular manifestation.

And even if such aggressive action is successful, and I am sure it would be, we shall have to maintain thereafter eternal vigilance: vigilance against the intrusion of the second-rate; vigilance against the compartmentation of knowledge in the interests of what the military people call "cryptographic security" but what is more likely to yield ignorant insecurity; vigilance against encroachments on freedom to possess, to display, and to circulate each and every book which has any scholarly significance, regardless of how unfashionable may be the cause it espouses—remembering always that judgments are not best formed by reading a completely fair middle-of-the-road account but rather by reading completely unfair but brilliantly telling arguments from both sides of the road.

If we keep this vigil, we need not be afraid. If we do not keep it, we may expect to find early symptoms of our decay in what we hold and circulate in our libraries. And as the books are closed, the candles of freedom will also begin to flicker out.

On the other hand, these magnificent surroundings give us cause for the utmost optimism. In the *Aeneid,* as Sir Richard Livingstone reminded us last April, Jupiter says of the Roman people:

> His ego nec metas rerum nec tempora pono;
> Imperium sine fine dedi.

> (For them I set no limits of circumstance or time.
> I have given them an empire without boundaries.)

This should be an attractive challenge in this almost boundless state, on this almost boundless campus. You have a tradition of freedom here in Texas. It seems certain to me that this library under its able librarian and in these ingratiatingly human surroundings will meet the challenge. I congratulate you on the opportunity. I congratulate you on having erected this stately pleasure-dome in which to realize it.

QUESTIONS

1. Comment on the tone of the entire essay.
2. What three dangers does the scholarly library face today?
3. What limitation should be placed on the publication of scientific knowledge?
4. What disposition should a librarian make of material that is obviously propaganda?
5. State concisely the central theme of this essay; explain the principle of organization by which Burchard develops this theme.

INTELLECTUAL FREEDOM
AND HIGHER EDUCATION
✐ R. A. Tsanoff

Our Student Forum has shown good judgment in bringing us together to consider the problem of intellectual freedom, for it concerns the very life and spirit to which a university community is dedicated. And in dealing with intellectual freedom, it is natural that we should emphasize especially its rights and its responsibilities in colleges and universities.

So now let us ask our question: "What is the freedom which we college and university students and faculty need and which we have a right to demand and a duty to defend?"

This so-called academic freedom is indicated by the very character of our institutions. A college or a university has as its chief function the preservation, the transmission, and the expansion of knowledge. Its main purpose is the attainment of truth.

It is not accidental that the two oldest American universities, Harvard and Yale, have the word "Truth," "*Veritas*," engraved on their seals. Now truth can be defended in only one way, by being proved and established in fair inquiry. And error is not destroyed by being prohibited, but only by being disproved and refuted.

Truth does not need police protection, but only support by adequate evidence. We need the truth, and so we must have the

An address to the Rice Institute Student Forum, April, 1953. Kindly revised by the author for this volume.

facts. Universities, real universities, are dedicated to this sort of fair inquiry. That is why we can call them temples of free minds, for the spirit of consecration to the truth is the surest guarantee of freedom. On the front of the Main Building at the University of Texas are engraved these words, and they come from the New Testament: "Ye shall know the truth, and the truth shall make you free." These words should be cherished as the charter of university education in a democratic society.

This unprejudiced pursuit of the truth has been opposed by dogmatic minds, who have feared that some cherished doctrines of theirs might be upset. In some periods of our civilization these dogmatists have been ecclesiastics, in other periods they have been political or social reactionaries.

When Galileo formulated his principles of modern astronomy, he was accused by the Inquisition of teaching doctrines contrary to God's truth. His answer to the judges should be remembered. He told the holy fathers that he was a scientist, and that the only way in which he could try not to disagree with God's truth was to make his truth as true as possible. The judgment of posterity has sustained Galileo.

In our day the government of communist Russia prohibited for several years the teaching of the generally accepted biological theory that acquired characteristics are not inheritable. Now it is conceivable that future scientific investigation may prove that this doctrine is an error, but this could not be achieved by prohibition, but in only one way, by investigation. Such legislation in matters of scientific truth is a scandal and a disaster to Russian science. And it would be a disaster to us, too, if we were to follow in our education the communist policy of intellectual repression in any field. The best way to preserve ourselves from communist corruption is not to imitate the communist policies. The rule is very simple: Do not repeat the communist evils.

This principle of intellectual freedom applies in college teaching just as truly as it does in scientific or scholarly research. If ecclesiastic or civil authorities or well-organized factions in our society should succeed in enforcing on teachers the obligation to teach certain definite ideas and to oppose certain other books, then the whole process of education would be compromised. No real training of young minds in the pursuit of truth would be possible, if the students saw in their teachers men who were obliged to teach them the way they did, for otherwise they would lose their jobs and get into further trouble. The cornerstone of a real university is intellectual integrity.

You can see, then, why free inquiring minds resist curbs and shackles. The spirit of resistance to compulsion in thinking is a bulwark to our democratic freedom all around and especially in a period of crisis like the present. The way to safeguard our young minds, and our old minds too, from pernicious errors, is to examine and understand those errors, to see why they are errors and pernicious. It has been well said that the first foreign language which a people should learn is the language of their chief enemies. So it is also important for us to understand thoroughly the doctrines and the propaganda of communism. There are some people among us who think that if our college students should read a communist book they would be converted to communism. We on the other hand believe that erroneous and false doctrines have to be understood in order to be really rejected. The better we understand the communist teachings and the communist practices, the more clearly we can see how communism threatens our whole democratic civilization and its great human values, the more intelligently we can then resist its insidious influence.

I have endeavored so far to give my reasons for my firm belief in intellectual freedom. Now, however, I am bound to consider the other aspect of this problem, as I see it, in our university life: namely, the responsibilities of academic freedom.

A great modern liberal expressed a profound truth which is relevant to our discussion. He wrote: "A man has a moral right to that freedom which he requires for the performance of his duties." Why do I demand freedom of teaching and research? Because I need that freedom in order to live a life of intellectual integrity, to seek and find the truth. Therefore, in my classes and in my writings, I should examine and discuss all ideas fairly. Surely I should not take advantage of my students' trust in me, I should not give them a biased account of the facts and the ideas with which I am dealing. As all of us know, even with the most fair-minded intentions a professor is apt to convey in his teaching his own partiality to some ideas rather than to others. But just on that account, I say, I should always try to be as objective as possible. What is most important is that I give my students good evidence of the spirit of fair inquiry, both in what I advocate and in what I oppose.

Another important responsibility of academic freedom is that university minds, both professors and students, should never lose sight of the social-practical power of ideas, their bearing on men's daily lives. We should do our thinking with responsible socially-minded regard for the security and the well-being of the people and not betray their trust in us. Ideas are not mere playthings for academic minds. The social acceptance or rejection of them may spell blessing or disaster for our nation. The issue between communism and American democracy is not just a pair of alternatives for idle debaters. It is an issue of life or death for our civilization. In dealing with this issue, or with the related ideas of social-political order, or of moral principles, or religious problems, those of us who rightly demand intellectual freedom should never forget the responsibilities which that freedom entails.

Let me read to you the words of a great American, Thomas Jefferson, from his Presidential Inaugural Address of 1801. Jefferson said: "If there be any among us who would wish to dissolve this Union or change its republican form, let them stand undisturbed as monuments of the safety with which error of opinion may be tolerated where reason is left free to combat it."

Note Jefferson's keen insight into the range and also the limits of democratic tolerance: "Error of opinion may be tolerated where reason is left free to combat it." Take, for instance, this meeting. We have no doubt persons of different opinions in our audience. I say, let them stand up freely and express their ideas. But we cannot allow any of them to conspire and break up our meeting of free discussion. We shall tolerate disagreement of opinion, but we shall not tolerate organized intolerance and disruption, whether it be communist or fascist disruption or any other kind.

There should be no misunderstanding here. The protection of intellectual freedom in our universities from communist agents or any other conspirators and traitors is a task for university faculties and administrators. Colleges and universities are not irresponsible institutions. They are chartered by the states; they know their men much better than any outsiders can know them and they are quite able and resolved to maintain their integrity.

But whenever any individual faces a charge of being a member of the communist party conspiracy, he should have a full trial in the courts, with the same legal provisions for his defense which our laws accord even to the worst criminals. Outside pressure groups should not be allowed to invade our educational system and, under the pretense of rooting out communism in the schools, undertake to repress liberal critical thinking on the part of teachers and students. We do not protect our American democracy but, on the contrary, we undermine it, when we allow lawful trial by jury to be replaced by high-handed practices of slanderous accusations and smears. These were the tactics of Hitler: they are the tactics of the communists.

We should not imitate the enemies of our American freedom. We do not want aggressive reactionaries to control our universities for the same reason for which we do not want communist agents on our faculties. They are both marked by the same un-American activities of dictatorial opposition to free inquiry and discussion. We cherish and we seek to preserve in our schools the truly American activities of freedom of thought, freedom of speech, freedom of fair discussion.

In resisting communism we should know what we are resisting. We must resist its tyrannical spirit and policies, its oppression of men's minds and lives. Therefore we should try to resist the spirit of oppression in ourselves, lest it corrupt us. Of what avail would it be to have defeated Hitler's armies on the field of battle, if the spirit of Hitler should enter your soul and mind, if you and I in our turn should adopt Hitler's policy of book-burning and witch-hunting and intolerance and oppression? As with Hitler, so with Stalin, and so with their successors. We abhor their names, for we understand the perversity of their doctrines and their practices. And therefore we should be resolved not to imitate their oppressive policies. We do not want any iron curtain in our beloved American land.

And if you want a vow in the spirit to which the true universities are dedicated, here is one, again by Thomas Jefferson: "I have sworn upon the altar of God eternal hostility against every form of tyranny over the mind of man."

QUESTIONS

1. After reading Tsanoff's essay, write a few paragraphs explaining what you think academic freedom is.
2. What would be the result of a system in which teachers were compelled to teach certain ideas and reject certain others? How far can ecclesiastic or civil authorities go in enforcing such a policy?
3. What ideological parallels can be drawn between this essay and that by Burchard?
4. List several of the responsibilities that academic freedom entails.
5. Into what two main sections can this essay be divided? Make an outline of the essay showing its logical development.

LEHRFREIHEIT AND *LERNFREIHEIT*

✒ Richard Hofstadter
and Walter P. Metzger

All through the nineteenth century, but particularly after the establishment of the Empire, German scholars boasted of their academic freedom and brought it to the attention of the scholarly world. And the scholarly world, in the habit of paying homage to the German universities, agreed that freedom was triumphant there, the proof and cause of their superiority. In recent times, it is worth noting, the reality of this vaunted freedom has been sharply questioned. With the recent capitulation of the German universities to pseudo-science and the totalitarian state, doubt has arisen as to whether, at any time in the pre-Hitler period, they had ever truly been free. It is pointed out that professors as civil servants had been subject to a special disciplinary code; that under the Kaisers, Social Democrats, Jews, and other minorities had been discriminated against in appointments; that on most questions of national honor and interest (witness the performance of the German professors during the First World War), the academic corps had docilely taken its place in the chauvinistic chorus. It is also pointed out that the German universities were state uni-

From *The Development of Academic Freedom in the United States* (New York, Columbia University Press, 1955). [We have omitted all references to sources.]

versities in an undemocratic state, dependent upon the uncertain good will of the minister of education and on a dynasty far more autocratic than the constitutional forms reveal. Granting all this to be true, however, there remains the question of what was the basis of the boast that the German universities were free.

Two factors point to the answer. The first is the greater independence enjoyed by the universities under the Empire than at any time before. The Reformation had fixed the universities in the theology of the territorial ruler. Though test oaths for students had been abolished in the Protestant universities during the eighteenth century, and speculative philosophy and theological skepticism had flourished at the expense of orthodoxy, it was not until complete separation of church and state was achieved under the Hohenzollerns that the universities were finally free from church control. Likewise punitive action by the state became comparatively rare after unification. The German states lost much of their cameralistic urge to regulate everything directly. The territorial oaths and religious tests in force in the seventeenth century, such as the official resolution of the University of Marburg in 1653 to ban Cartesian philosophy, the capricious absolutism of the eighteenth century, revealed in Frederick William I's expulsion of Christian Wolff and the reprimand of Kant by Prime Minister Wollner, and the repressive censorship of the early and middle nineteenth century, exemplified by the Carlsbad Decrees and the dismissal of the Göttingen Seven, all seemed part of an inglorious but forever finished past. The provision in the Prussian Constitution of 1850 that "science and its teaching shall be free" epitomized the more permissive attitude of the new order. Finally, the German universities were not directly affected by public opinion under the Empire. Public opinion in general never reached the degree of crystallization, organization, and articulation that it achieved in England, France, or the United States. Like the army, the universities belonged to the state, which protected them against local and sectarian pressures.

The German system of control allowed the universities considerable corporate autonomy. The states drew up the budgets, created new chairs, appointed professors, and framed the general scheme of instruction. But the election of academic officials, the appointment of lecturers or *Privatdocenten,* and the nomination of professors were powers enjoyed by the faculty. No lay board of control was interposed between the ultimate authority of the state and the plenary powers of the professors. No elaborate administrative structure was required; no office of the president was established. Each faculty was presided over by a dean elected by and chosen from that faculty; each university was represented by a rector chosen from and elected by the whole professorial corps. The German universities were state institutions, but the combination of governmental restraint, cultural isolation, limited professorial co-option, and elected administrators gave them the appearance of self-governing bodies.

The German definition of academic freedom offers the second clue. When the German professor spoke of academic freedom, he referred to a condition summed up by two words: *Lernfreiheit* and *Lehrfreiheit.* By *Lernfreiheit* he meant the absence of administrative coercions in the learning situation. He referred to the fact that German students were free to roam from place to place, sampling academic wares; that wherever they lighted, they were free to determine the choice and sequence of courses, and were responsible to no one for regular attendance; that they were exempted from all tests save the final examination; that they lived in private quarters and controlled their private lives. This freedom was deemed essential to the main purposes of the German university: to forward research and to train researchers. By *Lehrfreiheit,* the German educator meant two things. He meant that the university professor was free to examine bodies of evidence and to report his findings in lecture or published form—that he enjoyed freedom of teaching and freedom of inquiry. This, too, was thought to follow from the searching function, from the presumption that knowledge was not fixed or final, from the belief, as Paulsen put it, that *Wissenschaft* knew no "statute of limitation," no authoritative "law of prescription," no "absolute property right." This freedom was not, as the Germans conceived it, an inalienable endowment of all men, nor was it a superadded attraction of certain universities and not of others; rather, it was the distinctive prerogative of the academic profession, and the essential condition of all universities. Without it, no institution had the right to call itself a "university." In addition, *Lehrfreiheit*, like *Lernfreiheit*, also denoted the paucity of administrative rules within the teaching situation: the absence of a prescribed syllabus, the freedom from tutorial duties, the opportunity to lecture on any subject according to the teacher's interest. Thus, academic freedom, as the Germans defined it, was not simply the right of professors to speak without fear or favor, but the atmosphere of consent that surrounded the whole process of research and instruction.

The German's pride in these two freedoms can be attributed in part to the status they conferred and to their significance as patriotic symbols. To the university student, coming from the strict and formal *Gymnasium*, *Lernfreiheit* was a precious privilege, a recognition of his arrival at man's estate. To the university professor, extremely sensitive to considerations of social esteem, *Lehrfreiheit* was a dispensation that set him apart from the ordinary civil servant. In a nation still aristocratic and feudalistic in its mores, caste considerations thus underlay the loyalty to academic freedom. In addition, *Lern-* and *Lehrfreiheit* had patriotic associations. They were identified with the national revival. The renewal of student peregrinations in the eighteenth century symbolized the breakdown of territorial exclusiveness and the growth of national consciousness. The University of Berlin, dedicated to academic freedom, was a phoenix that had arisen from the ashes of military defeat. The denial of academic freedom in the Metternich era had been the work of Catholic dogmatism, Protestant particularism, petty absolutism—all enemies of a united Reich. Moreover, after unification, academic freedom was thought to atone for the lack of political freedoms and to prove the special virtue of the Fatherland. The romantic nineteenth century was given to equating freedom and nationality, but it was a peculiarity of German thought that it made academic freedom one of the major terms in this equation.

The German conception of academic freedom, reflecting the philosophical temper of German academic thought, distinguished sharply between freedom *within* and freedom *outside* the university. Within the walls of academe, a wide latitude of utterance was allowed, even expected. With Fichte's heroic scholar as their model, university professors saw themselves, not as neutral observers of life, but as the diviners and spokesmen of absolutes, as oracles of transcendent truths. In the normative sciences particularly, "professing" in Germany tended to be the presentation with aggressive finality of deep subjective convictions. Among certain professors, to be sure, there were proponents of a more restrained and cautious conception. In 1877, in the heat of the Darwinian controversy, Rudolph Virchow, the great German pathologist, argued that unproved hypotheses should never be taught as true, that professors should stay within their spheres of competence, that they should consult the *consensus gentium* before expressing possibly dangerous beliefs. But in a famous reply to Virchow, Ernst Haeckel, the biologist, contended that no line between objective and subjective knowledge could or ought to be drawn, that science advances only through the open clash of wrong and correct opinions, that the obligation of the professor to adhere to indubitable facts or to defer to existing opinion would relinquish the field of education to the religious infallibilists. The leading theorists of academic freedom in this period adhered to the latter position—Max Müller of St. Gallen, Georg Kaufmann, von Helmholtz, Friedrich Paulsen. Reasoning from rationalistic or idealistic premises, they believed that the only alternative to the presentation of personal convictions was the prescription of authoritative dogma, that the only alternative to polemical controversy was the stoppage of academic inquiry. Recognizing that there were dangers in subjective and polemical teaching, they thought there were adequate safeguards in the freedom and maturity of the student, who was neither captive nor unprimed. As Paulsen put it:

The content of instruction is not prescribed for the academic teacher; he is, as searcher as well as teacher, attached to no authority; he himself answers for his own instruction and is responsible to no one else. Opposite him is his student with complete freedom to accept or to reject; he is not a pupil but has the privilege of the critic or the improver. There is only one aim for both:

the truth; only one yardstick: the agreement of thought with reality and with no other outside authority.

To Helmholtz,

Whoever wants to give his students complete conviction about the accuracy of his statements must first of all know from his own experience how one wins conviction, and how one does not. Thus he must have had to know how to struggle for this by himself when no predecessor had yet come to his aid; this means that he must have worked on the boundaries of human knowledge and conquered new realms for it. A teacher who imparts convictions that are not his own is sufficient for students who are to be directed by authority as the source of their knowledge, but it is not for such as those who demand a foundation for their conviction down to the very last fundamentals. . . . The free conviction of scholars is only to be won if the free expression of conviction on the part of the teacher, freedom of teaching, is assured.

But outside the university, the same degree of freedom was not condoned. Though quite a few German professors played prominent political roles in the nineteenth century, and a number of these—notably Mommsen and Virchow—were outspoken critics of Bismarck, it was not generally assumed that *Lehrfreiheit* condoned or protected such activities. Rather, it was generally assumed that professors as civil servants were bound to be circumspect and loyal, and that participation in partisan politics spoiled the habits of scholarship. Even so firm a libertarian as Paulsen held that

the scholars cannot and should not engage in politics. They cannot do it if they have developed their capacities in accordance with the demands of their calling. Scientific research is their business, and scientific research calls for constant examination of thoughts and theories to the end of harmonizing them with the facts. Hence those thinkers are bound to develop a habit of *theoretical indifference* with respect to the opposing sides, a readiness to pursue any other path in case it promises to lead to a theory more in accordance with the facts. Now every form of practical activity, and practical politics particularly, demands above everything else a determination to follow *one* path that one has chosen. . . . Political activity . . . produces a habit that would prove fatal to the theorist, the habit of *opportunism*.

A university teacher who violated this canon by working for the Social Democratic Party (a legal party after 1890) might find the temporal power rigid and severe. The removal of Dr. Leo Arons, *Privatdocent* at the University of Berlin, for having delivered speeches for the Social Democratic Party is a case in point. The Prussian Minister of Education declared, in removing him, that every teacher "must defend the existing order against all attacks." The philosophical faculty of Berlin had admonished Arons some years before "to cease from such agitation . . . as may bring . . . the good name of the university into obloquy." When, however, their power to discipline the *Privatdocenten* was infringed upon by the Prussian Minister, they defended Arons and demanded that he be retained. Their verdict, which was overruled, contained the statement that university professors "were not strictly comparable to other officials" and that they should enjoy "a wider realm of utterance." But they did concede that professors were not "free and independent citizens," and that professors were obliged, as members of state institutions, to adhere to a special code of decorum. What was noticeably missing from their statement was any assertion that professors, as citizens, enjoyed an uninfringeable right to freedom of extramural speech. The issue was debated on the ground of prerogative, not on the ground of civil liberty.

In this dichotomy between freedom within and freedom without, we perceive, in transmuted form, some of the classic dualities in German philosophy. The assumption that there were two realms of professorial existence—the one, within the university, the realm of freedom; the other, outside the university, the realm of legal compulsion—suggests Kant's division of the noumena and the phenomena, of the world of free will and the world of causal necessity. The limitation of freedom to the inner realm suggests Luther's formula of spiritual freedom combined with temporal obedience. And the injunction that the scholar withdraw from the sphere of practical matters to the anchorite's world of contemplation suggests Fichte's distinction between the true student and the false one, between him who is dedicated to truth and him who seeks selfish advantage.

The American reaction to the German universities' concept

of academic freedom again shows striking evidences of dependence, selectivity, and modification. Dependence appeared from the days of the first expatriates, when the freedom of the German professor in theological affairs gripped the attention and won the admiration of Americans. Ticknor wrote from Göttingen:

No matter what a man thinks, he may teach it and print it; not only without molestation from the government but also without molestation from publick opinion. . . . The same freedom in France produced the revolution and the same freedom in England would now shake the deep foundations of the British throne—but here it passes as a matter of course. . . . If truth is to be attained by freedom of inquiry, as I doubt not it is, the German professors and literati are certainly on the high road, and have the way quietly open before them.

Considerably cooler to the skepticism and impiety of the Göttingen theologians, George Bancroft also marveled at the fact that

the German literary world is a perfect democracy. No man acknowledges the supremacy of another, and everyone feels himself perfectly at liberty to follow his own inclinations in his style of writing and in his subject. . . . No laws are acknowledged as limiting the field of investigation or experiment.

Decades later, William Graham Sumner, no Germanophile, paid tribute to the freedom and courage of the German scholar in an area designated as sacrosanct in America:

I have heard men elsewhere talk about the nobility of that spirit [the seeking of truth]; but the only *body* of men whom I have ever known who really lived by it, sacrificing wealth, political distinction, church preferment, popularity, or anything else for the truth of science, were the professors of biblical science in Germany. That was precisely the range of subjects which in this country was then treated with a reserve in favor of tradition which was prejudicial to everything which a scholar should value.

After the Civil War, when theological freedom under university auspices no longer occasioned surprise, American economists, psychologists, and philosophers sang the praises of German freedom. "The German University is to-day the freest spot on earth," wrote G. Stanley Hall, the psychologist; the German university made him "free intellectually, free spiritually," attested Paul Russell Pope, professor of German at Cornell; "we were impressed in the German university by a certain largeness and freedom of thought," said Richard T. Ely, speaking for himself and for other founders of the American Economic Association.

Since the propensity of Americans to acknowledge that others are free is not usually great, we are led to seek the reason for the lavishness of this praise. As far as the earlier enthusiasts are concerned, the reason may lie in the fact that most of them attended the freest of the German universities, Göttingen and Berlin. This was not by chance: at these universities they did not have to take the religious oaths that would have tried their consciences at the South German Catholic universities or at the universities of Oxford and Cambridge. In addition, it should be recalled that most of the Americans who went to Germany throughout the century were young men who were suddenly projected into an older and more permissive culture than their own. Temperament decided how this situation would be used, but we can assume that it would be an American in whom the asceticism of Calvin and the prudishness of Victoria were deeply and ineradicably ingrained who would resist the blandishments of the carefree German Sabbath, the *Kneipe* in the afternoon, and perhaps an innocent, initiating love affair. Biography and autobiography are not very revealing on this score, but it is not unlikely that many an American small-town boy shared, with G. Stanley Hall, a sense of deliverance from "the narrow, inflexible orthodoxy, the settled lifeless *mores*, the Puritan eviction of joy." "Germany almost remade me," the president of Clark University wrote in his candid autobiography. "It gave me a new attitude toward life. . . . I fairly revelled in a freedom unknown before." To an unmeasurable degree, the German university's reputation rested on the remembrance of freedoms enjoyed that were not in any narrow sense academic. Needless to say, this did not diminish its reputation.

"To the German mind," wrote James Morgan Hart, "if either freedom of teaching or freedom of learning is wanting, that institution, no matter how richly endowed, no matter how numerous its students, no matter how imposing its buildings, is not . . . a *University.*" If one were to single out the chief German contribution to the American conception of academic freedom, it would be the assumption that academic freedom, like academic searching, *defined* the true university. This simple though signally imporant idea fastened itself upon American academic thought. It became an idea to which fealty had to be expressed. It took hold in the rhetoric of academic ceremonials, a rhetoric that, for all its flamboyance, tells much about underlying assumptions. Charles W. Eliot in his 1869 inaugural address decked this idea with memorable words:

A university must be indigenous; it must be rich; and above all, it must be free. The winnowing breeze of freedom must blow through all its chambers. It takes a hurricane to blow wheat away. An atmosphere of intellectual freedom is the native air of literature and science. This university aspires to serve the nation by training men to intellectual honesty and independence of mind. The Corporation demands of all its teachers that they be grave, reverent and high-minded; but it leaves them, like their pupils, free.

Not since Jefferson had an academic leader acclaimed academic freedom so aphoristically and from so high a tribunal. But where Jefferson's tribute to the "illimitable freedom of the human mind" spoke for a waning hope, Eliot's words were harbingers of a mood that would thoroughly conquer. Again and again, high-placed figures in the academic world gave this idea their support. Gilman, at his inauguration, asserted that freedom for teachers and students was essential to a true university. Andrew Dickson White, commenting on the Winchell case, declared that "an institution calling itself a university thus violated the fundamental principles on which any institution worthy of the name must be based." William Rainey Harper of Chicago spoke these glowing words:

When for any reason, in a university on private foundation or in a university supported by public money, the administration of the institution or the instruction in any one of its departments is changed by an influence from without, when an effort is made to dislodge an officer or a professor because the political sentiment or the religious sentiment of the majority has undergone a change, at that moment the institution has ceased to be a university, and it cannot again take its place in the rank of universities so long as there continues to exist to any appreciable extent the factor of coercion. . . . Individuals or the state or the church may found schools for propagating certain special kinds of instruction, but such schools are not universities, and may not be so denominated.

Nor did these hosannas swell from the throats of reformers alone: a president of a small church-related college, a trustee to whom Ricardo was the last word in economics, an alumnus proud of his university's achievement at games, were also willing choristers.

It need hardly be said that a gap existed between these words and their implementation. Early in his regime, Charles W. Eliot told a professor to omit a doctrine offensive to Boston businessmen from his projected book, or else erase any reference to his Harvard connection from the title page: the Harvard president was to regret his arbitrary imposition. Andrew Dickson White's understanding of the principle of tenure was so underdeveloped when he took office that he proposed an annual scrutiny of the performance of each professor by the trustees, with dismissal to follow upon a sufficient number of unsatisfactory ballots. . . . William Rainey Harper's statement on behalf of academic freedom was preceded some years before by the dismissal of the economist Edward W. Bemis on what appeared to be ideological grounds. And many a eulogy to academic freedom was followed by a contradictory recitative proclaiming the absolute right of trustees to hire and fire whomsoever they pleased. Nevertheless, the idea that academic freedom was part of the definition of a university was new and consequential. It was a norm from which the distance to practice could be measured. It was a belief which, in entering the ambit of good form, more easily won advocates and an audience. It was an ideal that elevated academic freedom from an undefined and unconscious yearning to a conscious and declared necessity of academic existence.

The contribution to the development of academic freedom in America made by German-trained scholars was more than oratorical. From the nineties to the First World War, a good proportion of the leaders and targets in academic-freedom

cases had studied in Germany: Richard T. Ely, E. Benjamin
Andrews, Edward A. Ross, John Mecklin, J. McKeen Cattell.
Others—E. R. A. Seligman, Arthur O. Lovejoy, and Henry W.
Farnam—worked on behalf of embattled colleagues. Eight of
the thirteen signers of the 1915 "Report on Academic Freedom" of the American Association of University Professors had
studied in Germany: Seligman, Farnam, Ely, Lovejoy, U. G.
Weatherly, Charles E. Bennett, Howard Crosby Warren, Frank
A. Fetter. Some of the leaders in the fight for professorial self-
government were German university alumni: Cattell, Joseph
Jastrow, and George T. Ladd. That the attitudes of these prominent professors were formed solely by their sojourn abroad is
not, of course, certain. It is possible that their very prominence,
combined with their interest in the threatened social sciences,
placed them in the forefront of battle. But it is not too fanciful
to see also in their remarkable showing a pattern of with-
drawal-and-return wherein American scholars, temporarily
abandoning their world and drawing courage from alien
springs, returned to dispense their inspiration.

This much we take to be the direct German contribution. But
evidence of selection and modification can also be perceived.
The 1915 "Report on Academic Freedom" of the AAUP opened
with the statement that " 'academic freedom' has traditionally
had two applications—to the freedom of the teacher and to
that of the student, to *Lehrfreiheit* and *Lernfreiheit*." This was
a gracious acknowledgement of the influence the Germans
exerted. When, however, one reads further in that classic document, it soon becomes apparent that the American conception was no literal translation from the German. The idea had
changed its color, its arguments, and its qualifications in the
process of domestication. All the peculiarities of the American
university—its inclusion of a college, its eclectic purposes, its
close ties to the community—and all the peculiarities of American culture—its constitutional provision for free speech, its
empiricist traditions, its abundant pragmatic spirit—contributed to a theory of academic freedom that was character-
istically American.

One obvious difference was the dissociation of *Lernfreiheit*
and *Lehrfreiheit* in the American pattern of argument. "It need

scarcely be pointed out," wrote the authors of the 1915 report, "that the freedom which is the subject of this report is that of the teacher." The frame of reference had not always been so limited. Indeed, before the nineties, "academic freedom" had alluded primarily to student freedoms, particularly the freedom to elect courses. In 1885, when Dean Andrew F. West of Princeton wrote an article asking "What Is Academic Freedom?" he answered: the elective system, scientific courses, voluntary chapel attendance. But once the battle for elective courses had been won, and attention came to be focused on the collision of social ideologies that was leading to faculty dismissals, the phrase came to be applied to professorial freedoms, to the producer rather than the consumer in education. The new reference became fixed in the nineties, when, at the nearest hint of a violation of professorial freedom, "academic freedom" and *Lehrfreiheit* were invoked, as though merely to sound the phrases had a certain incantational value. In 1899, when Professor Albion W. Small of Chicago wrote an article entitled "Academic Freedom," he made no mention of student freedoms. After that date, only one of the important documents of academic freedom linked *Lernfreiheit* with *Lehrfreiheit;* this was Charles W. Eliot's 1907 Phi Beta Kappa address. Under the heading of "Academic Freedom," the septuagenarian Harvard president included the student's freedom to choose his studies, to refuse to attend chapel, to compete on even terms for scholarships, and to choose his own friends, as well as the professor's freedom to teach in the manner most congenial to him, to be free from harassing routines, to enjoy a secure tenure, and to receive a fixed salary and a retirement allowance. But this catholic approach was exceptional.

A close reading of Eliot's Phi Beta Kappa address provides the reason for the subordination or exclusion of student freedoms in later definitions. Eliot's discussion of *Lehrfreiheit* was almost entirely given over to administrative issues: to the hazardous relations of professors with nonprofessional boards of trustees, to the friction between professors and dictatorial presidents. He made a point of the fact that "so long as . . . boards of trustees of colleges and universities claim the right to dismiss at pleasure all the officers of the institutions in their charge, there will be no security for the teachers' proper freedom," that "it is easy for a department to become despotic, particularly if there be one dominant personage in it." The status of the American professor in the university organization presented a unique set of problems. He was an employee of a lay board of control; he was not, as in Germany, a civil servant of the state or, as in England, a director in a self-governing corporation. Further, he was governed by an administrative hierarchy which possessed the power to make important decisions; not by officials elected from the professors' ranks, as in Germany and England, or by a Ministry of Education removed from the scene, as in Germany. To resolve the anomaly of being at one and the same time an employee and a scientific researcher, to cope with the problem of maintaining spontaneity in a highly bureaucratized system—these problems absorbed the interest of American theorists. Faced with the task of adorning, democratizing, and protecting the academic job, they lost sight of the goal of *Lernfreiheit*. The focus of the problem of academic freedom in this country became institutional, not primarily educational.

Another difference between the American and the German theories of academic freedom lay in their arguments for the defense of the independence of the university. German theorists leaned on the protective power of the state and on traditional gild prerogatives. Neither of these was meaningful on the American scene. Here government by trustees not only prevented professorial independence, but encouraged the widespread notion that professors were incapable of self-government. The state was an unreliable mainstay. The tradition of local sponsorship in American education made federal intervention—assuming that it might have improved the position of the university—impossible. The courts were unwilling to upset decisions of the administrative authorities save when these clearly conflicted with the university's charter. To appeal to state legislatures was hazardous, since their members were so often no better disposed toward intellectual freedom or academic independence than were trustees or private pressure groups. Thus, American theorists, unable to appeal with practical effect to the lawmakers or the courts, yet searching for

some authority which could be used to check continual encroachments, appealed to the will of the whole community.
They asserted that all universities, private or state, belonged to
the people as a whole; that the trustees were merely public
servants, the professors public functionaries, the universities
public properties. Hence, regardless of legal provisions for control, to treat the universities as though they were private possessions, to tie them to a particular faith or ideology, to bend
them to the interest of a class or sect or party, was to violate
a public trust. At this point, American theorists faced a further problem. What if, as so often happened, the public should
consent to the violation of that trust? What if crusading newspapers or patriotic groups, presuming to speak for the whole
community, should try to warp the university toward their particular goals? American theorists had to maintain that the real
public interest was not the same as the public opinion of the
moment. Indeed, from Tocqueville to Lippmann, no group was
more critical of the workings of public opinion in democracy
than the theorists of academic freedom. In America, where the
university presented such diverse and irreconcilable aspects,
academic freedom was too new an idea to arouse patriotic
feelings, too exclusive to prompt mass support. In sponsoring
the public interest, therefore, American theorists were sponsoring something that transcended all the current and ephem-
eral forms of its expression. Like Rousseau, they found the
true will and need of the public to lie not in the public's own
transient notions, but in something more nebulous and abstract. They fell back in the last resort upon a *mystique* of the
general will.

We come to the heart of the difference when we compare
the American and German conceptions of inner and outer freedom. We need not assume that the lines of each were exactly
drawn in order to assert that the areas they covered were incongruous. The German idea of "convincing" one's students,
of winning them over to the personal system and philosophical
views of the professor, was not condoned by American academic opinion. Rather, as far as classroom actions were concerned, the proper stance for American professors was thought
to be one of neutrality on controversial issues, and silence on

substantive issues that lay outside the scope of their competence. Innumerable statements affirmed these limitations.
Eliot, in the very address that so eloquently declared that the
university must be free, made neutrality an aspect of that
freedom:

Philosophical subjects should never be taught with authority.
They are not established sciences; they are full of disputed matters,
open questions, and bottomless speculations. It is not the function
of the teacher to settle philosophical and political controversies for
the pupil, or even to recommend to him any one set of opinions as
better than any other. Exposition, not imposition, of opinions is the
professor's part. The student should be made acquainted with all
sides of these controversies, with the salient points of each system;
he should be shown what is still in force of institutions or philosophies mainly outgrown, and what is new in those now in vogue.
The very word "education" is a standing protest against dogmatic
teaching. The notion that education consists in the authoritative
inculcation of what the teacher deems true may be logical and
appropriate in a convent, but it is intolerable in universities and
the public schools, from primary to professional.

The norm of competence was neatly summarized in President
Harper's convocation address, cited above:

A professor is guilty of an abuse of his privilege who promulgates
as truth ideas or opinions which have not been tested scientifically
by his colleagues in the same department of research or investigation. . . .

A professor abuses his privilege who takes advantage of a classroom exercise to propagate the partisan views of one or another of
the political parties.

A professor abuses his privilege who in any way seeks to influence his pupils or the public by sensational methods.

A professor abuses his privilege of expression of opinion when,
although a student and perhaps an authority in one department
or group of departments, he undertakes to speak authoritatively on
subjects which have no relationship to the department in which
he was appointed to give instruction.

A professor abuses his privilege in many cases when, altho shut
off in large measure from the world and engaged within a narrow
field of investigation, he undertakes to instruct his colleagues or

the public concerning matters in the world at large in connection
with which he has had little or no experience.

These were not merely the cautious constructions of conservative elements in education. If they were narrowly interpreted by certain members of boards of trustees to prevent professors from criticizing the social order, if they were invoked
by university presidents to justify disciplinary action against
nonconformist professors, they were also upheld by liberal professors like Howard Crosby Warren and John Dewey, and by
progressive college presidents like Alexander Meiklejohn of
Amherst. The liberal wing of the academic community, like
every other, still believed that college students were in constant danger of mental seduction by their teachers. The old
fear that students were easy prey to heretical doctrine became
the new fear that students had but fragile defenses against
subtle insinuation of "propaganda." The norms of "neutrality"
and "competence" constituted a code of fair practices in ideas,
and as such won assent from all sides.

Of course, the roots of these norms went deeper still. "Neutrality" and "competence" describe not only the limits of American academic freedom, but the very temper of American
academic thought. They reflect, in the first place, the empiricist
bias of that thought. Even in the ante-bellum period the main
accent of American philosophy, sounded by the Scottish school,
was empirical, realistic, commonsensical. No invading Napoleon in that period forced our professors to seek refuge in
thought against disturbing realities. The transcendental philosophy, the American version of German idealism, generally could
not breach the academic barrier. Its intuitionism was opposed
by our clerics, lest each man disclose his own religion and
become unto himself a church; its idealism was resisted by our
philosophers, lest mind or nature be deified, and atheism or
pantheism result. With the advent of the university, the triumph of science-oriented philosophies deepened the commitment to empiricism. Kant and Hegel had a brilliant revival, yet
their luster was dimmed somewhat by the more effulgent light
of evolutionary pragmatism and positivism. Most Americans
who went to study in Germany in this period took home the

methods of her seminars and laboratories, but left the *Anschauung* of idealism behind. To this empiricist heritage, one must add the influence of Darwinism on American academic thought. In Germany, the first success in the attack upon religious authority was achieved by philosophy; in America, as we have seen, the hold of religious authority was broken by the advocates of science. The empiricist heritage fostered the belief that facts must be the arbiters between competing notions of truth, thus strengthening the standard of neutrality; that universal and synthetic speculation must give way to specialized knowledge, thus promoting the standard of competence. The Darwinian influence, as we have noted, fostered the belief that certainty was as alien to inquiry as immutability was to the processes of life (neutrality); that the right to pass judgment on scientific questions was reserved to those who possessed special credentials (competence). The German and American theories of intramural freedom thus reflected different philosophical traditions.

These theories, it should be emphasized, were concerned with norms for intramural utterance, for the utterances of professors in their role as teachers. Outside the university, for professors in their civil roles, the American norm was more permissive than the German, because it reflected a stronger social and constitutional commitment to the idea of freedom of speech. The connections between free speech and academic freedom are many and subtle. One thing is clear as far as their historical linkages are concerned: the advance of the one has not automatically produced a comparable advance of the other. We have seen, for example, that academic freedom scored victories in which freedom of speech did not share. The masters of the North European medieval universities won a measure of philosophical freedom without like benefits being conferred on the laity; Halle and Göttingen in the eighteenth century were islands of intellectual freedom amid seas of petty despotism; Imperial Germany was far less free in the political sphere than in the sphere of academic education. Conversely, freedom of speech has made gains while academic freedom stood still. Thus, the abolition of the Alien and Sedition laws coincided with the expansion of denominational colleges and the sectarianizing of the state universities. One may therefore conclude that the two freedoms develop independently for different reasons, or that they are causally related to a common long-term factor, such as the diffusion of political power or the growth of the habit of tolerance.

Nevertheless, it can also be demonstrated that, under certain favorable conditions, these two freedoms do affect one another directly, and that the secure position of the one may improve the position of the other and deepen and broaden its meaning and potency. Free speech was protected in America; the post-bellum university presented the favorable conditions. First, the university granted its teachers the time to engage in outside activities: it removed the old residence requirement, it ended the boarding-house vigil. Secondly, the university appointed men whose interests were not engrossed by campus duties. It brought in the professional scholar, whose works were appraised by other specialists; it brought in the new-style president, a man of wide affairs; it brought in the technical expert, available for outside consultation. Thirdly, the university professor began to give up the quiet retreat of moral philosophy for the more worldly concerns of social science. This movement was accelerated by a fourth development, the rise of the philosophy of pragmatism, which sanctioned the application of the trained intelligence to the varied problems of life. For these reasons, the American university professor, much more than his German counterpart, functioned in the arena of social and political action. In that arena, he demanded the prerogative of free speech that was given to other citizens. There he felt that he had the right to express his opinion even on controversial subjects, even on matters outside his scholarly competence. There academic freedom became an aspect of the struggle for civil liberty.

And it was precisely in that arena that the greatest amount of academic friction was generated. The attempt to assimilate the doctrine of free speech into the doctrine of academic freedom aroused hostility in certain quarters. It seemed to demand a special protection for professors when they engaged in the rough give-and-take of politics. To argue that the institutional position of professors should not be affected by what they said as citizens was to urge immunity for them from the economic penalties that may repay unpopular utterances—the dwindling of clients, the boycott of subscribers, the loss of a job. Such a demand for immunity, exceeding anything provided by the constitutional safeguard of free speech, going even further than the "free-market" conceptions of the great philosophers of intellectual liberty, was bound to strain the less tensile tolerance of American trustees and administrators. A barrage of argument was touched off by this demand. In its favor, professors and certain presidents mustered methodological arguments: "ideas must be tested in action," the function of philosophy "is to clarify men's ideas as to the social and moral strifes of their own day"; administrative arguments: "If a university or college censors what its professors may say . . . it thereby assumes responsibility for that which it permits them to say . . . a responsibility which an institution of learning would be very unwise in assuming"; pedagogical arguments: what young men need "are not hermit scholars, but active zealous citizens, with opinions to express upon public questions, and power to express them." The answering volleys were usually, but not exclusively, returned by presidents and trustees. They too used methodological arguments: when a teacher enters politics, he acts "as a partisan and [loses his] place as a judge and an unbiased individual"; administrative arguments: "to use this institution and the funds so contributed for a purpose foreign and contrary to the ideas both of the contributors and of the whole community, and appropriate them to the propaganda of the exceptional ideas of a single individual, is a perversion of public trust"; pedagogical arguments: the professor who uses his university position as "an object of political purpose" destroys his educational effectiveness. And the salvos resound to this day.

The second source of friction was the closely allied problem of professional ethics in the public forum. Despite the invocation of the right of free speech, it was generally conceded by the academic fraternity that professors reached a limiting line of professional propriety long before they approached the boundary of libel, slander, or sedition. But where was that line to be drawn? Was it proper for a professor to run for political

office or to work actively for a political party? The academic
community spoke with two voices on this point. Was it proper
for a professor publicly to criticize the actions of a colleague or
a superior? In this most bureaucratically controlled of all the
professions, it was not easy to decide where free speech left
off and insubordination began. Was the professor's relation to
his trustees analogous to the relation of the judiciary to the
executive power? The analogy was useful in suggesting that the
trustees could not remove their appointee at will, but it was a
two-edged sword, for it also suggested that professors were
bound by the staid public ethics of judges. Again, the conflict
between free speech and professional ethics created a storm
center which has never lifted.

QUESTIONS

1. Why do these authors maintain that Americans are usually
   loath to admit the freedoms of citizens in other countries? Is
   it true?
2. Distinguish between the German attitude toward freedom within
   and freedom outside the university.
3. Do you feel that you are in danger of "mental seduction" by
   your professors? Can you be sure that those who give the appearance of such attempts are not making use of legitimate
   pedagogical techniques?
4. Define "effulgent," "pragmatism," "positivism."
5. Does the growth of academic freedom always parallel that of
   freedom of speech? Have the same factors governed the development of each?

QUESTIONS ON PART V

1. Why must universities be free to seek the truth no matter where
   the argument may lead?
2. Burchard's essay deals largely with freedom to read, Tsanoff's
   with freedom to teach. Explain carefully how these comple-
   mentary aspects of academic freedom have arisen.
3. Write an essay relating academic freedom to the general freedoms guaranteed in a democracy.
4. Write an essay in which you define extensively the idea of "the
   intellectual enterprise." Use whatever concepts seem relevant
   from the essays of this Part.

VI ✒ Freedom of Religion

A LETTER CONCERNING TOLERATION

✎ John Locke

. . . That any man should think fit to cause another man
—whose salvation he heartily desires—to expire in torments,
and that even in an unconverted state, would, I confess, seem
very strange to me, and, I think, to any other also. But nobody,
surely, will ever believe that such a carriage can proceed from
charity, love, or good-will. If any one maintain that men ought
to be compelled by fire and sword to profess certain doctrines,
and conform to this or that exterior worship, without any regard had unto their morals; if any one endeavour to convert
those that are erroneous unto the faith, by forcing them to profess things that they do not believe, and allowing them to practise things that the Gospel does not permit, it cannot be
doubted indeed but such a one is desirous to have a numerous
assembly joined in the same profession with himself; but that
he principally intends by those means to compose a truly Christian church, is altogether incredible. It is not, therefore, to be
wondered at if those who do not really contend for the advancement of the true religion, and of the church of Christ, make use
of arms that do not belong to the Christian warfare. If, like the
Captain of our salvation, they sincerely desired the good of
souls, they would tread in the steps and follow the perfect example of that Prince of peace, who sent out his soldiers to the

Published 1689. From the text of J. W. Gough (Oxford, 1946), by permission of B. H. Blackwell Ltd.

subduing of nations, and gathering them into his church, not armed with the sword, or other instruments of force, but prepared with the Gospel of peace, and with the exemplary holiness of their conversation. This was his method. Though if infidels were to be converted by force, if those that are either blind or obstinate were to be drawn off from their errors by armed soldiers, we know very well that it was much more easy for him to do it with armies of heavenly legions, than for any son of the church, how potent soever, with all his dragoons.

The toleration of those that differ from others in matters of religion, is so agreeable to the Gospel of Jesus Christ, and to the genuine reason of mankind, that it seems monstrous for men to be so blind as not to perceive the necessity and advantage of it in so clear a light. I will not here tax the pride and ambition of some, the passion and uncharitable zeal of others. These are faults from which human affairs can perhaps scarce ever be perfectly freed; but yet such as nobody will bear the plain imputation of, without covering them with some specious colour; and so pretend to commendation, whilst they are carried away by their own irregular passions. But, however, that some may not colour their spirit of persecution and unchristian cruelty with a pretence of care of the public weal and observation of the laws; and that others, under pretence of religion, may not seek impunity for their libertinism and licentiousness; in a word, that none may impose either upon himself or others, by the pretences of loyalty and obedience to the prince, or of tenderness and sincerity in the worship of God, I esteem it above all things necessary to distinguish exactly the business of civil government from that of religion, and to settle the just bound that lie between the one and the other. If this be not done, there can be no end put to the controversies that will be always arising between those that have, or at least pretend to have, on the one side, a concernment for the interest of men's souls, and, on the other side, a care of the commonwealth.

The commonwealth seems to me to be a society of men constituted only for the procuring, preserving, and advancing their own civil interests.

Civil interests I call life, liberty, health, and indolency of body; and the possession of outward things, such as money, lands, houses, furniture, and the like.

It is the duty of the civil magistrate, by the impartial execution of equal laws, to secure unto all the people in general, and to every one of his subjects in particular, the just possession of these things belonging to this life. If any one presume to violate the laws of public justice and equity, established for the preservation of those things, his presumption is to be checked by the fear of punishment, consisting of the deprivation or diminution of those civil interests, or goods, which otherwise he might and ought to enjoy. But seeing no man does willingly suffer himself to be punished by the deprivation of any part of his goods, and much less of his liberty or life, therefore is the magistrate armed with the force and strength of all his subjects, in order to the punishment of those that violate any other man's rights.

Now that the whole jurisdiction of the magistrate reaches only to these civil concernments, and that all civil power, right, and dominion, is bounded and confined to the only care of promoting these things; and that it neither can nor ought in any manner to be extended to the salvation of souls, these following considerations seem unto me abundantly to demonstrate.

First, because the care of souls is not committed to the civil magistrate, any more than to other men. It is not committed unto him, I say, by God; because it appears not that God has ever given any such authority to one man over another, as to compel any one to his religion. Nor can any such power be vested in the magistrate by the consent of the people, because no man can so far abandon the care of his own salvation as blindly to leave to the choice of any other, whether prince or subject, to prescribe to him what faith or worship he shall embrace. For no man can, if he would, conform his faith to the dictates of another. All the life and power of true religion consist in the inward and full persuasion of the mind; and faith is not faith without believing. Whatever profession we make, to whatever outward worship we conform, if we are not fully satisfied in our own mind that the one is true, and the other well pleasing unto God, such profession and such practice, far from being any furtherance, are indeed great obstacles to our salvation. For in this manner, instead of expiating other sins by the exercise of religion, I say, in offering thus unto God Almighty such a worship as we esteem to be displeasing unto him, we add unto the number of our other sins those also of hypocrisy, and contempt of his Divine Majesty.

In the second place, the care of souls cannot belong to the civil magistrate, because his power consists only in outward force; but true and saving religion consists in the inward persuasion of the mind, without which nothing can be acceptable to God. And such is the nature of the understanding, that it cannot be compelled to the belief of anything by outward force. Confiscation of estate, imprisonment, torments, nothing of that nature can have any such efficacy as to make men change the inward judgment that they have framed of things.

It may indeed be alleged that the magistrate may make use of arguments, and thereby draw the heterodox into the way of truth, and procure their salvation. I grant it; but this is common to him with other men. In teaching, instructing, and redressing the erroneous by reason, he may certainly do what becomes any good man to do. Magistracy does not oblige him to put off either humanity or Christianity; but it is one thing to persuade, another to command; one thing to press with arguments, another with penalties. This civil power alone has a right to do; to the other good-will is authority enough. Every man has commission to admonish, exhort, convince another of error, and, by reasoning, to draw him into truth; but to give laws, receive obedience, and compel with the sword, belongs to none but the magistrate. And upon this ground, I affirm that the magistrate's power extends not to the establishing of any articles of faith, or forms of worship, by the force of his laws. For laws are of no force at all without penalties, and penalties in this case are absolutely impertinent, because they are not proper to convince the mind. Neither the profession of any articles of faith, nor the conformity to any outward form of worship (as has been already said), can be available to the salvation of souls, unless the truth of the one, and the acceptableness of the other unto God, be thoroughly believed by those that so profess and practise. But penalties are no way capable to produce such belief. It is only light and evidence that can work a change in men's opinions; which light can in no manner proceed from corporal sufferings, or any other outward penalties.

In the third place, the care of the salvation of men's souls cannot belong to the magistrate; because, though the rigour of laws and the force of penalties were capable to convince and change men's minds, yet would not that help at all to the salvation of their souls. For there being but one truth, one way to heaven, what hope is there that more men would be led into it if they had no rule but the religion of the court, and were put under the necessity to quit the light of their own reason, and oppose the dictates of their own consciences, and blindly to resign themselves up to the will of their governors, and to the religion which either ignorance, ambition, or superstition had chanced to establish in the countries where they were born? In the variety and contradiction of opinions in religion, wherein the princes of the world are as much divided as in their secular interests, the narrow way would be much straitened; one country alone would be in the right, and all the rest of the world put under an obligation of following their princes in the ways that lead to destruction; and that which heightens the absurdity, and very ill suits the notion of a Deity, men would owe their eternal happiness or misery to the places of their nativity.

These considerations, to omit many others that might have been urged to the same purpose, seem unto me sufficient to conclude that all the power of civil government relates only to men's civil interests, is confined to the care of the things of this world, and hath nothing to do with the world to come.

Let us now consider what a church is. A church, then, I take to be a voluntary society of men, joining themselves together of their own accord in order to the public worshipping of God in such manner as they judge acceptable to him, and effectual to the salvation of their souls.

I say it is a free and voluntary society. Nobody is born a member of any church; otherwise the religion of parents would descend unto children by the same right of inheritance as their temporal estates, and every one would hold his faith by the same tenure he does his lands, than which nothing can be imagined more absurd. Thus, therefore, that matter stands.

No man by nature is bound unto any particular church or sect, but every one joins himself voluntarily to that society in which he believes he has found that profession and worship which is truly acceptable to God. The hope of salvation, as it was the only cause of his entrance into that communion, so it can be the only reason of his stay there. For if afterwards he discover anything either erroneous in the doctrine or incongruous in the worship of that society to which he has joined himself, why should it not be as free for him to go out as it was to enter? No member of a religious society can be tied with any other bonds but what proceed from the certain expectation of eternal life. A church, then, is a society of members voluntarily uniting to that end.

It follows now that we consider what is the power of this church, and unto what laws it is subject.

Forasmuch as no society, how free soever, or upon whatsoever slight occasion instituted, whether of philosophers for learning, of merchants for commerce, or of men of leisure for mutual conversation and discourse, no church or company, I say, can in the least subsist and hold together, but will presently dissolve and break in pieces, unless it be regulated by some laws, and the members all consent to observe some order. Place and time of meeting must be agreed on; rules for admitting and excluding members must be established; distinction of officers, and putting things into a regular course, and suchlike, cannot be omitted. But since the joining together of several members into this church-society, as has already been demonstrated, is absolutely free and spontaneous, it necessarily follows that the right of making its laws can belong to none but the society itself; or, at least (which is the same thing), to those whom the society by common consent has authorised thereunto.

Some, perhaps, may object that no such society can be said to be a true church unless it have in it a bishop or presbyter, with ruling authority derived from the very apostles, and continued down to the present times by an uninterrupted succession.

To these I answer: In the first place, let them show me the edict by which Christ has imposed that law upon his church.

And let not any man think me impertinent, if in a thing of this consequence I require that the terms of that edict be very express and positive; for the promise he has made us (Matt. xviii. 20), that wheresoever two or three are gathered together in his name, he will be in the midst of them, seems to imply the contrary. Whether such an assembly want anything necessary to a true church, pray do you consider. Certain I am that nothing can be there wanting unto the salvation of souls, which is sufficient to our purpose.

Next, pray observe how great have always been the divisions amongst even those who lay so much stress upon the divine institution and continued succession of a certain order of rulers in the church. Now, their very dissension unavoidably puts us upon a necessity of deliberating, and, consequently, allows a liberty of choosing that which upon consideration we prefer.

And, in the last place, I consent that these men have a ruler in their church, established by such a long series of succession as they judge necessary, provided I may have liberty at the same time to join myself to that society in which I am persuaded those things are to be found which are necessary to the salvation of my soul. In this manner ecclesiastical liberty will be preserved on all sides, and no man will have a legislator imposed upon him but whom himself has chosen.

But since men are so solicitous about the true church, I would only ask them here, by the way, if it be not more agreeable to the church of Christ to make the conditions of her communion consist in such things, and such things only, as the Holy Spirit has in the Holy Scriptures declared, in express words, to be necessary to salvation; I ask, I say, whether this be not more agreeable to the church of Christ than for men to impose their own inventions and interpretations upon others as if they were of divine authority, and to establish by ecclesiastical laws, as absolutely necessary to the profession of Christianity, such things as the Holy Scriptures do either not mention, or at least not expressly command? Whosoever requires those things in order to ecclesiastical communion, which Christ does not require in order to life eternal, he may, perhaps, indeed constitute a society accommodated to his own opinion and his own advantage; but how that can be called the church of Christ which is established upon laws that are not his, and which excludes such persons from its communion as he will one day receive into the kingdom of heaven, I understand not. But this being not a proper place to inquire into the marks of the true church, I will only mind those that contend so earnestly for the decrees of their own society, and that cry out continually, The church! the church! with as much noise, and perhaps upon the same principle, as the Ephesian silversmiths did for their Diana; this, I say, I desire to mind them of, that the Gospel frequently declares that the true disciples of Christ must suffer persecution; but that the church of Christ should persecute others, and force others by fire and sword to embrace her faith and doctrine, I could never yet find in any of the books of the New Testament.

The end of a religious society (as has already been said) is the public worship of God, and, by means thereof, the acquisition of eternal life. All discipline ought therefore to tend to that end, and all ecclesiastical laws to be thereunto confined. Nothing ought nor can be transacted in this society relating to the possession of civil and worldly goods. No force is here to be made use of upon any occasion whatsoever. For force belongs wholly to the civil magistrate, and the possession of all outward goods is subject to his jurisdiction.

But, it may be asked, by what means then shall ecclesiastical laws be established, if they must be thus destitute of all compulsive power? I answer: They must be established by means suitable to the nature of such things, whereof the external profession and observation—if not proceeding from a thorough conviction and approbation of the mind—is altogether useless and unprofitable. The arms by which the members of this society are to be kept within their duty are exhortations, admonitions, and advices. If by these means the offenders will not be reclaimed, and the erroneous convinced, there remains nothing further to be done but that such stubborn and obstinate persons, who give no ground to hope for their reformation, should be cast out and separated from the society. This is the last and utmost force of ecclesiastical authority. No other punishment can thereby be inflicted than that, the relation ceasing between

the body and the member which is cut off. The person so condemned ceases to be a part of that church.

These things being thus determined, let us inquire, in the
next place: How far the duty of toleration extends, and what
is required from every one by it?

And, first, I hold that no church is bound, by the duty of toleration, to retain any such person in her bosom as, after admoni-
tion, continues obstinately to offend against the laws of the
society. For these being the condition of communion and the
bond of the society, if the breach of them were permitted without any animadversion the society would immediately be
thereby dissolved. But, nevertheless, in all such cases care is to
be taken that the sentence of excommunication, and the execution thereof, carry with it no rough usage of word or action
whereby the ejected person may any wise be damnified in body
or estate. For all force (as has often been said) belongs only to
the magistrate, nor ought any private persons at any time to
use force, unless it be in self-defence against unjust violence.
Excommunication neither does, nor can, deprive the excommunicated person of any of those civil goods that he formerly
possessed. All those things belong to the civil government, and
are under the magistrate's protection. The whole force of excommunication consists only in this: that the resolution of the
society in that respect being declared, the union that was between the body and some member comes thereby to be dissolved; and that relation ceasing, the participation of some
certain things which the society communicated to its members, and unto which no man has any civil right, comes also
to cease. For there is no civil injury done unto the excommunicated person by the church minister's refusing him that
bread and wine, in the celebration of the Lord's Supper, which
was not bought with his but other men's money.

Secondly, no private person has any right in any manner
to prejudice another person in his civil enjoyments because
he is of another church or religion. All the rights and fran-
chises that belong to him as a man, or as a denizen, are invio-
lably to be preserved to him. These are not the business of religion. No violence nor injury is to be offered him, whether he
be Christian or Pagan. Nay, we must not content ourselves with

the narrow measures of bare justice; charity, bounty, and liberality must be added to it. This the Gospel enjoins, this reason directs, and this that natural fellowship we are born into requires of us. If any man err from the right way, it is his own misfortune, no injury to thee; nor therefore art thou to punish him in the things of this life because thou supposest he will be miserable in that which is to come.

What I say concerning the mutual toleration of private persons differing from one another in religion, I understand also of particular churches which stand, as it were, in the same relation to each other as private persons among themselves: nor has any one of them any manner of jurisdiction over any other; no, not even when the civil magistrate (as it sometimes happens) comes to be of this or the other communion. For the civil government can give no new right to the church, nor the church to the civil government. So that whether the magistrate join himself to any church, or separate from it, the church remains always as it was before—a free and voluntary society. It neither requires the power of the sword by the magistrate's coming to it, nor does it lose the right of instruction and excommunication by his going from it. This is the fundamental and immutable right of a spontaneous society—that it has power to remove any of its members who transgress the rules of its institution; but it cannot, by the accession of any new members, acquire any right of jurisdiction over those that are not joined with it. And therefore peace, equity, and friendship are always mutually to be observed by particular churches, in the same manner as by private persons, without any pretence of superiority or jurisdiction over one another. . . .

Nobody, therefore, in fine, neither single persons nor churches, nay, nor even commonwealths, have any just title to invade the civil rights and worldly goods of each other upon pretence of religion. Those that are of another opinion would do well to consider with themselves how pernicious a seed of discord and war, how powerful a provocation to endless hatreds, rapines, and slaughters they thereby furnish unto mankind. No peace and security, no, not so much as common friendship, can ever be established or preserved amongst men so long as this opinion prevails, that dominion is founded in grace and that religion is to be propagated by force of arms.

In the third place, let us see what the duty of toleration requires from those who are distinguished from the rest of mankind (from the laity, as they please to call us) by some ecclesiastical character and office; whether they be bishops, priests, presbyters, ministers, or however else dignified or distinguished. It is not my business to inquire here into the original of the power or dignity of the clergy. This only I say, that whencesoever their authority be sprung, since it is ecclesiastical, it ought to be confined within the bounds of the church, nor can it in any manner be extended to civil affairs, because the church itself is a thing absolutely separate and distinct from the commonwealth. The boundaries on both sides are fixed and immovable. He jumbles heaven and earth together, the things most remote and opposite, who mixes these two societies, which are in their original, end, business, and in everything perfectly distinct and infinitely different from each other. No man, therefore, with whatsoever ecclesiastical office he be dignified, can deprive another man that is not of his church and faith either of liberty or of any part of his worldly goods upon the account of that difference between them in religion. For whatsoever is not lawful to the whole church cannot by any ecclesiastical right become lawful to any of its members.

But this is not all. It is not enough that ecclesiastical men abstain from violence and rapine and all manner of persecution. He that pretends to be a successor of the apostles, and takes upon him the office of teaching, is obliged also to admonish his hearers of the duties of peace and good-will towards all men, as well towards the erroneous as the orthodox; towards those that differ from them in faith and worship as well as towards those that agree with them therein. And he ought industriously to exhort all men, whether private persons or magistrates (if any such there be in his church), to charity, meekness, and toleration, and diligently endeavour to allay and temper all that heat and unreasonable averseness of mind which either any man's fiery zeal for his own sect or the craft of others has kindled against dissenters. I will not undertake to represent how happy and how great would be the fruit, both in church and state, if the pulpits everywhere sounded with this doctrine of peace and toleration, lest I should seem to reflect too severely upon those men whose dignity I desire not to detract from, nor would have it diminished either by others or themselves. But this I say, that thus it ought to be. And if any one that professes himself to be a minister of the word of God, a preacher of the gospel of peace, teach otherwise, he either understands not or neglects the business of his calling, and shall one day give account thereof unto the Prince of peace. If Christians are to be admonished that they abstain from all manner of revenge, even after repeated provocations and multiplied injuries, how much more ought they who suffer nothing, who have had no harm done them, forbear violence and abstain from all manner of ill-usage towards those from whom they have received none! This caution and temper they ought certainly to use towards those who mind only their own business, and are solicitous for nothing but that (whatever men think of them) they may worship God in that manner which they are persuaded is acceptable to him, and in which they have the strongest hopes of eternal salvation. In private domestic affairs, in the management of estates, in the conservation of bodily health, every man may consider what suits his own convenience, and follow what course he likes best. No man complains of the ill-management of his neighbour's affairs. No man is angry with another for an error committed in sowing his land or in marrying his daughter. Nobody corrects a spendthrift for consuming his substance in taverns. Let any man pull down, or build, or make whatsoever expenses he pleases, nobody murmurs, nobody controls him; he has his liberty. But if any man do not frequent the church, if he do not there conform his behaviour exactly to the accustomed ceremonies, or if he brings not his children to be initiated in the sacred mysteries of this or the other congregation, this immediately causes an uproar. The neighbourhood is filled with noise and clamour. Every one is ready to be the avenger of so great a crime, and the zealots hardly have the patience to refrain from violence and rapine so long till the cause be heard, and the poor man be, according to form, condemned to the loss of liberty, goods, or life. Oh, that our ecclesiastical orators of every sect would apply themselves with all the strength of arguments that they are able to the confounding of men's errors! But let them spare their persons. Let them not supply their want of reasons with the instruments of force, which belong to another jurisdiction, and do ill become a churchman's hands. Let them not call in the magistrate's authority to the aid of their eloquence or learning, lest perhaps, whilst they pretend only love for the truth, this their intemperate zeal, breathing nothing but fire and sword, betray their ambition and show that what they desire is temporal dominion. For it will be very difficult to persuade men of sense that he who with dry eyes and satisfaction of mind can deliver his brother to the executioner to be burnt alive, does sincerely and heartily concern himself to save that brother from the flames of hell in the world to come.

In the last place, let us now consider what is the magistrate's duty in the business of toleration, which certainly is very considerable.

We have already proved that the care of souls does not belong to the magistrate. Not a magisterial care, I mean (if I may so call it), which consists in prescribing by laws and compelling by punishments. But a charitable care, which consists in teaching, admonishing, and persuading, cannot be denied unto any man. The care, therefore, of every man's soul belongs unto himself, and is to be left unto himself. But what if he neglect the care of his soul? I answer: What if he neglect the care of his health or of his estate, which things are nearlier related to the government of the magistrate than the other? Will the magistrate provide by an express law that such a one shall not become poor or sick? Laws provide, as much as is possible, that the goods and health of subjects be not injured by the fraud and violence of others; they do not guard them from the negligence or ill-husbandry of the possessors themselves. No man can be forced to be rich or healthful whether he will or no. Nay, God himself will not save men against their wills. Let us suppose, however, that some prince were desirous to force his subjects to accumulate riches, or to preserve the health and strength of their bodies. Shall it be provided by law that they must consult none but Roman physicians, and shall every one be bound to live according to their prescriptions? What, shall

no potion, no broth, be taken, but what is prepared either in
the Vatican, suppose, or in a Geneva shop? Or, to make these
subjects rich, shall they all be obliged by law to become merchants or musicians? Or, shall every one turn victualler, or
smith, because there are some that maintain their families
plentifully and grow rich in those professions? But, it may be
said there are a thousand ways to wealth, but one only way to
heaven. It is well said, indeed, especially by those that plead
for compelling men into this or the other way. For if there were
several ways that led thither, there would not be so much as a
pretence left for compulsion. But now if I be marching on with
my utmost vigour in that way which, according to the sacred
geography, leads straight to Jerusalem, why am I beaten and
ill-used by others because, perhaps, I wear not buskins; because
my hair is not of the right cut; because, perhaps, I have not
been dipped in the right fashion; because I eat flesh upon the
road, or some other food which agrees with my stomach; because I avoid certain by-ways, which seem unto me to lead into
briars or precipices; because, amongst the several paths that
are in the same road, I choose that to walk in which seems to
be the straightest and cleanest; because I avoid to keep company with some travellers that are less grave, and others that
are more sour than they ought to be; or, in fine, because I follow a guide that either is, or is not, clothed in white, or
crowned with a mitre? Certainly, if we consider right, we shall
find that, for the most part, they are such frivolous things as
these that (without any prejudice to religion or the salvation
of souls, if not accompanied with superstition or hypocrisy)
might either be observed or omitted. I say, they are such-like
things as these which breed implacable enmities amongst
Christian brethren, who are all agreed in the substantial and
truly fundamental part of religion.

But let us grant unto these zealots, who condemn all things
that are not of their mode, that from these circumstances are
different ends. What shall we conclude from thence? There is
only one of these which is the true way to eternal happiness:
but in this great variety of ways that men follow, it is still
doubted which is the right one. Now, neither the care of the
commonwealth, nor the right enacting of laws, does discover

this way that leads to heaven more certainly to the magistrate than every private man's search and study discovers it unto himself. I have a weak body, sunk under a languishing disease, for which (I suppose) there is one only remedy, but that unknown. Does it therefore belong unto the magistrate to prescribe me a remedy, because there is but one, and because it is unknown? Because there is but one way for me to escape death, will it therefore be safe for me to do whatsover the magistrate ordains? Those things that every man ought sincerely to inquire into himself, and by meditation, study, search, and his own endeavours, attain the knowledge of, cannot be looked upon as the peculiar possession of any sort of men. Princes, indeed, are born superior unto other men in power, but in nature equal. Neither the right nor the art of ruling does necessarily carry along with it the certain knowledge of other things, and least of all of true religion. For if it were so, how could it come to pass that the lords of the earth should differ so vastly as they do in religious matters? But let us grant that it is probable the way to eternal life may be better known by a prince than by his subjects, or at least that in this incertitude of things the safest and most commodious way for private persons is to follow his dictates. You will say, what then? If he should bid you follow merchandise for your livelihood, would you decline that course for fear it should not succeed? I answer: I would turn merchant upon the prince's command, because in case I should have ill-success in trade, he is abundantly able to make up my loss some other way. If it be true, as he pretends, that he desires I should thrive and grow rich, he can set me up again when unsuccessful voyages have broken me. But this is not the case in the things that regard the life to come; if there I take a wrong course, if in that respect I am once undone, it is not in the magistrate's power to repair my loss, to ease my suffering, nor to restore me in any measure, much less entirely to a good estate. What security can be given for the kingdom of heaven? . . .

But, after all, the principal consideration, and which absolutely determines this controversy, is this: Although the magistrate's opinion in religion be sound, and the way that he appoints be truly evangelical, yet, if I be not thoroughly persuaded thereof in my own mind, there will be no safety for me in following it. No way whatsoever that I shall walk in against the dictates of my conscience will ever bring me to the mansions of the blessed. I may grow rich by an art that I take not delight in, I may be cured of some disease by remedies that I have not faith in; but I cannot be saved by a religion that I distrust, and by a worship that I abhor. It is in vain for an unbeliever to take up the outward show of another man's profession. Faith only, and inward sincerity, are the things that procure acceptance with God. The most likely and most approved remedy can have no effect upon the patient if his stomach reject it as soon as taken; and you will in vain cram a medicine down a sick man's throat, which his particular constitution will be sure to turn into poison. In a word, whatsoever may be doubtful in religion, yet this at least is certain, that no religion which I believe not to be true can be either true or profitable unto me. In vain, therefore, do princes compel their subjects to come into their church communion, under pretence of saving their souls. If they believe, they will come of their own accord; if they believe not, their coming will nothing avail them. How great soever, in fine, may be the pretence of good-will and charity, and concern for the salvation of men's souls, men cannot be forced to be saved whether they will or no. And therefore, when all is done, they must be left to their own consciences. . . .

Concerning outward worship, I say, in the first place, that the magistrate has no power to enforce by law, either in his own church, or much less in another, the use of any rites or ceremonies whatsoever in the worship of God. And this, not only because these churches are free societies, but because whatsoever is practised in the worship of God is only so far justifiable as it is believed by those that practise it to be acceptable unto him. Whatsoever is not done with that assurance of faith is neither well in itself, nor can it be acceptable to God. To impose such things, therefore, upon any people, contrary to their own judgment, is in effect to command them to offend God, which, considering that the end of all religion is to please him, and that liberty is essentially necessary to that end, appears to be absurd beyond expression. . . .

In the next place: As the magistrate has no power to impose by his laws the use of any rites and ceremonies in any church, so neither has he any power to forbid the use of such rites and ceremonies as are already received, approved, and practised by any church; because, if he did so, he would destroy the church itself: the end of whose institution is only to worship God with freedom after its own manner.

You will say, by this rule, if some congregations should have a mind to sacrifice infants, or (as the primitive Christians were falsely accused) lustfully pollute themselves in promiscuous uncleanness, or practise any other such heinous enormities, is the magistrate obliged to tolerate them, because they are committed in a religious assembly? I answer, No. These things are not lawful in the ordinary course of life, nor in any private house; and therefore neither are they so in the worship of God, or in any religious meeting. But, indeed, if any people congregated upon account of religion should be desirous to sacrifice a calf, I deny that that ought to be prohibited by a law. Melibœus, whose calf it is, may lawfully kill his calf at home, and burn any part of it that he thinks fit. For no injury is thereby done to any one, no prejudice to another man's goods. And for the same reason he may kill his calf also in a religious meeting. Whether the doing so be well-pleasing to God or no, it is their part to consider that do it. The part of the magistrate is only to take care that the commonwealth receive no prejudice, and that there be no injury done to any man, either in life or estate. And thus what may be spent on a feast may be spent on a sacrifice. But if peradventure such were the state of things that the interest of the commonwealth required all slaughter of beasts should be forborne for some while, in order to the increasing of the stock of cattle that had been destroyed by some extraordinary murrain, who sees not that the magistrate, in such a case, may forbid all his subjects to kill any calves for any use whatsoever? Only it is to be observed that, in this case, the law is not made about a religious, but a political matter; nor is the sacrifice, but the slaughter of calves, thereby prohibited.

By this we see what difference there is between the church and the commonwealth. Whatsoever is lawful in the commonwealth cannot be prohibited by the magistrate in the church. Whatsoever is permitted unto any of his subjects for their ordinary use, neither can nor ought to be forbidden by him to any sect of people for their religious uses. If any man may lawfully take bread or wine, either sitting or kneeling in his own house, the law ought not to abridge him of the same liberty in his religious worship; though in the church the use of bread and wine be very different, and be there applied to the mysteries of faith and rites of divine worship. But those things that are prejudicial to the commonweal of a people in their ordinary use, and are therefore forbidden by laws, those things ought not to be permitted to churches in their sacred rites. Only the magistrate ought always to be very careful that he do not misuse his authority to the oppression of any church, under pretence of public good.

It may be said, what if a church be idolatrous, is that also to be tolerated by the magistrate? I answer, what power can be given to the magistrate for the suppression of an idolatrous church, which may not in time and place be made use of to the ruin of an orthodox one? For it must be remembered that the civil power is the same everywhere, and the religion of every prince is orthodox to himself. If, therefore, such a power be granted unto the civil magistrate in spirituals, as that at Geneva, for example, he may extirpate, by violence and blood, the religion which is there reputed idolatrous, by the same rule another magistrate, in some neighbouring country, may oppress the reformed religion, and, in India, the Christian. The civil power can either change everything in religion, according to the prince's pleasure, or it can change nothing. If it be once permitted to introduce anything into religion, by the means of laws and penalties, there can be no bounds put to it; but it will in the same manner be lawful to alter everything, according to that rule of truth which the magistrate has framed unto himself. No man whatsoever ought therefore to be deprived of his terrestrial enjoyments upon account of his religion. . . .

Thus far concerning outward worship. Let us now consider articles of faith.

The articles of religion are some of them practical and some speculative. Now, though both sorts consist in the knowledge of truth, yet these terminate simply in the understanding, those influence the will and manners. Speculative opinions, therefore, and articles of faith (as they are called) which are required only to be believed, cannot be imposed on any church by the law of the land. For it is absurd that things should be enjoined by laws which are not in men's power to perform. And to believe this or that to be true, does not depend upon our will. But of this enough has been said already. But (will some say) let men at least profess that they believe. A sweet religion, indeed, that obliges men to dissemble and tell lies, both to God and man, for the salvation of their souls! If the magistrate thinks to save men thus, he seems to understand little of the way of salvation. And if he does it not in order to save them, why is he so solicitous about the articles of faith as to enact them by a law?

Further, the magistrate ought not to forbid the preaching or professing of any speculative opinions in any church, because they have no manner of relation to the civil rights of the subjects. If a Roman Catholic believe that to be really the body of Christ, which another man calls bread, he does no injury thereby to his neighbour. If a Jew do not believe the New Testament to be the word of God, he does not thereby alter anything in men's civil rights. If a heathen doubt of both Testaments, he is not therefore to be punished as a pernicious citizen. The power of the magistrate and the estates of the people may be equally secure whether any man believe these things or no. I readily grant that these opinions are false and absurd. But the business of laws is not to provide for the truth of opinions, but for the safety and security of the commonwealth, and of every particular man's goods and person. And so it ought to be. For the truth certainly would do well enough if she were once left to shift for herself. She seldom has received, and I fear never will receive, much assistance from the power of great men, to whom she is but rarely known, and more rarely welcome. She is not taught by laws, nor has she any need of force to procure her entrance into the minds of men.

Errors indeed prevail by the assistance of foreign and borrowed succours. But if truth makes not her way into the understanding by her own light, she will be but the weaker for any borrowed force violence can add to her. Thus much for speculative opinions. Let us now proceed to practical ones.

A good life, in which consists not the least part of religion and true piety, concerns also the civil government; and in it lies the safety both of men's souls and of the commonwealth. Moral actions belong therefore to the jurisdiction both of the outward and inward court; both of the civil and domestic governor; I mean both of the magistrate and conscience. Here, therefore, is great danger, lest one of these jurisdictions intrench upon the other, and discord arise between the keeper of the public peace and the overseers of souls. But if what has been already said concerning the limits of both these governments be rightly considered, it will easily remove all difficulty in this matter.

Every man has an immortal soul, capable of eternal happiness or misery; whose happiness depending upon his believing and doing those things in this life which are necessary to the obtaining of God's favour, and are prescribed by God to that end. It follows from thence, first, that the observance of these things is the highest obligation that lies upon mankind, and that our utmost care, application, and diligence ought to be exercised in the search and performance of them; because there is nothing in this world that is of any consideration in comparison with eternity. Secondly, that seeing one man does not violate the right of another by his erroneous opinions and undue manner of worship, nor is his perdition any prejudice to another man's affairs, therefore, the care of each man's salvation belongs only to himself. But I would not have this understood as if I meant hereby to condemn all charitable admonitions, and affectionate endeavours to reduce men from errors, which are indeed the greatest duty of a Christian. Any one may employ as many exhortations and arguments as he pleases, towards the promoting of another man's salvation. But all force and compulsion are to be forborne. Nothing is to be done imperiously. Nobody is obliged in that matter to yield obedience unto the admonitions or injunctions of another,

further than he himself is persuaded. Every man in that has
the supreme and absolute authority of judging for himself.
And the reason is because nobody else is concerned in it, nor
can receive any prejudice from his conduct therein.

But besides their souls, which are immortal, men have also
their temporal lives here upon earth; the state whereof being
frail and fleeting, and the duration uncertain, they have need
of several outward conveniences to the support thereof, which
are to be procured or preserved by pains and industry. For
those things that are necessary to the comfortable support of
our lives are not the spontaneous products of nature, nor do
offer themselves fit and prepared for our use. This part therefore draws on another care, and necessarily gives another
employment. But the pravity of mankind being such that they
had rather injuriously prey upon the fruits of other men's
labours than take pains to provide for themselves, the necessity of preserving men in the possession of what honest industry has already acquired, and also of preserving their
liberty and strength, whereby they may acquire what they
farther want, obliges men to enter into society with one
another, that by mutual assistance and joint force they may
secure unto each other their properties, in the things that
contribute to the comfort and happiness of this life, leaving in
the meanwhile to every man the care of his own eternal
happiness, the attainment whereof can neither be facilitated
by another man's industry, nor can the loss of it turn to
another man's prejudice, nor the hope of it be forced from him
by any external violence. But, forasmuch as men thus entering into societies, grounded upon their mutual compacts of
assistance for the defence of their temporal goods, may, nevertheless, be deprived of them, either by the rapine and fraud of
their fellow citizens, or by the hostile violence of foreigners,
the remedy of this evil consists in arms, riches, and multitudes
of citizens; the remedy of the other in laws; and the care of
all things relating both to one and the other is committed by
the society to the civil magistrate. This is the original, this is
the use, and these are the bounds of the legislative (which is
the supreme) power in every commonwealth. I mean, that
provision may be made for the security of each man's private

possessions; for the peace, riches, and public commodities of the whole people; and, as much as possible, for the increase of their inward strength against foreign invasions.

These things being thus explained, it is easy to understand to what end the legislative power ought to be directed, and by what measures regulated; and that is the temporal good and outward prosperity of the society; which is the sole reason for men's entering into society, and the only thing they seek and aim at in it. And it is also evident what liberty remains to men in reference to their eternal salvation, and that is, that every one should do what he in his conscience is persuaded to be acceptable to the Almighty, on whose good pleasure and acceptance depends their eternal happiness. For obedience is due, in the first place, to God, and afterwards to the laws.

But some may ask, What if the magistrate should enjoin anything by his authority that appears unlawful to the conscience of a private person? I answer, that if government be faithfully administered, and the counsels of the magistrates be indeed directed to the public good, this will seldom happen. But if, perhaps, it do so fall out, I say, that such a private person is to abstain from the action that he judges unlawful, and he is to undergo the punishment which it is not unlawful for him to bear. For the private judgment of any person concerning a law enacted in political matters, for the public good, does not take away the obligation of that law, nor deserve a dispensation. But if the law indeed be concerning things that lie not within the verge of the magistrate's authority (as for example, that the people, or any party amongst them, should be compelled to embrace a strange religion, and join in the worship and ceremonies of another church), men are not in these cases obliged by that law, against their consciences. For the political society is instituted for no other end, but only to secure every man's possession of the things of this life. The care of each man's soul, and of the things of heaven, which neither does belong to the commonwealth nor can be subjected to it, is left entirely to every man's self. Thus the safeguard of men's lives, and of the things that belong unto this life, is the business of the commonwealth; and the preserving of those things unto their owners is the duty of the magistrate. And therefore the magistrate cannot take away these worldly things from this man or party, and give them to that; nor change propriety amongst fellow-subjects (no not even by a law), for a cause that has no relation to the end of civil government, I mean for their religion, which whether it be true or false does no prejudice to the worldly concerns of their fellow-subjects, which are the things that only belong unto the care of the commonwealth. . . .

QUESTIONS

1. Comment on Locke's use of the word "indolency" in the phrase "indolency of body." Comment also upon his use of the word "impertinent."
2. Summarize Locke's arguments for the separation of church and state.
3. Locke and Milton wrote in approximately the same period. Compare the tone of their two essays. What rhetorical devices does Milton make use of that Locke does not use?
4. Why is Locke apparently contemptuous of the use of the word "laity" by ecclesiastics?
5. Trace to their historical antecedents the allusions in this essay to specific questions of religious controversy.
6. Find in your library the historical occasion for Locke's essay.
7. Can you deduce from the essay what Locke's own religious position was? Does it prejudice his views on toleration?

OUR REGARD FOR FREEDOM OF CONSCIENCE

✐ Justice Charles Evans Hughes

I am unable to agree with the judgment in this case. It is
important to note the precise question to be determined. It is
solely one of law, as there is no controversy as to the facts. The
question is not whether naturalization is a privilege to be
granted or withheld. That it is such a privilege is undisputed.
Nor, whether the Congress has the power to fix the conditions
upon which the privilege is granted. That power is assumed.
Nor, whether the Congress may in its discretion compel service
in the army in time of war or punish the refusal to serve. That
power is not here in dispute. Nor is the question one of the
authority of Congress to exact a promise to bear arms as a
condition of its grant of naturalization. That authority, for the
present purpose, may also be assumed.

The question before the Court is the narrower one whether
the Congress has exacted such a promise. That the Congress
has not made such an express requirement is apparent. The
question is whether that exaction is to be implied from certain
general words which do not, as it seems to me, either literally
or historically, demand the implication. I think that the requirement should not be implied, because such a construction
is directly opposed to the spirit of our institutions and to the
historic practice of the Congress. It must be conceded that
departmental zeal may not be permitted to outrun the authority

283 U.S. 605, *United States Reports* (1930).

conferred by statute. If such a promise is to be demanded, contrary to principles which have been respected as fundamental, the Congress should exact it in unequivocal terms, and we should not, by judicial decision, attempt to perform what, as I see it, is a legislative function.

In examining the requirements for naturalization, we find that the Congress has expressly laid down certain rules which concern the opinions and conduct of the applicant. Thus it is provided that no person shall be naturalized "who disbelieves in or who is opposed to organized government, or who is a member of or affiliated with any organization entertaining and teaching such disbelief in or opposition to organized government, or who advocates or teaches the duty, necessity, or propriety of the unlawful assaulting or killing of any officer or officers, either of specified individuals or of officers generally, of the Government of the United States, or of any other organized government, because of his or their official character, or who is a polygamist." Act of June 29, 1906, c. 3592, § 7; 34 Stat. 596, 598; U. S. C. Tit. 8, § 364. The respondent, Douglas Clyde Macintosh, entertained none of these disqualifying opinions and had none of the associations or relations disapproved. Among the specific requirements as to beliefs, we find none to the effect that one shall not be naturalized if by reason of his religious convictions he is opposed to war or is unwilling to promise to bear arms. In view of the questions which have repeatedly been brought to the attention of the Congress in relation to such beliefs, and having regard to the action of the Congress when its decision was of immediate importance in the raising of armies, the omission of such an express requirement from the naturalization statute is highly significant.

Putting aside these specific requirements as fully satisfied, we come to the general conditions imposed by the statute. We find one as to good behavior during the specified period of residence preceding application. No applicant could appear to be more exemplary than Macintosh. A Canadian by birth, he first came to the United States as a graduate student at the University of Chicago, and in 1907 he was ordained as a Baptist minister. In 1909 he began to teach in Yale University and is now a member of the faculty of the Divinity School, Chaplain of the Yale Graduate School, and Dwight Professor of Theology. After the outbreak of the Great War, he voluntarily sought appointment as a chaplain with the Canadian Army and as such saw service at the front. Returning to this country, he made public addresses in 1917 in support of the Allies. In 1918, he went again to France where he had charge of an American Y.M.C.A. hut at the front until the armistice, when he resumed his duties at Yale University. It seems to me that the applicant has shown himself in his behavior and character to be highly desirable as a citizen and, if such a man is to be excluded from naturalization, I think the disqualification should be found in unambiguous terms and not in an implication which shuts him out and gives admission to a host far less worthy.

The principal ground for exclusion appears to relate to the terms of the oath which the applicant must take. It should be observed that the respondent was willing to take the oath, and he so stated in his petition. But, in response to further inquiries, he explained that he was not willing "to promise beforehand" to take up arms, "without knowing the cause for which my country may go to war" and that "he would have to believe that the war was morally justified." He declared that "his first allegiance was to the will of God"; that he was ready to give to the United States "all the allegiance he ever had given or ever could give to any country, but that he could not put allegiance to the Government of any country before allegiance to the will of God." The question then is whether the terms of the oath are to be taken as necessarily implying an assurance of willingness to bear arms, so that one whose conscientious convictions or belief of supreme allegiance to the will of God will not permit him to make such an absolute promise, cannot take the oath and hence is disqualified for admission to citizenship.

The statutory provision as to the oath which is said to require this promise is this: "That he will support and defend the Constitution and laws of the United States against all enemies, foreign and domestic, and bear true faith and allegiance to the same." Act of June 29, 1906, c. 3592, § 4,

34 Stat. 596, 598; U. S. C. Tit. 8, § 381. That these general words have not been regarded as implying a promise to bear arms notwithstanding religious or conscientious scruples, or as requiring one to promise to put allegiance to temporal power above what is sincerely believed to be one's duty of obedience to God, is apparent, I think, from a consideration of their history. This oath does not stand alone. It is the same oath in substance that is required by Act of Congress of civil officers generally (except the President, whose oath is prescribed by the Constitution). The Congress, in prescribing such an oath for civil officers, acts under Article VI, section 3, of the Constitution, which provides: "The Senators and Representatives before mentioned, and the Members of the several State Legislatures, and all executive and judicial Officers, both of the United States and of the several States, shall be bound by Oath or Affirmation, to support this Constitution; but no religious test shall ever be required as a Qualification to any Office or public Trust under the United States." The general oath of office, in the form which has been prescribed by the Congress for over sixty years, contains the provision "that I will support and defend the Constitution of the United States against all enemies, foreign and domestic; that I will bear true faith and allegiance to the same; that I take this obligation freely, without any mental reservation or purpose of evasion." (R. S. § 1757, U. S. C., Tit. 5, § 16.) It goes without saying that it was not the intention of the Congress in framing the oath to impose any religious test. When we consider the history of the struggle for religious liberty, the large number of citizens of our country, from the very beginning, who have been unwilling to sacrifice their religious convictions, and in particular, those who have been conscientiously opposed to war and who would not yield what they sincerely believed to be their allegiance to the will of God, I find it impossible to conclude that such persons are to be deemed disqualified for public office in this country because of the requirement of the oath which must be taken before they enter upon their duties. The terms of the promise "to support and defend the Constitution of the United States against all enemies, foreign and domestic," are not, I think, to be read as demanding any such result.

There are other and most important methods of defense, even in time of war, apart from the personal bearing of arms. We have but to consider the defense given to our country in the late war, both in industry and in the field, by workers of all sorts, by engineers, nurses, doctors and chaplains, to realize that there is opportunity even at such time for essential service in the activities of defense which do not require the overriding of such religious scruples. I think that the requirement of the oath of office should read in the light of our regard from the beginning for freedom of conscience. While it has always been recognized that the supreme power of government may be exerted and disobedience to its commands may be punished, we know that with many of our worthy citizens it would be a most heart-searching question if they were asked whether they would promise to obey a law believed to be in conflict with religious duty. Many of their most honored exemplars in the past have been willing to suffer imprisonment or even death rather than to make such a promise. And we also know, in particular, that a promise to engage in war by bearing arms, or thus to engage in a war believed to be unjust, would be contrary to the tenets of religious groups among our citizens who are of patriotic purpose and exemplary conduct. To conclude that the general oath of office is to be interpreted as disregarding the religious scruples of these citizens and as disqualifying them for office because they could not take the oath with such an interpretation would, I believe, be generally regarded as contrary not only to the specific intent of the Congress but as repugnant to the fundamental principle of representative government.

But the naturalization oath is in substantially the same terms as the oath of office to which I have referred. I find no ground for saying that these words are to be interpreted differently in the two cases. On the contrary, when the Congress reproduced the historic words of the oath of office in the naturalization oath, I should suppose that, according to familiar rules of interpretation, they should be deemed to carry the same significance.

The question of the proper interpretation of the oath is, as I have said, distinct from that of legislative policy in exacting military service. The latter is not dependent upon the former. But the long-established practice of excusing from military service those whose religious convictions oppose it confirms the view that the Congress in the terms of the oath did not intend to require a promise to give such service. The policy of granting exemptions in such cases has been followed from colonial times and is abundantly shown by the provisions of colonial and state statutes, of state constitutions, and of acts of Congress. See citations in the opinion of the Circuit Court of Appeals in the present case. 42 F. (2d) 845, 847, 848. The first constitution of New York, adopted in 1777, in providing for the state militia, while strongly emphasizing the duty of defense, added "That all such of the inhabitants of this state (being of the people called Quakers) as, from scruples of conscience may be averse to the bearing of arms, be therefrom excused by the legislature, and do pay to the state such sums of money, in lieu of their personal service, as the same may, in the judgment of the legislature, be worth." Art. XL. A large number of similar provisions are found in other States. The importance of giving immunity to those having conscientious scruples against bearing arms has been emphasized in debates in Congress repeatedly from the very beginning of our government, and religious scruples have been recognized in draft acts. Annals of Congress (Gales), 1st Congress, vol. I, pp. 434, 436, 729, 731; vol. II, pp. 1818–1827; Acts of February 24, 1864, 13 Stat. 6, 9; January 21, 1903, 32 Stat. 775; June 3, 1916, 39 Stat. 166, 197; May 18, 1917, 40 Stat. 76, 78. I agree with the statement in the opinion of the Circuit Court of Appeals in the present case that "This Federal legislation is indicative of the actual operation of the principles of the Constitution, that a person with conscientious or religious scruples need not bear arms, although as a member of society, he may be obliged to render services of a non-combatant nature."

Much has been said of the paramount duty to the State, a duty to be recognized, it is urged, even though it conflicts with convictions of duty to God. Undoubtedly that duty to the State exists within the domain of power, for government may enforce obedience to laws regardless of scruples. When one's belief collides with the power of the State, the latter is supreme within its sphere and submission or punishment follows. But, in the forum of conscience, duty to a moral power higher than the State has always been maintained. The reservation of that supreme obligation, as a matter of principle, would unquestionably be made by many of our conscientious and law-abiding citizens. The essence of religion is belief in a relation to God involving duties superior to those arising from any human relation. As was stated by Mr. Justice Field, in *Davis* v. *Beason*, 133 U.S. 333, 342: "The term 'religion' has reference to one's views of his relations to his Creator, and to the obligations they impose of reverence for his being and character, and of obedience to his will." One cannot speak of religious liberty, with proper appreciation of its essential and historic significance, without assuming the existence of a belief in supreme allegiance to the will of God. Professor Macintosh, when pressed by the inquiries put to him, stated what is axiomatic in religious doctrine. And, putting aside dogmas with their particular conceptions of deity, freedom of conscience itself implies respect for an innate conviction of paramount duty. The battle for religious liberty has been fought and won with respect to religious beliefs and practices, which are not in conflict with good order, upon the very ground of the supremacy of conscience within its proper field. What that field is, under our system of government, presents in part a question of constitutional law and also, in part, one of legislative policy in avoiding unnecessary clashes with the dictates of conscience. There is abundant room for enforcing the requisite authority of law as it is enacted and requires obedience, and for maintaining the conception of the supremacy of law as essential to orderly government, without demanding that either citizens or applicants for citizenship shall assume by oath an obligation to regard allegiance to God as subordinate to allegiance to civil power. The attempt to exact such a promise, and thus to bind one's conscience by the taking of oaths or the submission to tests, has been the cause of many deplorable conflicts. The Congress has sought to avoid such conflicts in this country by respecting our happy tradition. In no sphere of legislation has the intention to prevent such clashes been more conspicuous than in relation to the bearing of arms. It would require strong evidence that the Congress intended a reversal of its policy in prescribing the general terms of the naturalization oath. I find no such evidence.

Nor is there ground, in my opinion, for the exclusion of Professor Macintosh because his conscientious scruples have particular reference to wars believed to be unjust. There is nothing new in such an attitude. Among the most eminent statesmen here and abroad have been those who condemned the action of their country in entering into wars they thought to be unjustified. Agreements for the renunciation of war presuppose a preponderant public sentiment against wars of aggression. If, while recognizing the power of Congress, the mere holding of religious or conscientious scruples against all wars should not disqualify a citizen from holding office in this country, or an applicant otherwise qualified from being admitted to citizenship, there would seem to be no reason why a reservation of religious or conscientious objection to participation in wars believed to be unjust should constitute such a disqualification.

Apart from the terms of the oath, it is said that the respondent has failed to meet the requirement of "attachment to the principles of the Constitution." Here, again, is a general phrase which should be construed, not in opposition to, but in accord with, the theory and practice of our Government in relation to freedom of conscience. What I have said as to the provisions of the oath I think applies equally to this phase of the case.

The judgment in *United States* v. *Schwimmer*, 279 U.S. 644, stands upon the special facts of that case, but I do not regard it as requiring a reversal of the judgment here. I think that the judgment below should be affirmed.

QUESTIONS

1. Compare Hughes's position in this essay with Chafee's in regard to the question of hysteria in times of crisis.
2. Define what Hughes means by "our happy tradition" as it relates to questions in which conscience collides with the power of the state.

3. What is your response to a dissenting opinion of the Supreme Court when you may think it is more just than the majority opinion, which is legally binding? How may a free people act to change such law?
4. Study the essay to determine how Hughes makes clear to the reader the details of the case and the majority opinion without explicitly stating either.
5. Is it reasonable to use the word "essay" to describe such a legal document as this?

QUESTIONS ON PART VI

1. Write an essay in which you attack or defend the principle that men must be free to worship in their own way or not at all.
2. Justify Hughes's dissenting opinion and Locke's principal thesis by reference to the First Amendment to the Constitution.

Appendixes

I. THE CONSTITUTION OF THE UNITED STATES

We the People of the United States, in Order to form a more perfect Union, establish Justice, insure domestic Tranquility, provide for the common defence, promote the general Welfare, and secure the Blessings of Liberty to ourselves and our Posterity, do ordain and establish this Constitution for the United States of America.

ARTICLE. I.

SECTION. 1. All legislative Powers herein granted shall be vested in a Congress of the United States, which shall consist of a Senate and House of Representatives.

SECTION. 2. The House of Representatives shall be composed of Members chosen every second Year by the People of the several States, and the Electors in each State shall have the Qualifications requisite for Electors of the most numerous Branch of the State Legislature.

No person shall be a Representative who shall not have attained to the Age of twenty-five Years, and been seven Years a Citizen of the United States, and who shall not, when elected, be an Inhabitant of that State in which he shall be chosen.

Representatives and direct Taxes shall be apportioned among the several States which may be included within this Union, according to their respective Numbers, which shall be determined by adding to the whole Number of free Persons, including those bound to Service for a Term of Years, and excluding Indians not taxed, three fifths of all other Persons. The actual Enumeration shall be made within three Years after the first Meeting of the Congress of the United States, and within every subsequent Term of ten Years, in such Manner as they shall by Law direct. The Number of Representatives shall not exceed one for every thirty Thousand, but each

State shall have at Least one Representative; and until such enumeration shall be made, the State of New Hampshire shall be entitled to chuse three, Massachusetts eight, Rhode-Island and Providence Plantations one, Connecticut five, New-York six, New Jersey four, Pennsylvania eight, Delaware one, Maryland six, Virginia ten, North Carolina five, South Carolina five, and Georgia three.

When vacancies happen in the Representation from any State, the Executive Authority thereof shall issue Writs of Election to fill such Vacancies.

The House of Representatives shall chuse their Speaker and other Officers; and shall have the sole Power of Impeachment.

SECTION. 3. The Senate of the United States shall be composed of two Senators from each State, chosen by the Legislature thereof, for six Years; and each Senator shall have one Vote.

Immediately after they shall be assembled in Consequence of the first Election, they shall be divided as equally as may be into three Classes. The Seats of the Senators of the first Class shall be vacated at the Expiration of the second Year, of the second Class at the Expiration of the fourth Year, and of the third class at the Expiration of the sixth Year, so that one third may be chosen every second Year; and if Vacancies happen by Resignation, or otherwise, during the Recess of the Legislature of any State, the Executive thereof may make temporary Appointments until the next Meeting of the Legislature, which shall then fill such Vacancies.

No Person shall be a Senator who shall not have attained to the Age of thirty Years, and been nine Years a Citizen of the United States, and who shall not, when elected, be an Inhabitant of that State for which he shall be chosen.

The Vice President of the United States shall be President of the Senate, but shall have no Vote, unless they be equally divided.

The Senate shall chuse their other Officers, and also a President pro tempore, in the Absence of the Vice President, or when he shall exercise the Office of President of the United States.

The Senate shall have the sole Power to try all Impeachments. When sitting for that Purpose, they shall be on Oath or Affirmation. When the President of the United States is tried, the Chief Justice shall preside: And no Person shall be convicted without the Concurrence of two thirds of the Members present.

Judgment in Cases of Impeachment shall not extend further than to removal from Office, and disqualification to hold and enjoy any Office of honor, Trust or Profit under the United States: but the Party convicted shall nevertheless be liable and subject to Indictment, Trial, Judgment and Punishment, according to Law.

SECTION. 4. The Times, Places and Manner of holding Elections for Senators and Representatives, shall be prescribed in each State by the Legislature thereof, but the Congress may at any time by Law make or alter such Regulations, except as to the Places of chusing Senators.

The Congress shall assemble at least once in every Year, and such Meeting shall be on the first Monday in December, unless they shall by Law appoint a different day.

SECTION. 5. Each House shall be the Judge of the Elections, Returns and Qualifications of its own Members, and a Majority of each shall constitute a Quorum to do Business; but a smaller Number may adjourn from day to day, and may be authorized to compel the Attendance of absent Members, in such Manner, and under such Penalties as each House may provide.

Each House may determine the Rules of its Proceedings, punish its Members for disorderly Behaviour, and, with the Concurrence of two thirds, expel a Member.

Each House shall keep a Journal of its Proceedings, and from time to time publish the same, excepting such Parts as may in their Judgment require Secrecy; and the Yeas and Nays of the Members of either House on any question shall, at the Desire of one fifth of those Present, be entered on the Journal.

Neither House, during the Session of Congress, shall, without the Consent of the other, adjourn for more than three days, nor to any other Place than that in which the two Houses shall be sitting.

SECTION. 6. The Senators and Representatives shall receive a Compensation for their Services, to be ascertained by Law, and paid out of the Treasury of the United States. They shall in all Cases, except Treason, Felony and Breach of the Peace, be privileged from Arrest during their Attendance at the Session of their respective Houses, and in going to and returning from the same; and for any Speech or Debate in either House, they shall not be questioned in any other Place.

No Senator or Representative shall, during the Time for which he was elected, be appointed to any civil Office under the Authority of the United States, which shall have been created, or the Emoluments whereof shall have been encreased during such time; and no Person holding any Office under the United States, shall be a Member of either House during his Continuance in Office.

SECTION. 7. All Bills for raising Revenue shall originate in the House of Representatives; but the Senate may propose or concur with Amendments as on other Bills.

Every Bill which shall have passed the House of Representatives and the Senate shall, before it become a Law, be presented to the President of the United States; If he approve he shall sign it, but if not he shall return it, with his Objections to that House in which it shall have originated, who shall enter the Objections at large on their Journal, and proceed to reconsider it. If after such Reconsideration two thirds of that House shall agree to pass the Bill, it shall be sent, together with the Objections, to the other House, by which it shall likewise be reconsidered, and if approved by two thirds of that House, it shall become a Law. But in all such Cases the Votes of both Houses shall be determined by yeas and Nays, and the Names of the Persons voting for and against the Bill shall be entered on the Journal of each House respectively. If any Bill shall not be returned by the President within ten Days (Sundays excepted) after it shall have been presented to him, the Same shall be a Law, in like Manner as if he had signed it, unless the Congress by their Adjournment prevent its Return, in which Case it shall not be a Law.

Every Order, Resolution or Vote to which the Concurrence of the Senate and House of Representatives may be necessary (except on a question of Adjournment) shall be presented to the President of the United States; and before the Same shall take Effect, shall be approved by him, or being disapproved by him, shall be repassed by two thirds of the Senate and House of Representatives, according to the Rules and Limitations prescribed in the Case of a Bill.

SECTION. 8. The Congress shall have Power: To lay and collect Taxes, Duties, Imposts and Excises, to pay the Debts and provide for the common Defence and general Welfare of the United States; but all Duties, Imposts and Excises shall be uniform throughout the United States;

To borrow Money on the credit of the United States;

To regulate Commerce with foreign Nations, and among the several States, and with the Indian Tribes;

To establish an uniform Rule of Naturalization, and uniform Laws on the subject of Bankruptcies throughout the United States;

To coin Money, regulate the Value thereof, and of foreign Coin, to fix the Standard of Weights and Measures;

To provide for the Punishment of counterfeiting the Securities and current Coin of the United States;

To establish Post Offices and post Roads;

To promote the Progress of Science and useful Arts, by securing for limited Times to Authors and Inventors the exclusive Right to their respective Writings and Discoveries;

To constitute Tribunals inferior to the supreme Court;

To define and punish Piracies and Felonies committed on the high Seas, and Offences against the Law of Nations;

To declare War, grant Letters of Marque and Reprisal, and make Rules concerning Captures on Land and Water;

To raise and support Armies, but no Appropriation of Money to that Use shall be for a longer Term than two Years;

To provide and maintain a Navy;

To make Rules for the Government and Regulation of the land and naval Forces;

To provide for calling forth the Militia to execute the Laws of the Union, suppress Insurrections and repel Invasions;

To provide for organizing, arming, and disciplining, the Militia, and for governing such Part of them as may be employed in the Service of the United States, reserving to the States respectively, the Appointment of the Officers, and the Authority of training the Militia according to the discipline prescribed by Congress;

To exercise exclusive Legislation in all Cases whatsoever, over such District (not exceeding ten Miles square) as may, by Cession of particular States, and the Acceptance of Congress, become the Seat of the Government of the United States, and to exercise like Authority over all Places purchased by the Consent of the Legislature of the Senate in which the Same shall be, for the Erection of Forts, Magazines, Arsenals, dock-Yards, and other needful Buildings;—And

To make all Laws which shall be necessary and proper for carrying into Execution the foregoing Powers, and all other Powers vested by this Constitution in the Government of the United States, or in any Department or Officer thereof.

SECTION. 9. The Migration or Importation of such Persons as any of the States now existing shall think proper to admit, shall not be prohibited by the Congress prior to the Year 1808, but a Tax or duty may be imposed on such Importation, not exceeding ten dollars for each Person.

The Privilege of the Writ of Habeas Corpus shall not be suspended, unless when in Cases of Rebellion or Invasion the public Safety may require it.

No Bill of Attainder or ex post facto Law shall be passed.

No Capitation, or other direct, Tax shall be laid, unless in Proportion to the Census or Enumeration herein before directed to be taken.

No Tax or Duty shall be laid on Articles exported from any State.

No Preference shall be given by any Regulation of Commerce or Revenue to the Ports of one State over those of another; nor shall Vessels bound to, or from, one State, be obliged to enter, clear, or pay Duties in another.

No Money shall be drawn from the Treasury, but in Consequence of Appropriations made by Law, and a regular Statement and Account of the Receipts and Expenditures of all public Money shall be published from time time.

No Title of Nobility shall be granted by the United States: And no Person holding any Office of Profit or Trust under them, shall, without the Consent of the Congress, accept of any present, Emolument, Office, or Title, of any kind whatever, from any King, Prince, or foreign State.

SECTION. 10.   No State shall enter into any Treaty, Alliance, or Confederation; grant Letters of Marque and Reprisal; coin Money; emit Bills of Credit; make any Thing but gold and silver Coin a Tender in Payment of Debts; pass any Bill of Attainder, ex post facto Law, or Law impairing the Obligation of Contracts, or grant any Title of Nobility.

No State shall, without the Consent of the Congress, lay any Imposts or Duties on Imports or Exports, except what may be absolutely necessary for executing its inspection Laws: and the net Produce of all Duties and Imposts, laid by any State on Imports or Exports, shall be for the Use of the Treasury of the United States; and all such Laws shall be subject to the Revision and Controul of the Congress.

No State shall, without the Consent of Congress, lay any Duty of Tonnage, keep Troops, or Ships of War in time of Peace, enter into any Agreement or Compact with another State, or with a foreign Power, or engage in War, unless actually invaded, or in such imminent Danger as will not admit of delay.

ARTICLE. II.

SECTION. 1.   The Executive Power shall be vested in a President of the United States of America. He shall hold his Office during the Term of four Years, and, together with the Vice President, chosen for the same Term, be elected, as follows:

Each State shall appoint, in such Manner as the Legislature thereof may direct, a Number of Electors, equal to the whole Number of Senators and Representatives to which the State may be entitled in the Congress: but no Senator or Representative, or Person holding an Office of Trust or Profit under the United States, shall be appointed an Elector.

The Electors shall meet in their respective States, and vote by Ballot for two persons, of whom one at least shall not be an Inhabitant of the same State with themselves. And they shall make a List of all the Persons voted for, and of the Number of Votes for each; which List they shall sign and certify, and transmit sealed to the Seat of the Government of the United States, directed to the President of the Senate. The President of the Senate shall, in the Presence of the Senate and House of Representatives, open all the Certificates, and the Votes shall then be counted. The Person having the greatest Number of Votes shall be the President, if such Number be a Majority of the whole Number of Electors appointed; and if there be more than one who have such Majority, and have an equal Number of Votes, then the House of Representatives shall immediately chuse by Ballot one of them for President; and if no Person have a Majority, then from the five highest on the List the said House shall in like Manner chuse the President. But in chusing the President, the Votes shall be taken by States, the Representation from each State having one Vote; A quorum for this Purpose shall consist of a Member or Members from two thirds of the States, and a Majority of all the States shall be necessary to a Choice. In every Case, after the Choice of the President, the Person having the greatest Number of Votes of the Electors shall be the Vice President. But if there should remain two or more who have equal Votes, the Senate shall chuse from them by Ballot the Vice President.

The Congress may determine the Time of chusing the Electors, and the Day on which they shall give their Votes; which Day shall be the same throughout the United States.

No Person except a natural born Citizen, or a Citizen of the United States, at the time of the Adoption of this Constitution, shall be eligible to the Office of President, neither shall any Person be eligible to that Office who shall not have attained to the Age of thirty-five Years, and been fourteen Years a Resident within the United States.

In Case of the Removal of the President from Office, or of his Death, Resignation, or Inability to discharge the Powers and Duties of the said Office, the Same shall devolve on the Vice President, and the Congress may by Law provide for the Case of Removal, Death, Resignation or Inability, both of the President and Vice President, declaring what Officer shall then act as President, and such Officer shall act accordingly, until the Disability be removed, or a President shall be elected.

The President shall, at stated Times, receive for his Services, a Compensation, which shall neither be encreased nor diminished during the Period for which he shall have been elected, and he shall not receive within that Period any other Emolument from the United States, or any of them.

Before he enter on the Execution of his Office, he shall take the following Oath or Affirmation: — "I do solemnly swear (or affirm) that I will faithfully execute the Office of President of the United States, and will to the best of my Ability, preserve, protect and defend the Constitution of the United States."

SECTION. 2. The President shall be Commander in Chief of the Army and Navy of the United States, and of the Militia of the several States, when called into the actual Service of the United States; he may require the Opinion, in writing, of the principal Officer in each of the executive Departments, upon any Subject relating to the Duties of their respective Offices, and he shall have Power to grant Reprieves and Pardons for Offences against the United States, except in Cases of Impeachment.

He shall have Power, by and with the Advice and Consent of the Senate, to make Treaties, provided two thirds of the Senators present concur; and he shall nominate, and by and with the Advice and Consent of the Senate, shall appoint Ambassadors, other public Ministers and Consuls, Judges of the supreme Court, and all other Officers of the United States, whose Appointments are not herein otherwise provided for, and which shall be established by Law; but the Congress may by Law vest the Appointment of such inferior Officers, as they think proper, in the President alone, in the Courts of Law, or in the Heads of Departments.

The President shall have Power to fill up all Vacancies that may happen during the Recess of the Senate, by granting Commissions which shall expire at the End of their next Session.

SECTION. 3. He shall from time to time give to the Congress Information of the State of the Union, and recommend to their Consideration such Measures as he shall judge necessary and expedient; he may, on extraordinary Occasions, convene both Houses, or either of them, and in Case of Disagreement between them, with Respect to the Time of Adjournment, he may adjourn them to such

Time as he shall think proper; he shall receive Ambassadors and other public Ministers; he shall take Care that the Laws be faithfully executed, and shall Commission all the Officers of the United States.

SECTION. 4.   The President, Vice President and all civil officers of the United States, shall be removed from Office on Impeachment for, and Conviction of, Treason, Bribery, or other high Crimes and Misdemeanors.

ARTICLE. III.

SECTION. 1.   The judicial Power of the United States, shall be vested in one supreme Court, and in such inferior Courts as the Congress may from time to time ordain and establish. The Judges, both of the supreme and inferior Courts, shall hold their Offices during good Behavior, and shall, at stated Times, receive for their Services, a Compensation, which shall not be diminished during their Continuance in Office.

SECTION. 2.   The judicial Power shall extend to all Cases, in Law and Equity, arising under this Constitution, the Laws of the United States, and Treaties made, or which shall be made, under their Authority;—to all Cases affecting Ambassadors, other public Ministers and Consuls;—to all Cases of admiralty and maritime Jurisdiction;—to Controversies to which the United States shall be a Party;—to Controversies between two or more States;—between a State and Citizens of another State;—between Citizens of different States;—between Citizens of the same State claiming Lands under Grants of different States, and between a State, or the Citizens thereof, and foreign States, Citizens or Subjects.

In all Cases affecting Ambassadors, other public Ministers and Consuls, and those in which a State shall be Party, the supreme Court shall have original Jurisdiction. In all the other Cases before mentioned, the supreme Court shall have appellate Jurisdiction, both as to Law and Fact, with such Exceptions, and under such Regulations as the Congress shall make.

The Trial of all Crimes, except in Cases of Impeachment, shall be by Jury; and such Trial shall be held in the State where the said Crimes shall have been committed; but when not committed within any State, the Trial shall be at such Place and Places as the Congress may by Law have directed.

SECTION. 3.   Treason against the United States, shall consist only in levying War against them, or in adhering to their Enemies, giving them Aid and Comfort. No Person shall be convicted of Treason unless on the Testimony of two Witnesses to the same overt Act, or on Confession in open Court.

The Congress shall have Power to declare the Punishment of Treason, but no Attainder of Treason shall work Corruption of Blood, or Forfeiture except during the Life of the Person attainted.

ARTICLE. IV.

SECTION. 1. Full Faith and Credit shall be given in each State to the public Acts, Records, and judicial Proceedings of every other State. And the Congress may by general Laws prescribe the Manner in which such Acts, Records and Proceedings shall be proved, and the Effect thereof.

SECTION. 2. The Citizens of each State shall be entitled to all Privileges and Immunities of Citizens in the several States.

A Person charged in any State with Treason, Felony, or other Crime, who shall flee from Justice, and be found in another State, shall on Demand of the executive Authority of the State from which he fled, be delivered up, to be removed to the State having Jurisdiction of the Crime.

No Person held to Service or Labour in one State, under the Laws thereof, escaping into another, shall, in Consequence of any Law or Regulation therein, be discharged from such Service or Labour, but shall be delivered up on Claim of the Party to whom such Service or Labour may be due.

SECTION. 3. New States may be admitted by the Congress into this Union; but no new State shall be formed or erected within the Jurisdiction of any other State; nor any State be formed by Junction of two or more States, or Parts of States, without the Consent of the Legislatures of the States concerned as well as of the Congress.

The Congress shall have Power to dispose of and make all needful Rules and Regulations respecting the Territory or other Property belonging to the United States; and nothing in this Constitution shall be so construed as to Prejudice any Claims of the United States, or of any particular State.

SECTION. 4. The United States shall guarantee to every State in this Union a Republican Form of Government, and shall protect each of them against Invasion; and on Application of the Legislature, or of the Executive (when the Legislature cannot be convened) against domestic Violence.

Article. V.

The Congress, wherever two thirds of both Houses shall deem it necessary, shall propose Amendments to this Constitution, or, on the Application of the Legislatures of two thirds of the several States, shall call a Convention for proposing Amendments, which, in either Case, shall be valid to all Intents and Purposes, as Part of this Constitution, when ratified by the Legislatures of three fourths of the several States, or by Conventions in three fourths thereof, as the one or the other Mode of Ratification may be proposed by the Congress; Provided that no Amendment which may be made prior to the Year One thousand eight hundred and eight shall in any Manner affect the first and fourth Clauses in the Ninth Section of the first Article; and that no State, without its Consent, shall be deprived of its equal Suffrage in the Senate.

Article. VI.

All Debts contracted and Engagements entered into, before the Adoption of this Constitution, shall be as valid against the United States under this Constitution, as under the Confederation.

This Constitution, and the Laws of the United States which shall be made in Pursuance thereof; and all Treaties made, or which shall be made, under the Authority of the United States, shall be the supreme Law of the Land; and the Judges in every State shall be bound thereby, any Thing in the Constitution or Laws of any State to the Contrary notwithstanding.

The Senators and Representatives before mentioned, and the Members of the several State Legislatures, and all executive and judicial Officers, both of the United States and of the several States, shall be bound by Oath or Affirmation, to support this Constitution; but no religious Test shall ever be required as a Qualification to any Office or public Trust under the United States.

Article. VII.

The Ratification of the Conventions of nine States, shall be sufficient for the Establishment of this Constitution between the States so ratifying the Same.

Done in Convention by the Unanimous Consent of the States present the Seventeenth Day of September in the Year of our Lord one thousand seven hundred and Eighty seven and of the Independence of the United States of America the Twelfth. In witness whereof We have hereunto subscribed our Names.

II. AMENDMENTS TO THE CONSTITUTION

Articles in addition to, and Amendment of the Constitution of the United States of America, proposed by Congress, and ratified by the Legislatures of the several States, pursuant to the fifth Article of the original Constitution.

ARTICLE I.

Congress shall make no law respecting an establishment of religion, or prohibiting the free exercise thereof; or abridging the freedom of speech, or of the press; or the right of the people peaceably to assemble, and to petition the Government for a redress of grievances.

ARTICLE II.

A well regulated Militia, being necessary to the security of a free State, the right of the people to keep and bear Arms, shall not be infringed.

ARTICLE III.

No Soldier shall, in time of peace be quartered in any house, without the consent of the Owner, nor in time of war, but in a manner to be prescribed by law.

ARTICLE IV.

The right of the people to be secure in their persons, houses, papers, and effects, against unreasonable searches and seizures, shall not be violated, and no Warrants shall issue, but upon probable cause, supported by Oath or affirmation, and particularly describing the place to be searched, and the persons or things to be seized.

ARTICLE V.

No person shall be held to answer for a capital, or otherwise infamous crime, unless on a presentment or indictment of a Grand Jury, except in cases arising in the land or naval forces, or in the Militia, when in actual service in time of War or public danger; nor shall any person be subject for the same offence to be twice put in jeopardy of life or limb; nor shall be compelled in any criminal case to be a witness against himself, nor be deprived of life, liberty, or property, without due process of law; nor shall private property be taken for public use, without just compensation.

ARTICLE VI.

In all criminal prosecutions, the accused shall enjoy the right to a speedy and public trial, by an impartial jury of the State and district wherein the crime shall have been committed, which district shall have been previously ascertained by law, and to be informed of the nature and cause of the accusation; to be confronted with the witnesses against him; to have compulsory process for obtaining witnesses in his favor, and to have the Assistance of Counsel for his defence.

ARTICLE VII.

In Suits at common law, where the value in controversy shall exceed twenty dollars, the right of trial by jury shall be preserved, and no fact tried by a jury, shall be otherwise re-examined in any Court of the United States, than according to the rules of the common law.

ARTICLE VIII.

Excessive bail shall not be required, nor excessive fines imposed, nor cruel and unusual punishments inflicted.

ARTICLE IX.

The enumeration in the Constitution, of certain rights, shall not be construed to deny or disparage others retained by the people.

ARTICLE X.

The powers not delegated to the United States by the Constitution, nor prohibited by it to the States, are reserved to the States respectively, or to the people. [The first ten amendments went into effect November 3, 1791.]

III. THE UNANIMOUS DECLARATION OF THE THIRTEEN UNITED STATES OF AMERICA (THE DECLARATION OF INDEPENDENCE)

When in the Course of human events, it becomes necessary for one people to dissolve the political bands which have connected them with another, and to assume among the powers of the earth, the separate and equal station to which the Laws of Nature and of Nature's God entitle them, a decent respect to the opinions of mankind requires that they should declare the causes which impel them to the separation.

We hold these truths to be self-evident, that all men are created equal, that they are endowed by their Creator with certain unalienable Rights, that among these are Life, Liberty and the pursuit of Happiness. —That to secure these rights, Governments are instituted among Men, deriving their just powers from the consent of the governed, —That whenever any Form of Government becomes destructive of these ends, it is the Right of the People to alter or to abolish it, and to institute new Government, laying its foundation on such principles and organizing its powers in such form, as to them shall seem most likely to effect their Safety and Happiness. Prudence, indeed, will dictate that Governments long established should not be changed for light and transient causes; and accordingly all experience hath shewn, that mankind are more disposed to suffer, while evils are sufferable, than to right themselves by abolishing the forms to which they are accustomed. But when a long train of abuses and usurpations, pursuing invariably the same Object evinces a design to reduce them under absolute Despotism, it is their right, it is their duty, to throw off such Government, and to provide new Guards for their future security. —Such has been the patient sufferance of these Colonies; and such is now the necessity which constrains them to alter their former Systems of Government. The history of the present King of Great Britain is a history of repeated injuries and usurpations, all having in direct object the establishment of an absolute Tyranny over these States. To prove this, let Facts be submitted to a candid world.

He has refused his Assent to Laws, the most wholesome and necessary for the public good.

He has forbidden his Governors to pass Laws of immediate and pressing importance, unless suspended in their operation till his Assent should be obtained; and when so suspended, he has utterly neglected to attend to them.

He has refused to pass other Laws for the accommodation of large districts of people, unless those people would relinquish the right of Representation in the Legislature, a right inestimable to them and formidable to tyrants only.

He has called together legislative bodies at places unusual, uncomfortable, and distant from the depository of their public Records, for the sole purpose of fatiguing them into compliance with his measures.

He has dissolved Representative Houses repeatedly, for opposing with manly firmness his invasions on the rights of the people.

He has refused for a long time, after such dissolutions, to cause others to be elected; whereby the Legislative powers, incapable of Annihilation, have returned to the People at large for their exercise; the State remaining in the mean time exposed to all the dangers of invasion from without, and convulsions within.

He has endeavoured to prevent the population of these States; for that purpose obstructing the Laws for Naturalization of Foreigners; refusing to pass others to encourage their migrations hither, and raising the conditions of new Appropriations of Lands.

He has obstructed the Administration of Justice, by refusing his Assent to Laws for establishing Judiciary powers.

He has made Judges dependent on his Will alone, for the tenure of their offices, and the amount and payment of their salaries.

He has erected a multitude of New Offices, and sent hither swarms of Officers to harrass our people, and eat out their substance.

He has kept among us, in times of peace, Standing Armies without the Consent of our legislatures.

He has affected to render the Military independent of and superior to the Civil power.

He has combined with others to subject us to a jurisdiction

foreign to our constitution and unacknowledged by our laws; giving his Assent to their Acts of pretended Legislation: —For quartering large bodies of armed troops among us: —For protecting them, by a mock Trial, from punishment for any Murders which they should commit on the Inhabitants of these States: —For cutting off our Trade with all parts of the world: —For imposing Taxes on us without our Consent: —For depriving us in many cases, of the benefits of Trial by Jury: —For transporting us beyond Seas to be tried for pretended offences: —For abolishing the free System of English Laws in a neighbouring Province, establishing therein an Arbitrary government, and enlarging its Boundaries so as to render it at once an example and fit instrument for introducing the same absolute rule into these Colonies: —For taking away our Charters, abolishing our most valuable Laws and altering fundamentally the Forms of our Governments: —For suspending our own Legislatures and declaring themselves invested with power to legislate for us in all cases whatsoever.

He has abdicated Government here, by declaring us out of his Protection and waging War against us.

He has plundered our seas, ravaged our Coasts, burnt our towns, and destroyed the lives of our people.

He is at this time transporting large Armies of foreign Mercenaries to compleat the works of death, desolation and tyranny, already begun with circumstances of Cruelty & perfidy scarcely paralleled in the most barbarous ages, and totally unworthy the Head of a civilized nation.

He has constrained our fellow Citizens taken Captive on the high Seas to bear Arms against their Country, to become the executioners of their friends and Brethren, or to fall themselves by their Hands.

He has excited domestic insurrections amongst us, and has endeavoured to bring on the inhabitants of our frontiers, the merciless Indian Savages, whose known rule of warfare, is an undistinguished destruction of all ages, sexes and conditions. In every stage of these Oppressions We have Petitioned for Redress in the most humble terms: Our repeated Petitions have been answered only by repeated injury. A Prince, whose character is thus marked by every act which may define a Tyrant, is unfit to be the ruler of a free people. Nor have We been wanting in attentions to our Brittish brethren. We have warned them from time to time of attempts by their legislature to extend an unwarrantable jurisdiction over us. We have reminded them of the circumstances of our emigration and settlement here. We have appealed to their native justice and magnanimity, and we have conjured them by the ties of our common kindred to disavow these usurpations, which would inevitably interrupt our connections and correspondence. They too have been deaf to the voice of justice and of consanguinity. We must, therefore, acquiesce in the necessity, which denounces our Separation, and hold them, as we hold the rest of mankind, Enemies in War, in Peace Friends.

We, therefore, the Representatives of the *united States of America,* in General Congress, Assembled, appealing to the Supreme Judge of the world for the rectitude of our intentions do, in the Name, and by Authority of the good People of these Colonies, solemnly publish and declare, That these United Colonies are, and of Right ought to be *Free and Independent States;* that they are Absolved from all Allegiance to the British Crown, and that all political connection between them and the State of Great Britain, is and ought to be totally dissolved; and that as Free and Independent States, they have full Power to levy War, conclude Peace, contract Alliances, establish Commerce, and to do all other Acts and Things which Independent States may of right do. —And for the support of this Declaration, with a firm reliance on the protection of divine Providence, we mutually pledge to each other our Lives, our Fortunes and our sacred Honor.

INDEX OF
AUTHORS AND TITLES

DESIGNED BY FAITH NELSON

SET IN PRIMER AT BROWN BROS. LINOTYPERS, INC.

MANUFACTURED BY HADDON CRAFTSMEN

HARPER & BROTHERS, PUBLISHERS, NEW YORK